Switched LANs
Implementation, Operation, Maintenance

Switched LANs
Implementation, Operation, Maintenance

John J. Roese

McGraw-Hill
New York • San Francisco • Washington, D.C. • Auckland • Bogotá
Caracas • Lisbon • London • Madrid • Mexico City • Milan
Montreal • New Delhi • San Juan • Singapore
Sydney • Tokyo • Toronto

Library of Congress Cataloging-in-Publication Data

Roese, John J.
    Switched LANs / John Roese.
        p. cm.
    Originally published under title: Implementing and operating switched
local area networks. Boston: International Thomson Computer Press, 1997.
    Includes bibliographical references and index.
    ISBN 0-07-053413-6
    1. Local area networks (Computer networks) 2. Computer network
protocols. I. Roese, John J. Implementing and operating switched local
area networks. II. Title.
    TK5105.7.R64 1998
    004.6'8--dc21   98-14473
                                                  CIP

McGraw-Hill

A Division of The McGraw·Hill Companies

1 2 3 4 5 6 7 8 9 0 DOC/DOC 9 0 3 2 1 0 9 8

ISBN 0-07-053413-6

The sponsoring editor for this book was Simon Yates and the production supervisor was Pamela A. Pelton. It was set in Vendome by Multiscience Press, Inc.

Printed and bound by R. R. Donnelley and Sons Company.

McGraw-Hill books are available at special quantity discounts to use as premiums and sales promotions, or for use in corporate training programs. For more information, please write to the Director of Special Sales, McGraw-Hill, 11 West 19th Street, New York, NY 10011. Or contact your local bookstore.

 This book is printed on recycled, acid-free paper containing a minimum of 50% recycled de-inked fiber.

All brand names and product names are the trademarks, registered trademarks, or trade names of their respective holders.

This book is dedicated to my parents, John and Patricia Roese. The work ethic and values they have instilled in me have made this project possible.

CONTENTS

PREFACE

Over the past several years, the Local Area Network (LAN) has become easily the single most critical company resource. It has evolved from a simple basic system to an extremely high capacity communications lifeline of business. This evolution has been driven by the increased complexity and communications demands of the applications we use daily: e-mail, databases, video conferencing, and so forth. As the demands for bandwidth capacity increased, the traditional legacy equipment used to build the LAN became overburdened. Attempts were made to increase capacity, but it has become obvious that even enhancements to the existing hub and router technology will not be enough. The result of this analysis has led to a fundamental change in the implementation of local area networks. It has led to the implementation of switch-based LANs.

Switched LANs: Implementation, Operation, Maintenance provides system administrators, network planners, and network technicians with a comprehensive overview of the technology involved in implementing switched LANs. This book examines the major issues involved in successfully designing and building large-scale switched systems. Unlike typical networking texts that focus on one element of the network system—a protocol or IEEE standard, for instance—this book addresses the complete system. Basic physical operation of the switched LAN is discussed, but the real focus is on the practical issues involved in structuring your network and its protocols and services for long-term successful operation.

The primary reason I have developed this book is simple. There has been a shift in the basic building blocks of LANs away from hubs and routers and towards switch-based systems. While the shift is underway, if not complete, the mind set and knowledge base of the networking community are still focused on the assumptions made in legacy networks. As a technology trainer tasked with providing my students with the skills necessary to implement and support quality networks, I have come to realize that there is a very real requirement for reference material and guides to assist in the reeducation of those transitioning from router- and hub-based networks to switch-based networks. My goal is to take my experience with switched network operation and codify the major areas of concern in an organized reference. I have personally dealt with the issues involved in implementing switch-based systems and "flattening" networks (flattening a network is the process of removing

some or all of the router-based protocol segmentation). More importantly, my position has allowed me to experience and identify the potential
implementation issues of switched networks and their solutions. Your
network is not a laboratory; it is a critical element of your business. As
such it is important to use proven implementation processes and have a
complete understanding of them when deploying switches into your
LAN. It is my sincere hope that *Switched LANs: Implementation, Operation,
Maintenance* will provide that knowledge and assist you in successfully
deploying and operating your switch-based network.

Acknowledgments

I would like to acknowledge and thank the many talented individuals
who have assisted me in the process of creating this book—specifically,
John Gorsky for his insight on network layer protocols; Mark Danckert,
Robert Allende, and the many other innovators of this technology that I
have worked with; and David Williams for his assistance in reviewing
the network management chapters. This topic is entirely new in the networking industry, and without the assistance of my colleagues, who
have led the way in switched LAN implementation, it would have been
impossible to provide the comprehensive proven processes contained
herein.

John J. Roese
(jjr@ctron.com)

INTRODUCTION

Designing, implementing, and operating networks is not simple. As the network becomes a more and more critical component of the business operations of almost every company, understanding its operation has become essential for system administrators. Unfortunately, with organizations' increased dependence on their networks come additional requirements for performance and reliability. Those additional demands have led to the implementation of far more complex networks. This book is devoted to a recent trend in network design: the Switched Local Area Network. In this book, you will find a complete reference for implementing a switched LAN. We will examine topics ranging from the definition and operation of LAN switches to proper methods of implementing several thousand node-switched networks. By examining the major aspects of switched LAN operation, implementation, and design a system administrator or network planner should have the necessary reference material to understand the compete switched LAN system.

The audience of this book is assumed to be familiar with the basic concepts of networking. If the reader is not familiar with the operation of core LAN technologies such as Ethernet or Internet protocols, the bibliography identifies appropriate reference material on the topics necessary for use of this book.

This book can be used in a number of ways, depending on readers' goals. If the goal is to understand switched LANs, it is recommended that the entire book be read in order. Reading this book in order will introduce the technology used in switched LANs and then provide design and implementation processes. The book examines the operation of specific protocols in switched LANs and concludes with additional assorted topics dealing with other miscellaneous features and tasks associated with building or operating a switched LAN. This sequence allows a reader who is unfamiliar with switched LANs to learn the basics before more complex protocol-related topics are introduced.

For current administrators of switched LANs, the book can be used as a reference guide. Most chapters are designed to stand alone and can be examined independently. If the reader is, for example, interested in the operation of a particular protocol over a switched LAN, or is planning the management strategy of a switched LAN, he or she should examine those specific chapters directly.

CHAPTER 1

LAN Switching
Defined

The word *switch* is possibly one of the most widely used terms in networking today. There are LAN switches, ATM switches, layer three switches, frame relay switches, phone switches, and many others. Unfortunately, the term *switch* has not been clearly defined in such a way as to fully define a type of device that accurately describes each of the technologies found in these various switches. Before a discussion of LAN switching can begin, an understandable definition of the term *switch* is necessary.

In order to freely use a definition of the term *switch* in describing the various types of switches, the definition must be suitably broad. It must also provide enough description of the components needed to be defined as a switch to be useful in comparison of various switching technologies. With these concerns in mind, the following definition of the term *switch* is proposed: *switch*—a device consisting of two components, input/output interfaces, and forwarding logic, capable of relaying data elements such as packets and cells.

This definition is illustrated in Figure 1.1.

This basic model of a switch provides a broad description of any type of switch. The two primary components are the forwarding logic and the input/output ports. The forwarding logic component describes the rules used by the switch technology to forward data units (packets and cells). These rules can be as simple as the transparent bridging mechanism used in LAN switches or as complex as those used by a multiprotocol router. The input/output ports are the physical or logical interfaces that connect to the communications network requiring data unit relaying. Examples include simple physical interfaces, such as LAN technologies including Ethernet, Token Ring, and FDDI. They can also include more abstract logical interfaces, such as emulated ATM LANs and fractionalized T1 interfaces. Even though this definition is very

Figure 1.1

Basic switch model.

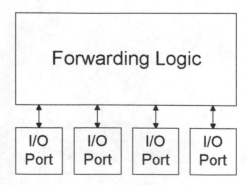

TABLE 1.1

Some Assorted
Switching
Technologies

Switch Type	Forwarding Logic	Input/Output Ports
ATM switch	Cell switching: virtual path and virtual circuit identifier remapping	OC-3/12/48 interfaces, T1/3, E1/3, TAXI, 25meg, fiber-optic and copper media
LAN switches	Transparent bridging (source address table)	Ethernet, Token Ring, FDDI, ATM ELANs, various WAN interfaces, spread spectrum, and other wireless technologies
Routers (layer three switches)	Protocol-based forwarding (network reachability)	Ethernet, Token Ring, FDDI, ATM ELANs, various WAN interfaces, spread spectrum, and other wireless technologies
Frame relay switches	DLCI forwarding	Various WAN interfaces

broad, it provides a framework in which different switching technologies can be evaluated. Table 1.1 describes the input/output ports and forwarding logic found in a variety of networking devices, all called switches.

Each of these technologies provides data relaying in its own way. Routers forward data based on protocol, while ATM switches care only about the VCI/VPI indicator in the header of the ATM cells. It is also true that many of these technologies share the same physical or logical input/output ports—for example, both LAN switches and routers can connect to Ethernet networks even though they do not share the same forwarding logic. Because they all meet the basic switch definition, all these technologies are correct in considering themselves switches.

The remainder of this chapter will focus primarily on one particular switch type: the LAN switch. This type of switch makes up the majority of local area networking switch ports. This technology, while not new, is allowing LANs to scale in size far beyond what was previously possible. We will first examine exactly what a LAN switch is and how it operates. We will then examine additional features, beyond the basic LAN switch definition, found in many LAN switches. The final section of this chapter will deal with the concept of layer three switching in terms of what it is and how it differs from LAN switching.

Basic Model of the LAN Switch

LAN switches are operationally equivalent to transparent bridges. That statement may offend some in the industry, but it is a fact. LAN switches forward data based on the mechanisms defined in the IEEE 801.1D specifications. This standard defines fundamental bridge operation, including elements such as source address tables, spanning tree algorithm, and transparent operation. Since both LAN switches and bridges adhere to the same architectural standard, they are operationally equivalent. It seems that in the networking industry, the term *bridge* became an offensive term, and all new bridges based on faster forwarding logic and having higher port density suddenly became known as switches, or LAN switches. This change in terminology caused a great deal of confusion in the industry, as system administrators and network planners struggled to understand what was different about these new switches and the "older" bridges. In reality, the only real noticeable difference was that these new switches were simply much larger, faster bridges. For the purposes of this book, the term *LAN switch* is used to describe a switch using the general forwarding rules defined in IEEE 801.1D.

Components

There are two major components to any switch. They are forwarding logic and input/output ports. Depending on the type of LAN switch, the input/output ports will vary to provide interfaces into many types of physical networks. Regardless of the physical input/output ports, the forwarding logic of all LAN switches will remain constant. It would be correct to state that it is the forwarding logic that defines the type of switch, rather than the physical interfaces.

Forwarding Logic Operation

The forwarding logic of a LAN switch is defined in IEEE 801.1D. The term used to describe the overall process is known as *transparent bridging*. This term refers to the fact that the forwarding logic should be transparent to the devices on the network. To understand how LAN switches can be technically invisible to the devices utilizing it, an understanding

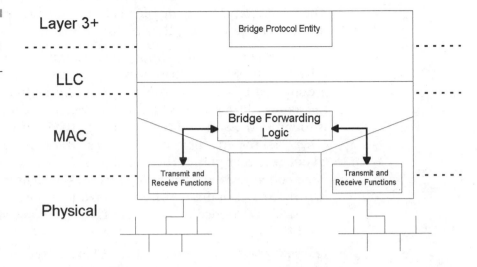

Figure 1.2

LAN switch (bridge)
logical model.

of the basic forwarding logic of the switch is needed. Figure 1.2 illustrates the logical model of the LAN switch (or bridge).

In this model, the switch is defined against the first three layers of the OSI model. Its basic operation is at layer two in the relaying of MAC layer packets. It must also have layer one physical interfaces to connect to the LAN and WAN technologies it is located between and must have a higher-layer existence to facilitate its management operations, such as the spanning tree algorithm discussed later in this chapter. The forwarding logic component exists at layer two and is illustrated in Figure 1.3.

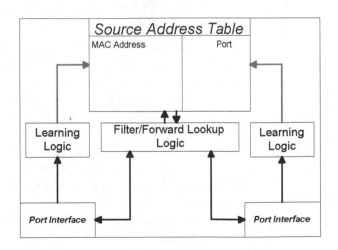

Figure 1.3

LAN switch (bridge)
forwarding logic.

There are several key components in the forwarding logic of a LAN switch, as defined in the following list.

Forward/filter logic: This component decides the fate of all packets received by the switch. When packets are seen, the destination address is examined by the forwarding logic and compared to the entries in the source address table (SAT). If the destination address of the packet is found in the SAT and the location of the destination is on a port other than the one the packet was received on, the packet is forwarded out only that port. If the SAT shows that the destination is on the same port as the current packet, this packet is filtered by discarding it. If the SAT contains no information about the destination address, the packet is flooded out all ports. These processes are shown in Figure 1.4.

Learning logic: The source address table is a dynamic entity. When the switch is first initialized, it contains no information about MAC addresses on the LAN. The learning logic enables the switch to gather end-system MAC addresses and locations to populate the SAT. This learning is done on every packet received, regardless of whether the packet will be ultimately filtered or forwarded. On each received packet, the learning logic examines the source address and either adds a new entry to the source address table for that end-system MAC address and its corresponding port or updates the aging timer for an existing entry for that MAC address.

Port interface: This component is the logical interface into the physical port. At the port interface all layer one and two packet functions are performed. These include packet translations between technologies and interfacing into the MAC layer rules of the technologies.

Source address table: LAN switches are able to intelligently control packet flow based on this table. The format of the table consists of a list of MAC addresses of end systems and the associated port where they were last heard. The table is populated by the learning logic and is then utilized by the forward and filter logic to decide the fate of any received packet. Entries in this table have an associated age, which, when expired, allows the switch to discard that MAC address information. This table defines the capability of the switch. Since the table is limited in size, that size limits the particular LAN switch to deployments on LANs with a total MAC address count of less than or equal to the source address table (or SAT). This concept will be discussed in Chapter 3.

Figure 1.4 shows the three options the LAN switch forwarding logic uses to determine the action to be taken with any packet. If the destination is known and is on a different port than the received packet, forwarding takes place. If the destination is on the same port that received the packet, filtering takes place. Finally, if the destination is unknown, the packet is flooded out to all interfaces. This flooding mechanism allows LAN switches to deliver packets to devices that have not communicated yet and as such are not placed in the SAT by the learning logic.

The forwarding logic of the LAN switch allows for two very significant features: transparent operation and plug-and-play operation. The forwarding logic is transparent in its operation, based on the fact that the switch forwards layer two packets without modification to the MAC layer destination either deliberately or by flooding. Since the original packet is delivered, the destination has no indication that a switch has handled the packet. This feature is very desirable, as it allows the switch to exist in a LAN without any end-system configuration requirements. The second feature of LAN switch forwarding logic is its plug-and-play configuration. Since the learning logic of the forwarding logic will automatically populate the SAT as MAC addresses are seen, there is no configuration needed to add a LAN switch to the network. In fact,

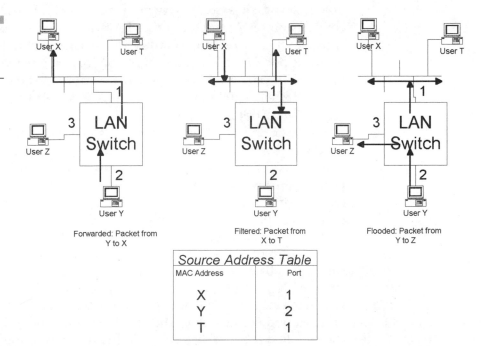

Figure 1.4

Forwarding logic options.

the longer a LAN switch exists on a network, the more intelligent it becomes, based on the information its learning logic has collected.

Input/Output Ports

The second major component of the LAN switch is its input/output ports. LAN switches are utilized in most situations to connect layer two networks together. Since there are many types of layer two networks, there are a great variety of physical interfaces available on LAN switches. What is significant about the input/output ports is not the wide variety available but the fact that the basic forwarding logic is unchanged, regardless of the physical interfaces to which it attaches. This book will not examine the various physical layer technologies that LAN switches can attach to, since there are many excellent books available on those subjects. Instead, we will examine two roles of interfaces that LAN switches must usually support. The two categories are termed *access* and *network uplink ports.*

Access ports are the physical interfaces a switch uses to connect to end systems on the LAN. The majority of any LAN switch's interfaces will be used in the access role. These ports must connect to the same LAN technology as the end system. Network uplink ports are those ports that will connect the LAN switch to other LAN switches in the switch fabric. It is usually desirable to have a higher-capacity technology used on the network ports than on access ports, because the network ports will be required to potentially transport the combined traffic of many access ports to other switches in the fabric. An example of this concept of access and network ports is shown in Figure 1.5.

The basic definition of a port used as a network uplink is that it must have adequate bandwidth capacity to forward the combined traffic from several of the switch's access ports. The definition of the access ports is simply that they must connect the switch, using the correct technology, to end systems or shared segments. Depending on the role a switch is to play in the network, the number of access and network uplink interfaces will vary.

The concepts of network uplink and access ports are purely logical, since it is absolutely possible to connect a server or end system to the 100Base-FX port of the switch in Figure 1.5 or even connect another switch to one of the 10Base-T interfaces. Generally these configurations are not good practice, since they could create bandwidth bottlenecks in the switched fabric. What is significant about defining ports as network

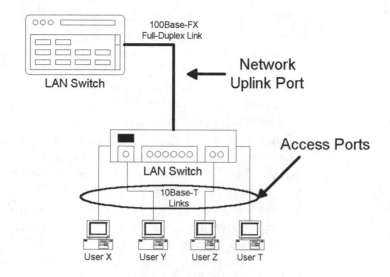

uplinks or access ports is that by identifying the roles of each, a proper switch can be utilized in areas requiring a known number of uplinks and end-system connections. If you were building a large switch-based network, you would wish to have core switches with mainly network ports, while your periphery switches may require only one network up-link interface.

Advantages of LAN Switches

Now that the basic forwarding logic of a LAN switch is understood, this device's role in networks today should be examined. LAN switches are now the primary building block of networks. The primary reason for this role is based on their transparent ability to increase capacity of a network for unicast communication. In Figure 1.4, it was seen that the LAN switch is able to make intelligent decisions about where a packet should be sent. As a replacement for the traditional Ethernet repeaters, which were the primary building blocks of networks in the past, the switch is able to keep communication between users away from other users on the network. The repeater did not have this capability, since its role was to assure that every device on a shared segment saw every pack-et. Since the cost of a switched port is not significantly higher than the cost of repeated ports, network planners are deploying LAN switches for direct connection to the end users on their networks. The LAN switches can also be used for connection between shared segments, but the industry direction is moving more towards direct user connection to a switch port.

The other appeal of LAN switches, beyond their ability to segment user traffic and increase capacity of the network, is the fact that these advantages are gained transparently. Routers provided segmentation of the network in the past, but they did so by forcing the end users to implement specific protocols and configurations in order to comply with the router-based hierarchy. This hierarchy was made up of the logical protocol-specific networks and subnetworks that formed the logical routed network. This is best seen by the fact that an end system wishing to speak to a particular protocol in a routed network must have a valid logical address. If the end system is misconfigured with the wrong logical network address, the routers will not deliver that system's packets correctly. Because the routers absolutely required that all end systems be configured with the proper logical address in order to coexist with the routed network, the routers forced the end systems to be configured to map to their place in the routed network. Once the routers were placed in a network, all devices, including both end systems and routers, were required to implement additional configurations in order to operate. Adding routers to a LAN did not just add router configuration complexity, it added additional configuration complexity to every end system. This end-user knowledge of routers made the use of routers for segmentation very time consuming and administrative intensive. With LAN switches, their operation is in layer two of the OSI model, so they are protocol independent and their operation is essentially transparent to the end users. To test this concept, add a LAN switch between two devices on your network and observe that its presence is not known to the end users and no network configuration is needed. Try the same test with a router and observe that if you don't complete the entire router and end-system configuration correctly, the users cease to communicate. Because the LAN switch brings significant performance and capacity improvement to a network without significant network reconfiguration, it is a very appealing element in almost all networks today.

Topology Rules

A LAN switch, based on 801.1D bridging technology, is governed by certain topology rules. These rules relate to the switch's forwarding logic operations not being able to understand multiple active paths in a LAN.

To understand this limitation, it is necessary to examine the operation of a LAN switch in a system that contains more than one path between segments.

Start with the switch topology illustrated in Figure 1.6. Two LAN switches are placed in parallel between two segments. Given the SATs of the switches as shown, when user X sends a packet to user Y, the switches on the local segment will learn the location of the source user by MAC address, X.

Based on the forwarding logic of each switch, the packet from X to Y must be flooded, as their SATs do not know the location of the destination. Figure 1.7 shows that one of the switches will flood the packet onto the other segment first—based on the access method of the second segment.

At this point, the original packet from X to Y is present on the second segment. That segment contains users, but it also contains the other switch. The second switch will see this packet and will examine it. During the learning process, the switch will add the source address of the packet to the SAT, indicating that user X is now on the second port of the switch. This information is incorrect, but the switch has no way of knowing that. Figure 1.8 shows this result.

Figure 1.6

Switch topology with parallel switches.

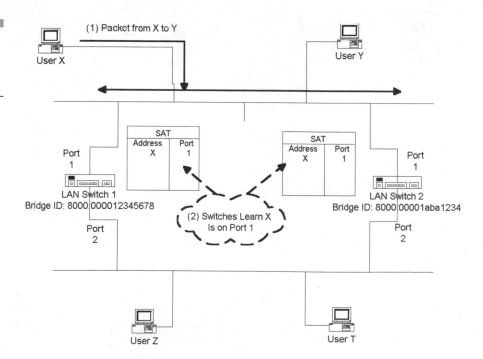

Figure 1.7

Packet flooded
onto second
segment.

Figure 1.7

Packet flooded
onto second
segment.

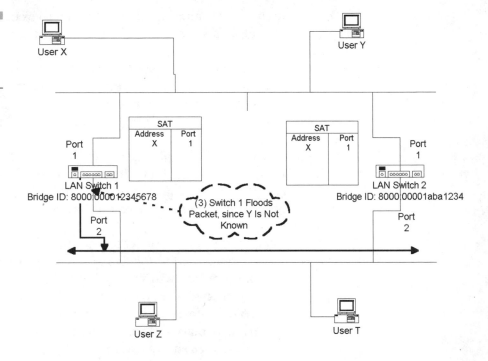

Figure 1.8

Incorrect source
address table
because of the
loop.

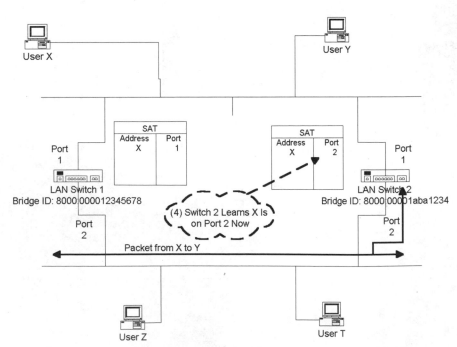

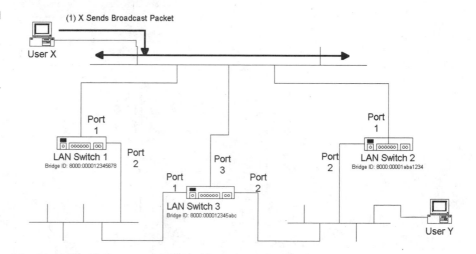

Figure 1.9

Broadcast sent into
a switched LAN
with several paths.

While this is obviously a potential problem, since the switches will
not have valid information in their source address tables, there is a far
worse impact to this configuration. In this and in more complex topologies the presence of broadcast packets can completely halt an SAT-
based switched network if loops are allowed to persist. Figure 1.9 shows
a configuration of switches with several paths that receives a broadcast
packet.

When the switches see the packet, they will all flood the packet to
their other ports. The logic for this is simply based on the fact that packets to unknown destinations are always flooded out to all other interfaces. Since a broadcast address can never be a source of a packet, the
learning logic will never add such an address to the SAT. As such, all
broadcasts and multicast packets are always flooded, just as unknown
destination unicast packets are. Since the packet will then be seen by
other interfaces of other switches on those segments, the packet is flooded out to more interfaces. Figure 1.10 shows the immediate result of the
broadcast being forwarded into the switched LAN.

Figure 1.10 shows that the broadcast is flooded by all three switches
into the lower segments, creating multiple copies of the packet on those
segments. The copies are then flooded back to the upper segment. This
process continues indefinitely, as the switches cannot filter the broadcast packets. Each time the packets are flooded, more copies are seen and
in just a short period of time the entire network is saturated with broadcast packets. In a minimal amount of time, the entire LAN stops functioning, because all bandwidth is occupied by the looping broadcast

Figure 1.10

Result of broadcast
packet sent into
multipath switched
LAN.

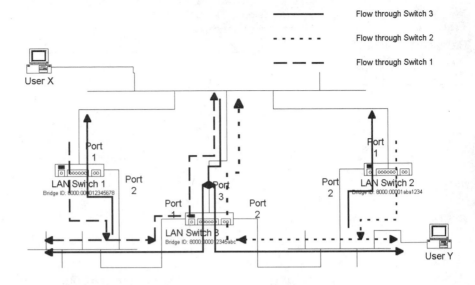

packets. This event could be considered a "broadcast storm" in the real sense of the term.

It is obvious that this type of event cannot be allowed to occur. In order to make this type of situation impossible, the 801.1D committee developed an algorithm to do one thing: Remove any loops in a bridged/switched LAN. That algorithm is known as the spanning tree algorithm. By eliminating loops in the network, there is no possibility of packets recirculating in the network.

The spanning tree algorithm, or STA, works on a simple principle. The network will build a single loop-free tree from some identified point known as the root. This single tree will be the data path for all traffic. Since it contains no loops but ultimately reaches all segments, it does not isolate or prevent any communication.

STA follows a simple set of processes to achieve this loop-free topology. The first process involves electing a root bridge on the LAN. In order to do this, all STA bridges/switches send out packets known as bridge protocol data units, or BDPUs. These messages are sent out to all interfaces every two seconds by default (a tunable parameter). They include information about the bridge and its configuration. The content of a BPDU is shown in Figure 1.11.

The BPDU message is transmitted in a MAC layer packet from the bridge/switch's source address to a specific destination multicast address. BPDUs operate using IEEE 802.2 LLC using an SAP value of 41. The first few fields are not really utilized (protocol type, version, and message

▬▬ ▬▬ ▬▬ ▬▬
Figure 1.11

Spanning tree
bridge protocol
data unit.

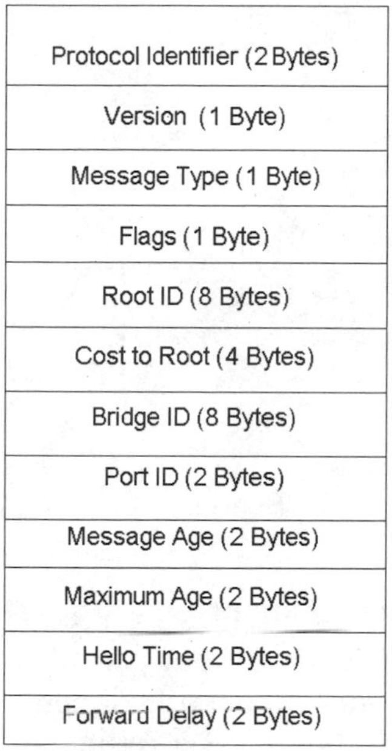

Protocol Identifier (2 Bytes)
Version (1 Byte)
Message Type (1 Byte)
Flags (1 Byte)
Root ID (8 Bytes)
Cost to Root (4 Bytes)
Bridge ID (8 Bytes)
Port ID (2 Bytes)
Message Age (2 Bytes)
Maximum Age (2 Bytes)
Hello Time (2 Bytes)
Forward Delay (2 Bytes)

type) at this time. The flags include several indicators related to topology changes. These are not very significant in understanding the spanning tree.

The interesting fields begin with the root ID. It is an eight-byte value, which indicates the current root bridge on the network. Its format includes two sections. The first is the bridge priority (two bytes) and the second is the bridge MAC address. These two fields combine to form the bridge identifier of the root bridge. The next field is the cost of the path to root. This field indicates the cost of the path from the bridge sending the BPDU to the root bridge indicated in the root ID field. Cost is based on the bandwidth of the links in the path to root. Generally, the higher the bandwidth of a link, the lower its cost.

The next fields, the bridge ID and port ID, indicate the bridge sending this BPDU and the port from where it was transmitted. Additionally, the port ID includes a port priority value. Following these fields is the information about the age of the BPDU and how old information should be allowed to get before a bridge discards it. The final fields indicate how often these messages are to be sent and how long a bridge is to remain in the listening and learning states before the bridge begins forwarding data.

Figure 1.12

BPDU transmission.

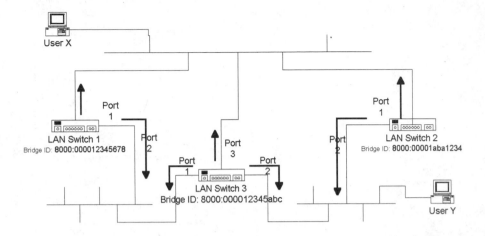

These BDPUs are used first to elect a root bridge on the LAN. The election is done as part of the normal transmission of BPDUs every two seconds by default. When a bridge first comes on line, it sends out BP-DUs indicating it is the root bridge. Since there may be other bridges on the network and only one root is needed, the bridges must decide which one is to be the root. Comparing the BPDUs received on a bridge's ports with their own configuration does this. In Figure 1.12, each of the LAN switches is sending out BPDUs on all of their interfaces.

As each of the LAN switches sees the BPDUs of other bridges on the segments, it must compare the contents to determine the root. The criteria for determining the root are based on comparing the root ID in the BPDU. If the received BPDU has a lower root ID, then it wins. If the

Figure 1.13

Switch 1 to switch 3 comparison for STA.

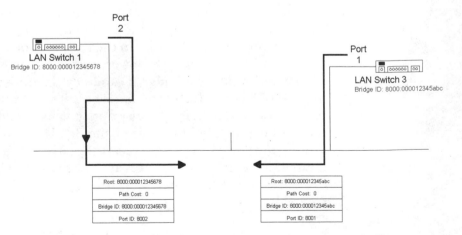

Figure 1.14

Switch 2 and switch
3 BPDU comparison.

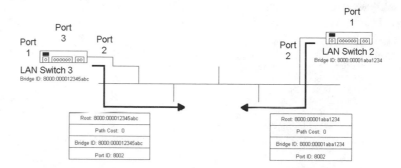

root ID is tied, then the cost to root is used, with the lower cost winning. If the cost is also tied, then the bridge ID of each bridge is compared, with the lower number winning. Finally, if all these are ties, the port ID field is used to break the tie, with the lower number winning. In most cases, the root ID, cost, and bridge ID should be enough to determine the root bridge and the shape of the spanning tree.

As an example, the network in Figure 1.12 would need several comparisons to determine the spanning tree. Figure 1.13 shows the BPDUs (in simplified form) sent between LAN switch 1 and LAN switch 3.

In this comparison, switch 1 has itself as the root ID with a value of 8000:000012345678, while switch 3 sees itself as the root with an ID of 8000:00001245abc. Since switch 1's root ID is lower, it wins this comparison. Now switch 3 and switch 2 compare their BPDUs. This comparison is seen in Figure 1.14.

In this comparison, switch 3 has a lower numerical root ID with 8000:000012345abc and as such wins this comparison. Recall though that we have already seen that switch 1 will win against switch 3. The final area to examine for comparison is the upper segment containing ports from all three switches. In Figure 1.15, that segment is displayed.

In this comparison, the root ID of switch 1 is lower than the other two switches. It will become the root switch on this LAN. At this time, the spanning tree must determine the single path to root from each segment. The spanning tree eliminates loops by forcing all parallel bridges to identify one active bridge with the other bridge ports on a given segment being placed in blocking mode. The bridges determine which one will be active by the same election process used to determine the root bridge. Now, each segment will identify a designated bridge for that segment based on cost to root and bridge ID. The final spanning tree configuration is seen in Figure 1.16.

Figure 1.15

Switches 1, 2, and 3 compared for STA.

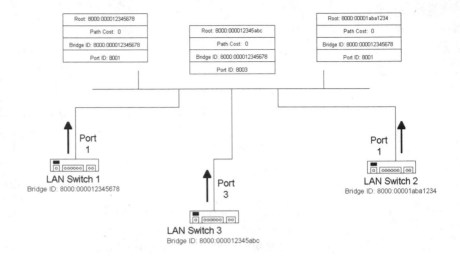

Note that switch 1 is the root bridge. As such it becomes the designated bridge for all segments it is attached to, because its cost to root is zero. That leaves the lower right-hand side segment with a need for a designated bridge. Switch 2 and switch 3 both have an equal cost to root. Using bridge ID, switch 3 becomes the designated switch, since its ID is lower than switch 2's. At that time, switch 2 places its second port into blocking mode to eliminate that possible loop. When the topology has finished spanning, the result is a network having a single path to all segments originating from the root. This path may not be the ideal conversation route for users such as X and Y, but it is absolutely necessary that

Figure 1.16

Final STA configuration.

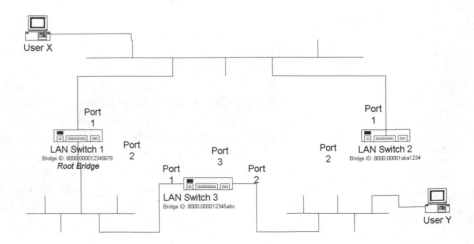

this be done. Without STA, the transparent bridging of these LAN switches would not function, as discussed previously.

The spanning process, known as listening, usually occurs in about 15 seconds. For the next 15 seconds, the switches will not forward data. This is known as the learning phase, in which they attempt to populate their SAT so there will be less flooding when they actually begin forwarding data. Once the network has spanned, several ports are in a mode called blocking. Once the switches begin forwarding, STA does not stop. Every two seconds (by default) each switch will generate BPDUs on all interfaces. These BPDUs are used to maintain the spanning tree and detect topology changes. If a switch leaves the network, the absence of its BPDUs will cause the network to respan to account for this topology change. During this topology change, the network forwarding operation of the switches is suspended.

In summary, the bridge/switch-based spanning tree algorithm provides a mechanism to protect these devices from loops in the network. The need for this protection is based on the fact that the bridges/switches forward data based on the contents of the source address table. Since this table can only understand each device existing through a single interface, loops are not allowed. While STA eliminates bridge loops very effectively, it does so at the expense of prohibiting communication through parallel paths. This limits the overall available bandwidth to that of a single path to the root of the network. The spanning tree algorithm can be viewed as a mechanism to create a single active data path, with other paths being placed in a nonactive, but redundant, state.

Additional Vendor Enhancements to LAN Switches

Most LAN switches operate in the manner described previously. The basic transparent bridge mode operation is functional in small-to-medium-sized LANs, but it may not scale to support large, active switched networks without some enhancements. Since 801.1D has not significantly evolved to address large-scale switched LANs, vendors of switches have added proprietary features to their devices to allow better scalability and control of switched LANs. Even though these enhancements are proprietary, they are usually necessary. If you have concerns about implementing any feature that is proprietary, you should evaluate the product feature carefully. If the feature prevents the switches from transparently delivering user data or will not operate with existing protocol stacks, then the feature may impact your network operation based on its proprietary nature. On the other hand, if the feature does operate and deliver data transparently to your users, regardless of protocol stack, then the implementation of this feature should be allowed, since it is providing a benefit without real cost. It is important to recognize that all networks have some proprietary components present in them. The key is to utilize only those proprietary components that add significant value to the network operation but appear transparent to the user community. This section will examine some of the proprietary enhancements to LAN switches widely implemented today.

Port Trunking

It is obvious that the spanning tree topologies may not be able to provide enough raw bandwidth to handle all traffic flowing through some parts of the switched LAN. The core of any switched LAN may aggregate hundreds of 10-megabit and 100-megabit links. In such a network, if spanning tree is in use and the core switches are to be connected using full-duplex 100-megabit links, this may not be enough bandwidth. This concept is shown in Figure 1.17. The core of the network, consisting of two large LAN switches, is oversubscribed, given the number of uplinks coming from other switches. With only one full-duplex 100-megabit

Figure 1.17

Oversubscribed LAN core.

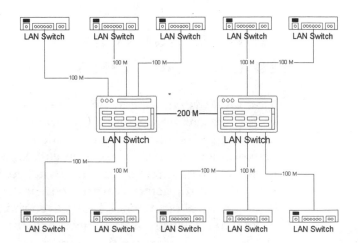

link (200 megabit total capacity) linking the switches, it is possible that not all traffic moving from one side of the network to the other will be able to be transported through the link. If this issue were addressed by simply adding another link between the core switches, the results would be the same, since the spanning tree algorithm would place one of the core switch ports into blocking mode to eliminate the loop.

A possible solution to this very real issue is to manipulate the topology rules of the network slightly by introducing a technology known as port trunking. Port trunking is a mechanism by which several physical links are made to appear as a single link to the spanning tree algorithm. The mechanisms to do this are very different, depending on the vendor, and are generally not supported on all LAN switches. Since no standard mechanism exists for port trunking, it is usually vendor specific. As such, only switches from the same vendor can connect using port trunking.

In the case of the network shown in Figure 1.17, port trunking between the two core switches may allow the initial bandwidth bottleneck to be relieved. If the core switches supported some form of port trunking, several 100-megabit links could be trunked together to allow more traffic to traverse the core network. Figure 1.18 shows this configuration.

The one concern regarding the use of port trunking is that all implementations are vendor specific. Most major switch vendors offer some form of trunking technology. The configuration and services provided by the vendor's trunking method will vary significantly. Some vendors will provide mechanisms for combining several ports using a manual

Figure 1.18

Port trunking to eliminate backbone congestion.

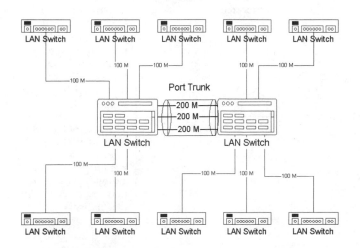

configuration method, while others may provide more automated methods. It is important to understand exactly what the characteristics of any vendor's trunking technology are. Table 1.2 lists several considerations comparing trunking schemes.

TABLE 1.2

Criteria Used in Evaluating Vendor-Specific Trunking Technologies

Consideration	Notes
Number of links in each trunk?	Most trunking technologies have some limit in the number of physical links that can be supported inside a single port trunk between two switches. If the number supported is low, the technology may not provide enough capacity for future LAN traffic growth.
Number of trunk groups per switch?	It may be necessary to trunk to several peer switches in the network. If the trunking technology only supports a small number of trunk groups per switch, that technology may prevent proper core network construction. In most cases, only one or two trunk groups are needed on any switch.
Configuration interface?	Is the trunking configuration interface simple to use? Some trunking technologies are plug and play, while others require complex command-line-driven configuration. While the configuration interface should not be the only factor in determining the technology to use, it is significant, since a complex interface requires more time and training expense to use.
Physical interfaces supported?	Does the trunking technology support the physical interfaces required? If your network requires an FDDI core because of distance requirements, for example, the trunking technology must operate over FDDI. Most vendors' trunking will support fast Ethernet. If your network requires 10 megabit Ethernet, FDDI, Token Ring, or any other technology in trunk groups, verify that the vendor's mechanism supports this.
Mesh topology?	While most trunking technologies are limited to two switches directly connected together and are still limited to a single spanning tree topology, some vendors are introducing more advanced topologies. If a single spanning tree significantly affects your network design, evaluate vendors offering alternative mechanisms that support more meshed topologies.

Port Mirroring

Port mirroring defines a troubleshooting and monitoring tool for switched LANs. By adding switching to a LAN, the performance and capacity have dramatically increased, but the troubleshooting tools and interfaces used in shared access environments are also changed. In a shared access environment, common troubleshooting techniques involve use of LAN analyzers on segments with problems. These analyzers can capture all communication on the segment to allow the troubleshooter some insight into the operation of the segment. In switched LANs (especially those utilizing per port switching with each user on a dedicated switch port), the analyzer cannot gather all packets, as the filtering operation of the LAN switch is designed to keep packets not destined to a port from being transmitted out of that port.

Most vendors offer a tool known as port mirroring, or traffic redirection, to examine the data traversing a switched LAN. These tools allow the troubleshooter to redirect traffic from a port or a user conversation to another location in the switched LAN for further analysis using any type of LAN analyzer. Since the technologies behind this process are all proprietary, the degree of functionality will be very different between vendors. In Table 1.3, several types of port mirroring technologies are listed, along with comments on their relative usefulness.

TABLE 1.3

*Some Port
Mirroring
Technologies*

Technology	Notes
Bit-level port mirror	This technology allows one or more ports on a switch to be redirected to another port on the same switch. This redirection is done at the bit level. Because of this, all packets are forwarded to the mirror port, including packets containing physical layer errors. This technology is generally redundant and less useful than other types of port mirrors for several reasons. First, the embedded remote monitoring (RMON) statistics on the switch (if it has them) will identify errors and other layer one issues, so there is no need to send the errors to another port to be logged by an external analyzer. The second reason this tool is less useful is that it can only copy bits from ports that share the same technology as the mirror port. It is not possible to perform a bit-level copy from a 100Base-T link to a 10Base-T segment, because the bits are physically different. The problem becomes more exaggerated when Token Ring and FDDI are introduced into the system.

TABLE 1.3

(continued)

Technology	Notes
Conversation taps	Some more advanced systems are offering the ability to mirror just a single conversation. This tool allows individual connections to be mapped to an analyzer port elsewhere on the network. This technology is usually able to redirect the conversation to any location on the LAN, not just the switch where the users are located. In order to use this type of tool, a new set of troubleshooting skills is needed, since this is radically different from the shared segment analysis methods used previously. Now, the troubleshooter must identify the conversation having the difficulty before looking for the packets involved. In the past, that process was reversed, with the entire segment being viewed and the results filtered to identify the potential problem communications.
Packet-level port mirror	This technology is used on most LAN switches for port mirroring. It allows the troubleshooter to redirect one or more ports' packets to a mirror port. Since the copy is done at the link layer, errors are not propagated and conversions from other technologies can take place. This port mirroring is generally limited mirroring from only one port on the switch to another port on the same switch. This tool can be useful, but, since it allows multiple ports to be mirrored to a single analyzer port, it can be subject to overload. Consider the situation in which three 10Base-T segments are mirrored to a single 10Base-T segment. If the sum of the traffic on the three ports exceeds 10 megabits per second, the mirror port will not be able to receive all the data. Additionally, consider the situation when a 100Base-T link is mirrored to a 10Base-T port. If the 100Base-T link operates at over 10 percent load, the mirror port will be saturated. It is critical that these limits be recognized when using port mirrors of any type.

Since each of the technologies listed in Table 1.3 is implemented as proprietary vendor-specific features, the availability of such features will depend on your particular vendor. It is critical that the vendor be able to provide some set of troubleshooting tools for use in the switched LAN. The more advanced the tools, the easier time you will have managing this LAN.

Alarm Limits

With the introduction of larger, flat-switched networks, the potential effect of a single station failing may be increased. These failures may be stations generating excessive invalid broadcasts and multicasts or may simply be excessive traffic generated from the station. When routers were segmenting LANs, single station failure would only affect the small number of users located in the same logical network or subnet bounded by the router interface. In a large switched network that router boundary is no longer present. It is possible to have thousands of users in one switched area. While the advantages of switched LANs include greatly simplified user configuration and extremely high performance levels, these advantages may not be justified if the switched LAN cannot provide some protection from station failure. To provide this protection, many vendors have introduced features known as alarm limits on their LAN switches.

An alarm limit is a simple mechanism in which the LAN switch monitors ports for various statistics, such as broadcast rate, errors, and so on. If that statistic reaches a certain level, known as an alarm limit, the switch can automatically take some defined action. Usually the actions include sending notification to a management console via an SNMP trap. More advanced switches can be configured not only to notify the network administrator but also to execute actions on the switch hardware. The typical actions include enabling and disabling the ports violating the threshold. An example of this type of alarm limit might be a switch that watched its ports for high broadcast rates. If the rate crosses that high-water mark, the switch disables the port and then notifies the administrator. If the high rate then stops, the switch can automatically reenable the port and also notify the administrator of this action. This type of proactive management operation allows the problem to be isolated immediately in order to protect the rest of the switched network. It also provides the administrator with a history of these events, so that the user on the port affected can be further troubleshot to determine the real cause of the high broadcast traffic.

It is very important to understand that the use of alarm limits requires proper networking baselining. If you are planning to use alarm limits on your network, it is highly recommended that you read Chapter 8, which discusses baselining and troubleshooting switched LANs. After you have baselined your LAN, you will be armed with the proper values against which you can set your alarm limits. If those values are wisely chosen for your LAN, the alarm limits feature of your switches can introduce a very effective management and fault protection tool into your network.

In evaluating switches with alarm limit features there are several components that should be examined. Table 1.4 lists the features and what functions they should contain.

Please refer to Chapter 8 for more information about how to set your alarm limits and how to properly implement thresholds. If they are not implemented correctly, there is a significant danger that they can gen-

TABLE 1.4

Alarm Limit
Characteristics

Feature	Notes
What statistics are monitored by the alarm limits?	It is important to monitor statistics that can cause potential problems on a switched LAN. These include broadcast rate, multicast rate, and traffic rate. It is also useful to monitor statistics that indicate error conditions and overload. These include traffic rate and error rates.
Does the alarm limit send notification when the limit is reached, and does the alarm limit interface offer the option of disabling the port affected?	Alarm limits require two actions in most cases. They must always notify the network administrator through a trap message. This is vital so that further troubleshooting can be performed as time allows. They should also allow the switch to automatically isolate the port experiencing the fault condition in order to restore the rest of the network.
If the alarm limit can disable ports reaching a threshold, can it also reenable them once the fault condition is finished?	Some more advanced alarm limits can reenable the ports once a falling threshold is reached that indicates the fault condition is no longer present. This tool is very useful in eliminating manual intervention once the failing device is removed from the network. Since the falling alarm should also generate a trap message to your network management platform, the rising alarm and falling alarm can be used together to indicate the duration of the failure.

erate excessive trap messages or even disable switch ports that are not experiencing any type of real fault condition.

Integrated RMON

Remote monitoring (RMON) is the single most useful tool in managing switched ports. The details of RMON are discussed in Chapter 10. If you are not familiar with RMON and how to utilize it, please refer to that chapter to gain an understanding of its capabilities. RMON provides a significant set of statistics for any switched segment that allow easy physical and data link layer troubleshooting via remote management. Since switches have extremely high port densities and are less and less connected to shared segments where RMON probes may exist, integration of the RMON probe into the switch is a vital addition.

Most LAN switches today implement some or all of the RMON version 1 groups. When evaluating a switch, however, it is important to understand that all nine groups of RMON version 1 are not necessary on all ports. Chapter 8 describes which groups should be used on which links in order to gain a complete understanding of the traffic and operational statistics on the switched LAN. In the implementation plan, it is shown that RMON statistics, history, alarms, and events groups should be implemented on all interfaces in order to monitor their stability and load characteristics. Periphery switches should also implement host, HostTopN, and matrix groups on their uplink ports into the core in order to track traffic matrixes from users to other resources, and packet capture and filter should be used on an as-needed basis near the resources under examination. The rationale for these suggestions is based on the fact that RMON was designed to gather local statistics on a single segment. Because LAN switches isolate unicast traffic from ports not involved in the conversation, an RMON probe at any one port cannot provide global information. Figure 1.19 shows a typical small switched LAN consisting of dedicated switch ports and shared segments.

In Figure 1.19, no one RMON probe can provide all information about all users. This is because each probe only monitors one segment, and, since each switch port is its own segment, the probe's data do not provide accurate information about multiple switch ports. It is best to always assume that an RMON probe has data that are only of local significance, which means that these data only relate to the users and links to which they are attached. Given this assumption, one matrix group implemented at each server port will tell us exactly what the traffic pat-

Figure 1.19

Example switched
network RMON
probes.

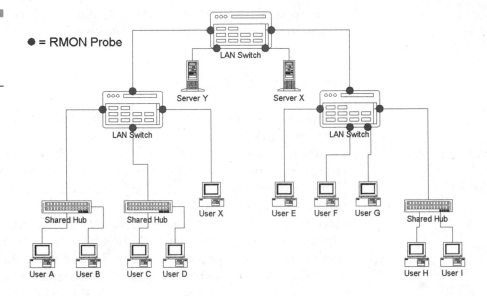

terns of all clients to that server are. Also, a host group at the uplink of the switches will provide host information of all traffic passing into or out of that switch involving all the users by MAC address on that switch. It should also be obvious that a host group on both interfaces on the interswitch links is not needed, since the data would be redundant. The key to proper RMON deployment is understanding what the groups provide and where the data are significant. Once that is known, choosing switches with the proper groups or deploying external RMON probes can be done intelligently.

Store and Forward versus Cut Through

When the term *switch* first emerged to describe high-density bridges, there was a very contentious debate about a new option to the basic forwarding logic of bridging. That option was called cut-through switching. Today, this debate is largely over, with cut-through switching being properly identified as a technology whose place is in low-end workgroup switching. Even though the debate is over, switches exist today using this feature, so an examination of its operation is worthwhile.

A traditional bridge/switch uses a forwarding logic known as store and forward. Using this logic, a bridge/switch will receive and buffer the entire packet before forwarding it on to its destination segment.

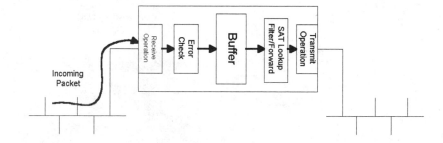

Figure 1.20

Store and forward logic.

This operation allows the bridge/switch to identify errored packets and discard them before they are delivered to other segments. This method also allows disparate technologies to be interconnected. By buffering the entire frame, it can be converted to other MAC layer media such as Token Ring, FDDI, and fast Ethernet. This basic process is shown in Figure 1.20.

In Figure 1.20, the process of store-and-forward logic is shown. Received packets are first error checked as they are fully buffered. Once in the packet buffer, the SAT is consulted to determine their destination and the complete packet is forwarded out of the appropriate port(s) or filtered. These processes are happening in series, with storing and error checking of the packet occurring before the forwarding logic is applied. This is beneficial in case the received packet has an error. If the error check fails, the packet is discarded at this switch without being seen by any other segments. This process usually takes an amount of time equal to the time needed to receive the entire packet (about .1 us per bit for 10 megabit Ethernet) plus a small delay due to the forwarding logic (typically measured at under 50 us). This is the standard forwarding logic choice of most switches today.

The other option introduced for switch forwarding logic is known as cut through. This option was meant to reduce the latency introduced into the communication by the store-and-forward logic. The way cut-through switching operates is by eliminating the complete buffering of the packets as they are switched. A cut-through switch will only store the header of the frame in order to determine its destination. At that point, the packet will be redirected to the correct out port. The result will be that even as the packet is being received on one port, earlier portions of the packet will be forwarded out of another interface. This results in only a small portion of the packet being buffered in the switch at any given time. Figure 1.21 illustrates this concept.

Figure 1.21

Cut-through
forwarding logic.

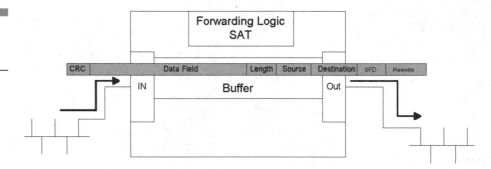

With cut-through switches, the entire packet is not buffered before forwarding begins. While this usually results in a much lower latency for a single packet forwarding operation than the store-and-forward option, this lack of buffering also eliminates the error isolation capabilities of switches. In Figure 1.21, if this packet contained an error, the cut-through switch would have already propagated the bad packet to other segments before it could examine the CRC (located at the end of the packet) to determine if it was a bad packet. This fundamental flaw of cut-through switches has generally resulted in them being excluded from roles in networks requiring fault tolerance and high reliability.

It should be noted that the makers of cut-through switches recognized this flaw and attempted to correct it with a modified cut-through algorithm. This algorithm calculates the CRC for all packets being switched in cut-through mode. If the calculation reveals that the switch has forwarded more than some defined threshold of bad packets to other segments, it reverts to store-and-forward operation until the bad packet rate drops below some other defined threshold. This may sound like a good solution, but, in reality, it still allows the switch to forward a reasonable number of bad packets to other segments before the store-and-forward mode becomes operational.

In general, the advantage of lower latency gained by cut-through switches is not significant enough to outweigh the harm caused by propagation of bad packets. The latency seen in store-and-forward switches is usually insignificant to any protocol, especially those using a windowing mechanism such as TCP and LLC2. The final reason for the lack of usefulness of cut-through switches is based on the fact that you cannot cut through between segments using different technologies or bandwidths. It is not possible to do cut-through switching between such combinations as Token Ring and Ethernet or Ethernet and FDDI.

These connections require frame translation, which must be done in buffers on the switch on the entire packet. Even more limiting is the fact that cut through does not work between different bandwidths. It is not possible to cut through between 10Base-T Ethernet and 100Base-T Ethernet. Even though the frame format is the same, the 100Base-T segment is delivering bits at ten times the rate of the 10Base-T segments. Simple math shows that the 10-megabit segment cannot provide enough bits to the 100-megabit link to build real packets.

In general, cut-through switches are used in small workgroup solutions where no uplink is required. In most cases these switches will be very inexpensive, based on the lack of large buffer memory. In real, large-scale switched LANs, the majority of switches will utilize store-and-forward switches only, since they provide the necessary error isolation and uplink capabilities to build a reliable, scalable switched LAN.

Virtual LANs

Virtual LANs (VLANs) will be covered in much greater detail in Chapter 9. While basic LAN switching does not deal with the concept of logical VLANs, it is important to recognize some of their potential values to your network design. Please refer to Chapter 9 for more detail on this topic.

Layer Three Switches

This book is about devices known as LAN switches. When we first defined the term *switch*, it was obvious that many devices can be called switches. The LAN switch is defined as a switch operating at layer two of the OSI model, following the same basic operation as defined by transparent bridging. This existence at layer two resulted in the device being transparent and high performance, because it was not concerned with the operation of upper-layer protocols. Understanding the operation of a LAN switch is fairly easy and implementing it into your network is also fairly simple. Unfortunately, vendors have once again confused the definition of LAN switching by introducing a vaguely defined new derivative called a layer three switch.

Definition

Layer three switches are defined generally as devices that forward data packets with knowledge of layer three and above protocols. If that definition sounds vague, it is. The term *layer three switch* has been applied to everything from LAN switches with some filtering capabilities to traditional routers. In fact, there are so many different types of devices known as layer three switches that it is not really possible to establish a functional model that fits the term. Instead, this section will examine several categories of devices, all calling themselves layer three switches. From this discussion, you should be able to identify the functions and role of the layer three switch a vendor offers.

Pure Routers

The first type of device that terms itself a layer three switch is the traditional router. It seems that routers have developed a bad name. The term *router* is usually and correctly, in most cases, associated with low performance. Since fundamental router operation is complex and will always be lower performance than LAN switching, the industry adopted the term *layer three switching* to describe what the router does. This term definitely sounds faster, but, in reality, the operation of the router/layer three switch has not changed. Figure 1.22 illustrates the process of moving data through a router.

The process of moving a packet from one port on a router to another is much more complex than the same process in a LAN switch. The main reason for this complexity is that the forwarding operations of routers are done in terms of layer three protocols such as IP, IPX, AppleTalk, and others. Figure 1.22 shows that when packets are received by a router, all MAC layer fields are removed, since they serve no purpose to the

Figure 1.22

Router forwarding logic abstraction.

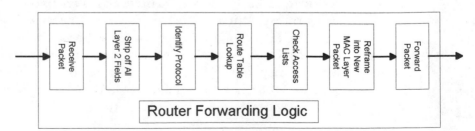

Receive Packet → Strip off All Layer 2 Fields → Identify Protocol → Route Table Lookup → Check Access Lists → Reframe into New MAC Layer Packet → Forward Packet

Router Forwarding Logic

router forwarding logic. Then the router must identify which protocol the packet contains. Every layer three protocol has a unique frame format and its own forwarding rules. Since routers usually handle many protocols, the router must determine which protocol this packet contains. Once the protocol is identified, the destination must be determined and a routing table calculation must be performed. Many high-end routers can cache these route table lookups to improve performance at this step. Once a destination has been determined, the router may apply any access lists or other policy or accounting services to the packet. Once all internal operations are complete, the router can build a new MAC layer packet and deliver it to the next hop in the path. Since the router is connectionless (treating each packet individually), this process must be repeated for every packet sent to any router interface.

By our basic definition of a switch, this is a switch. Its forwarding logic is based on protocol-specific rules, and it does have input and output ports. The significant issue is that this device is a router and not a LAN switch. As such, it suffers from higher latency and lower performance, and it does require specific protocol configuration before it operates (not plug and play). When a product is positioned as a layer three switch, a simple question can determine if it is really better termed a router: Does this layer three switch terminate the MAC layer communications in order to forward packets?

This question describes the fact that in traditional routers, the end users speak at layer two to the router's address even if the layer three communication is destined to a device located through the router. To identify traditional routing, simply examine the destination and source addresses of MAC layer packets involved in a conversation between two end users. If the MAC addresses used are not exclusively those of the two end devices, but instead include the MAC addresses of a device in the path, then that device is a router.

If the answer is yes, than the device is a router and should be considered one for the purposes of network design. If the answer is no, then the device is a LAN switch with some layer three services.

Embedded Routers

A second type of device defined as a layer three switch is those LAN switches with embedded router functions. What this really means is that the vendor has simply taken a LAN switch and placed a router in

Figure 1.23

Embedded routing
in a LAN switch.

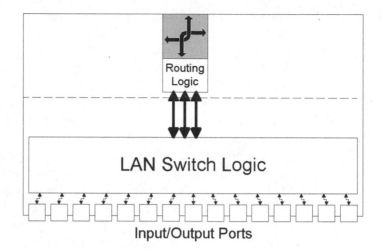

the same box. The device is both a LAN switch and a router. What determines which role it will play is based on who is communicating. If the communication is between users on the switch, the switch acts as a LAN switch and forwards at layer two. If the communication is between users in different logical areas or on different switches in some cases, the device acts as a router and routes the packets. This dual functionality makes it very difficult to design a large switched LAN. The switches with embedded routers act as routers and therefore limit the layer two communications, just as a stand-alone router would do. This type of switch is shown in Figure 1.23. Note that the device is really just a router embedded in the same case as a LAN switch.

This type of device usually supports a very simple set of routing services in its routing logic. Most vendors limit this type of switch to just routing IP, IPX, and maybe a few other protocols. By limiting the protocols, the vendor is able to optimize the routing logic in hardware to gain significant performance improvements over traditional, multiprotocol routers.

For the purpose of this book, this kind of switch should be treated as a router if any of its routing functions are applied to communication between ports in the switched fabric. If the device only acts as a router with respect to ports leaving or entering the switched fabric, it can be treated as a LAN switch.

Hybrid Layer Three Switches

The third category of layer three switches is those devices that are inherently layer two switches but utilize some layer three knowledge to make forwarding decisions. The key component in this kind of switch is that all communication is done at layer two, based on MAC layer address. The device does not manipulate the packet, other than necessary media type conversions, as it passes through the switch. Its layer three services are based on its ability to understand certain MAC layer broadcasts as specific layer three functions. It is then able to utilize the information contained in the layer three portion of the packet to make some decisions as to where the packet should be sent.

An example of this kind of logic would be a switch that recognizes IP ARP protocol and understands the layer three addresses of end systems and IP networks. This kind of switch could intercept the ARPs sent by IP devices and use the layer three information (the target IP address) to forward the packet to only that IP user. This kind of service can be added for any protocol as long as the switches can identify the protocol-based addresses of the end users and recognize the packets used to establish communication. This kind of hybrid LAN switch is to be considered a LAN switch for the purposes of this book, since it does not terminate the MAC layer conversations that pass through it. A simple illustration of this kind of hybrid operation is shown in Figure 1.24.

In Figure 1.24, the hybrid switch is shown to maintain some upper-layer understanding of the MAC layer end systems in the switched LAN. When the hybrid switch sees broadcasts, it is able to make more intelligent decisions about their destination. In this case, user X has ARPed for user 178.18.1.234. The switch is able to identify the ARP request and resolve it to only one of its switch ports—the one that has seen that IP address associated with the MAC layer user Z. In some cases, the switch may even be able to convert the broadcast ARP into a unicast message destined to user Z specifically. This type of hybrid operation defines the hybrid switch as primarily a LAN switch with some additional layer three capabilities. This model of LAN switch is a very new concept, but it has very real uses in broadcast traffic management on large-scale switched LANs.

Figure 1.24

Hybrid switch
operation.

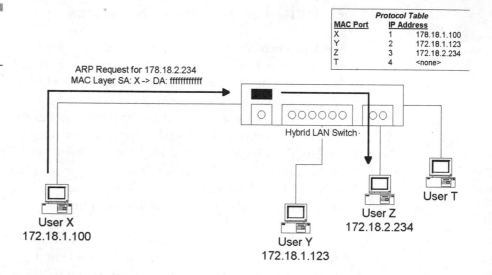

Summary

The basic role of a LAN switch is to forward user data at layer two of the OSI model, based on MAC layer addressing. Most LAN switches follow the forwarding rules defined in the IEEE 801.1D specification to achieve this task. The primary rationale for deploying LAN switches is that by acting as high-density "bridges" they allow significant end-user traffic segmentation transparently. Because they achieve the traffic segmentation needed to increase LAN bandwidth capacity without end-system impact, they are simple to use (plug and play) and usually reasonably cost effective.

LAN switches today are more than traditional bridges. They have higher performance and port density levels. They have been enhanced with many vendor-specific features (RMON, port trunking, analysis tools, VLANs) to allow far greater scalability than the traditional bridge of the 1980s. Because of these enhancements, it is much more difficult to choose the correct LAN switch for your network. From this chapter's examination of some of these enhancements, you should be better able to identify the role of additional features in LAN switches you are evaluating.

Finally, the term *layer three switch* has added an additional complexity in understanding LAN switching. Vendors are positioning everything from legacy traditional routers to cutting-edge hybrid switches as layer three switches. While this book is not specifically about layer three switches, this chapter should give you the information required to identify the role the layer three switch offered by a vendor will fill. It should be identified as either a router or as a LAN switch in terms of the designs and implementations in this book.

CHAPTER 2

Design Rules of Switched LANs

From the previous chapter it is obvious that a LAN switch is a fairly simple device. It operates at layer two of the OSI model and generally follows the well-defined operational process of IEEE 801.1D. While the devices individually are relatively simple, the proper combination of LAN switches to form a network is slightly more complex. This chapter will examine the design rules used in today's switched LANs. Through this discussion, a proper model of a large switched LAN should be detailed. While your particular network may not fit exactly into the design examples shown in this chapter, the principles involved in design should be applicable for any switched LAN.

Areas of the Switched LAN

The first principle of design that must be understood is the concept of areas. This refers to the fact that all LAN switches are not created equally and as such the role one LAN switch plays in the network may not be suitable for another kind of LAN switch. As a basic design rule of LAN switches, the network should consist of three major areas: the core, the periphery, and the centralized resources areas. Each of these three areas has a specific role in the overall operation of the switched LAN and additionally places certain requirements on the switches that will be utilized in each role. This model of areas is shown in the sample network in Figure 2.1.

The network shown in Figure 2.1 demonstrates a possible configuration of a large-scale switched network. It provides connectivity to large numbers of users using its periphery switches and then aggregates the user traffic to the network core using higher-speed links and larger switches. The final component addresses the needs of the centralized resources, such as superservers, Internet gateways, and mainframes. These devices are connected to the core via the centralized resources area of the switched LAN. Since these devices generally are more critical to business operations than the periphery devices and generally require more bandwidth, they are provided higher-performance switched connections using more fault-tolerant switches. The resultant network design should provide an extremely high capacity network for possibly thousands of periphery users.

Figure 2.1

Switched network areas.

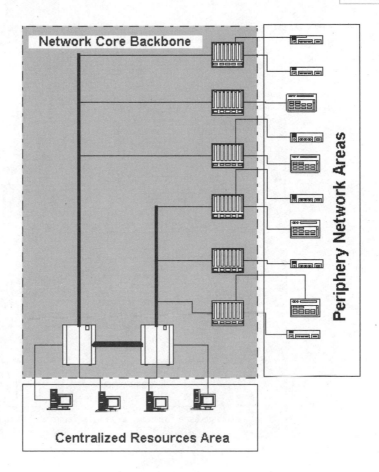

Core Area

The core area of any network is the most critical component. The core is the aggregation point of almost all traffic. As such the core must be built to provide two major features: extremely high performance and extremely high levels of redundancy and fault tolerance. Because of these requirements, it is probable that the switches deployed in the core will be more costly than the ones used in other areas of the network. Figure 2.2 shows an example of a core design.

In the example core shown in Figure 2.2, the network construction consists of several backbone switches, which act as the center of the switched network, or the Main Distribution Frame (MDF). Attached to

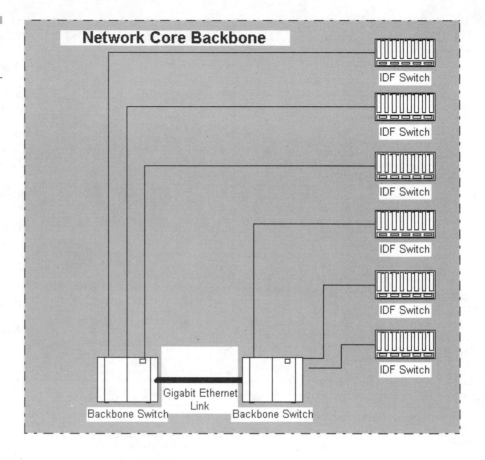

these switches using high-speed links are several Intermediate Distribution Frame (IDF) switches, which connect to the periphery areas of the network. For those unfamiliar with the terms MDF and IDF, they simply refer to areas of your cable system, with the MDF being the central connection point and the IDFs being additional fan-out points closer to the end users. An MDF is usually your central computer room, while an IDF may be a building's or floor's wiring closet. Between the backbone switches and the IDF switches, the core of the network is constructed. The backbone switches are your most critical component in this design. They must be as fault tolerant and reliable as possible. In this design, there are two backbone switches sharing the load of the IDF switches. In order to provide maximum capacity, the backbone switches are connected using gigabit Ethernet links. If gigabit Ethernet is not available, other options include port trunking of several full-duplex 100Base-TX or FX or even ATM OC12 622-megabit links. The requirement is that there be more capacity between the backbone switches than between the backbone and IDF switches. Additional requirements of the backbone switch include full redundancy, high port density, and extremely high scalable internal forwarding capacity.

Full redundancy exhibits itself in features such as N + 1 power supply redundancy, distributed processing, and no architectural single point of failure in the switch. High port density is required in most cases, so that the number of backbone switches needed to connect all IDFs is limited. The rationale for this requirement is based on the fact that the switches' internal backplanes are generally in the multigigabit per second range, while external links are generally limited to one gigabit per second or less. As such, it is desirable to connect IDFs using the faster internal switch capacity rather than crossing additional lower-speed external links. Additionally, the cost of high-capacity links to connect backbone switches is much higher than the cost for the links used for IDF to backbone connections. The final requirement of the backbone switch is that its architecture be scalable. As your network grows, and as faster technologies are introduced, the backbone should be able to scale to handle the additional performance requirements. This scalability is best achieved in switches that utilize distributed architectures in which each additional port group adds additional capacity. The primary reason to insist that the backbone switches deployed in your network be scalable is based on the principle that you will not be able to replace your backbone easily in the future. Once your network is in place, the core should be expandable but should not require downtime to upgrade its capacity. A scalable switch that can be expanded without replacing the entire device is most desirable in this situation. Table 2.1 lists these backbone switch requirements to assist in backbone switch evaluation.

The second component of the core is the IDF switches. These switches link the core switches to the periphery switches or hubs. The performance requirements of these switches are not as great as the backbone switches, but, nevertheless, these switches should be high capacity. As shown in Figure 2.2, the IDF switches are located closer to the periphery areas and are connected to the core switches using high-speed links. Any IDF switch must be able to support at least one high-speed technology for connection to the backbone switches. Possible options include full-duplex 100 megabit Ethernet or FDDI, ATM OC3 155 megabit, or even trunk groups of several 100-megabit links. The exact capacity required depends on the number of users in the periphery areas using this IDF switch to reach the core. The ideal IDF switch is one that can expand its capacity to the backbone switches as needed through the additional

TABLE 2.1

Backbone
Switch
Requirements

Requirement	Notes
Supports high-capacity links between backbone switches	This is achieved either through support of gigabit Ethernet, ATM OC12, or a port trunking technology.
N + 1 power supplies	The switch should always have enough power supplies to fully operate even if one supply completely fails.
No single point of failure	The switch should not have any true single point of failure. This includes such components as a single processor for all forwarding.
High port density of high-speed links	The switch should have a high port density of high-speed links to connect to IDF switches. This eliminates the need for excessive numbers of backbone switches in your core and maximizes the use of the internal backplanes of the backbone switches.
Scalable design	The switch must be able to scale as network demands increase and port density increases. This scalability is best achieved by expansion of the existing backbone switches rather than replacement of those switches or the addition of more switches to the core. Generally, large modular distributed backbone switches best fulfill this requirement.

links. Chapter 8 discusses how to measure link capacity in order to judge when increased capacity may be necessary.

The IDF switches, as part of the core, still require a high level of fault tolerance in the form of N + 1 power supplies, no single point of failure, and even distributed processing. The level of redundancy required is entirely dependent on what user communities are connected through this IDF switch. If the user community is noncritical, then the IDF switch may be less fault tolerant. If the user community is extremely critical to the business operations of your organization, then the additional expense of greater reliability is justified. In general, the more reliability you can build into your design, the more satisfaction you will have as you deal with less support-related issues.

An additional requirement of the IDF switches is greater network management capabilities. The backbone switches are usually able to provide some statistics on capacity and errors but are operating at such high speeds that more complex management tasks may degrade their performance. Since the backbone is not the correct place to be doing complex packet analysis, the backbone switches are usually not placed in that role. The IDF switch, having less of a performance requirement, is able to provide greater detail into the operation of the network. IDF switches should be able to provide alarm limits against their ports' activities and baselining information about network utilization. They may also be able to provide some advanced RMON tools such as host group analysis, but that requirement is usually placed on the periphery switches where the statistics have more relevance.

Periphery Areas

The second major area of any switched LAN is the periphery areas. These areas are the primary locations of end users. Since the network will potentially service thousands of end users, the periphery areas will require the largest number of switched ports. Since user requirements will vary in most networks, there are many options available for design of the periphery areas of a switched LAN. The basic structure of the periphery areas is shown in Figure 2.3. The IDF switches of the core area are connected to a variety of workgroup switches and shared access hubs. Each of these configurations will be examined more fully later in this chapter.

Within the periphery areas of the switched LAN there are two types of devices. The first category of periphery device is known as the workgroup switch. This type of switch is usually used to directly connect end users to switch ports. Depending on the number of end users requiring direct connection to switched ports and their location, this type of switch may be stackable or modular chassis based. The general role of a workgroup switch is to provide connectivity between end users and IDF switches in the network core. Usually the workgroup switch is a device separate from the IDF switch, but in some smaller networks, or in networks with high-density IDF switches, the roles of workgroup and IDF switches may be filled by the same device. Table 2.2 describes the general features a workgroup switch must provide to fulfill its role.

The second type of device in the periphery area of a switched network is shared access hubs. These devices are typically repeaters having either a stackable or modular form factor. In many networks, the repeaters have always been the devices connecting users to the network and now, with the introduction of switches, the repeaters continue to be used. The use of repeaters attached to switched ports is known as MicroLAN segmentation. This term refers to the fact that now the shared

Figure 2.3

Switched LAN
periphery area
example.

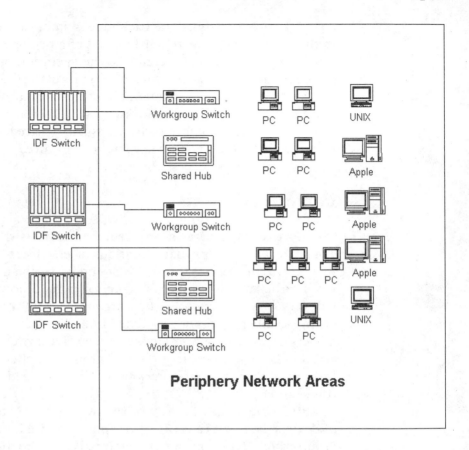

Periphery Network Areas

TABLE 2.2

Workgroup
Switch
Requirements

Feature	Description
Access port density	The workgroup switch must usually have high port density to accommodate many directly attached segments of users. When evaluating a workgroup switch, it is critical to understand how many ports will be required for user connectivity. If a group requires 22 connections, it is very wise to purchase a switch with at least that many ports rather than purchasing several lower-port density switches. The rationale for this decision, even if the higher-density switch is more expensive, is based on the fact that with additional workgroup switches, more IDF switch ports will be required to connect them to the core. While workgroup ports are usually very inexpensive, IDF switch ports for high-speed network uplinks are not.

TABLE 2.2

(continued)

Feature	Description
Cost per port	In most switched networks, the periphery switches will account for the majority of switch ports. As such, the cost per port can be a significant factor in determining which switch to utilize. While lower cost per port is desirable, be very careful that the switch chosen for lower cost per port does not lack some feature that will result in the requirement for additional components elsewhere in the switched network that negate the cost advantage. An example of this is switches with low cost but low port density that require additional IDF switch interfaces to connect multiple switches to the core. Other hidden cost-related issues are switches with no analysis tools (RMON/port and traffic mirror), which will ultimately require that you install external RMON or analyzer probes.
Expandability	The workgroup switches must be able to expand as users are added to the switched LAN. Modular chassis-based and stackable switches may be required in areas of the network where you predict dramatic increases in user count. Be sure that the workgroup switch not only expands its access ports but also allows for increased network uplink port density and capacity to accommodate the new end users.
Management	One of the best locations in a switched network to do complex traffic analysis is in the periphery of the switched LAN. Specifically, the best location for advanced RMON analysis is on the uplinks of periphery switches. The reason for this statement is simple, based on two facts. First, these complex tasks require processing resources that are generally more readily available on the periphery switches, since they are responsible for switching for a limited number of end users. Second, the uplinks are the conduit for all user traffic from the workgroup to the rest of the network. Since most computing resources (servers, proxies to the Internet, mainframes) are located through the uplinks, monitoring just those ports gives a complete set of data about the traffic flow from the workgroup users to their resources. The alternative to this is advanced RMON probes on every switched port in the switch, which would just duplicate the data an uplink would have collected.

TABLE 2.2

(continued)

Feature	Description
Network uplink port capacity	A workgroup switch provides connectivity for end users to the network core. As such, most of the user traffic will pass through the switch and be ultimately destined for servers and other resources located elsewhere on the switched LAN. Because of this, the workgroup switches should be able to provide enough bandwidth capacity into the IDF switch to support all of the attached users' demands. A general rule is that there should be no more than a 3:1 ratio between total access port capacity and network uplink capacity.
	An example of this could be the situation where a switch has 20 10 megabit Ethernet access ports and one 100Base-T uplink. This switch configuration has 200 megabits of total capacity in its access ports and 100 megabits of uplink capacity. This results in a 2:1 ratio between access and uplink ports on the switch. From an initial design perspective this seems acceptable, since it assumes that the access ports will operate at less than 50 percent capacity as an average. Once the design is in place, the switch's uplinks must be monitored to determine if the assumptions were correct. If the load on the uplink is not saturating its capacity, the design is acceptable. If baselining demonstrates the link is saturated often, a higher-speed technology or additional uplinks (using trunking) should be implemented. The main requirement is that the switch has uplink capacity that is not extremely overloaded in a basic configuration but also is expandable if the links do become saturated.

segments are limited in size to a small number of users. This group of shared users exists on a MicroLAN. Each MicroLAN is attached to the rest of the network using a switch port, which provides traffic segmentation between the user groups.

With the presence of shared MicroLANs on the switch periphery, the network designer must decide how to best utilize two options for user placement. The users can either be located in a MicroLAN or be given a direct connection to a workgroup switch port. In most situations, average users who already exist on shared segments in the existing network configurations should remain in MicroLANs. Users who utilize more network bandwidth or use multimedia or other bandwidth-intensive applications should be evaluated for placement on a switched port. Using the RMON HostTopN group, it is relatively simple to determine which users would best be suited for their own switch port. Simply run a HostTopN for the top byte count generators over a few days. The list of addresses returned indicates who, in an existing shared segment, is generating the most traffic over a given time frame. Those users would be best served by being connected directly to a switch port. Additionally, moving the highest traffic generators from the shared segment to a dedicated switch port provides the remaining shared MicroLAN users with more available bandwidth for their uses.

Shared Resources Area

The third area of a typical switched LAN is the area known as the shared resources area. This area identifies the location or locations in the switched network that provide connectivity to the centralized shared resources of the network. These resources include such devices as servers, routers, Internet firewalls, mainframes, and any other device utilized by many end systems. Figure 2.4 illustrates the structure of a shared resources area.

This portion of the network is similar to the periphery areas described above in that the servers and other centralized devices are really just end users in the switched network. While this is true, the requirements of these devices are significantly different from the requirements a typical end user places on the network. While the periphery area provided connectivity, which was a mix of shared and switched ports and focused on cost per port, the centralized resources area has an entirely different set of priorities. Servers and firewalls and other centralized resources require more than simple connectivity. They require high bandwidth capacity, extremely high reliability, and some level of traffic analysis and manageability. Because of these requirements, the switches used to connect the centralized resources to the network must be significantly more capable than the average workgroup switch.

Some requirements for a centralized resources area switch are listed in Table 2.3. They reflect the need for capacity and reliability in this critical area of your network.

In most switched networks, these three areas will exist in some form. Later in this chapter we will examine several case studies describing example networks built from these three areas.

Figure 2.4

Shared resources
area.

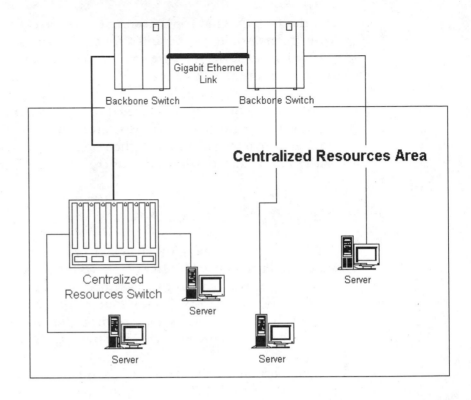

Centralized Resources Area

Gigabit Ethernet
Link

Backbone Switch   Backbone Switch

Centralized
Resources Switch

Server

Server

Server

Server

TABLE 2.3

Centralized
Resources
Area Switch
Requirements

Feature	Description
Advanced management	Advanced RMON and alarm limits are placed on centralized resources area switches. While these switches must focus on high performance, they should also provide a high level of information about traffic patterns and link capacity. By gathering traffic statistics at the server location, it is possible to understand the network utilization of that resource. For instance, if a server port provides the RMON matrix group, it is possible to see who on the network is using that server and how much data are being exchanged. While these data could be gathered by examining every uplink from every periphery switch for the server's address, this is far more work than simply examining the traffic matrix at the server's port.

TABLE 2.3

(continued)

Feature	Description
Full-duplex support	Since very large amounts of traffic may pass through these switches, the use of full-duplex technologies is very desirable. Full duplex is available on 10 and 100 megabit Ethernet and as a vendor-specific FDDI option. By using full-duplex operation, the typical access methods of Ethernet and FDDI are suspended, and the devices on the point-to-point link are able to simultaneously transmit and receive data. This has two effects. First, it doubles the overall capacity of the link, which is very useful for connections into the core of the network. The second advantage is that there is no longer a possibility of a collision on 10/100 megabit Ethernet. This allows for far fewer retransmissions and higher overall capacity. If your servers are able to handle full-duplex connections (given a fast internal I/O system), this feature should be used.
High-speed port density	The switch connecting your centralized resources to the network core will generally require a significant number of high-speed interfaces. This is necessary because it is now very common for high-end servers and other centralized resources to have 100-megabit connectivity (Ethernet or FDDI) internal to them. Since these resources have 100-megabit connectivity, the switch they connect to must also support this bandwidth rate. Because there will be several centralized servers in each centralized resources area, the switch requires many high-speed interfaces. Most switches in this role will have ten or more 100Base-T interfaces or FDDI interfaces. Several of these interfaces will connect to servers and other centralized resources, while other interfaces will connect the switch to the network core.
System reliability	If a periphery switch fails, the end users in that particular area of the network are affected. If a server's switch fails, anyone in the entire LAN using that resource is affected. It is very important that these switches do not fail. In order to accomplish this, these switches should be as reliable as those used in the network core. They should have N + 1 redundant power systems, environmental monitoring, UPSs, and, if possible, use a distributed processing architecture. While these additions are more expensive, the cost is justified if system failures can be avoided.
Uplink trunking	Since these switches will be the focal point of large amounts of traffic, their connection to the core must be very high capacity. One method of achieving this is by utilizing vendor-specific trunking technologies. See the previous chapter for details regarding port trunking.

Design Issues

Using the principles outlined above for defining three major functional areas of a switched LAN, the next step in understanding the structure of this type of network is to understand its fundamental design rules. These rules relate to the functions of individual LAN switches and the dependencies they have on each other. In order to successfully build a switched LAN, the network must be viewed as a system of switches, with each providing some set of service. This section discusses the two major design rule areas of switched LAN systems. They are switch capacity and interswitch connectivity.

Switch Capacity and Table Size

In order for a switch to successfully fulfill its role in the network, it must have adequate capacity in all of its functions. Most vendors focus only on the capacity of the switch's forwarding logic in terms of packets per second when comparing various switches. In fact, this narrow focus does not cover all relevant elements of the switching function. It is vital that the entire switch capacity be examined to determine its capabilities. This section will first define which elements of switch capacity should be identified and then will relate those elements to switches placed in the three areas of a switched LAN.

The elements that define a switch's capacity include several independent functions. The primary element that is usually the focus of any switch evaluation is the raw packet per second forwarding rate of the device. Since implementing switching is done primarily to increase network capacity, the devices must exhibit very high forwarding rates. This measurement is usually based on testing, in which the device is sent streams of minimum-sized packets. The testing increases in packet rate until the device cannot continue to forward all packets offered to it. Most LAN switches today will forward hundreds of thousands of packets per second, with some forwarding millions. While this test is a good indicator that the device is able to pass packets, it by no means indicates that this is an exceptional switch. In fact, most switches today deliver packets at rates far in excess of any real-world traffic pattern. Performance in terms of raw packet per second throughput has become a commodity, with extremely high levels of performance being the norm.

Beyond the raw performance of any switch, other elements must be examined to determine its capacity. The second element is the switch's forwarding logic capacity. Switches are required to deliver packets intelligently. In the raw performance test, the switch is only dealing with a few end users. In the real world, the switch may have to understand thousands of end systems. In order for the switch to maintain a proper understanding of the network, its source address table, or SAT, must be large enough to understand the MAC layer addresses of all devices in the network. If it is not, the device may not be able to learn and retain all needed MAC addresses to make intelligent filter/forward decisions. In Chapter 1 we saw that if the SAT did not contain the destination address of a packet seen by a switch, it would flood out the packet to all of its ports. This flooding is normal for destination addresses that are truly unknown but should not occur if the destination address had to be discarded because the SAT was not large enough. As a general switch capacity rule, the switch's SAT must be large enough to understand all end systems on the switched LAN. Figure 2.5 shows the relationship a switch has with the end users on the network.

In Figure 2.5 the switches are represented as connecting four 500 user segments together physically. The figure then shows each switch's view of the complete network. Switch 1 understands the network as 500 users

Figure 2.5

Switch SAT logical and physical end-system views.

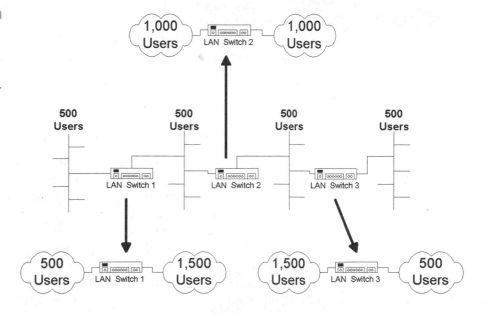

connected via its left side interface and 1,500 users connected via its right side interface. Switch 2 sees the network as two groups of 1,000 users, each connected to one of the switch's two interfaces. Finally, switch 3 sees the entire network as 1,500 users connected on its left and 500 users connected on its right. The reason the switches see the network in different ways is based on the individual switches' SATs having learned the source address of each end user from a specific port—for example, a user on the segment between switch 1 and switch 2 would be learned by switch 1 as being connected via its right interface, while switch 2 would learn that same user via its left side interface. Since every user may ultimately pass data through these switches, they must be capable of understanding all users on the switched network regardless of whether or not they are directly attached to a switch or actually attached to another switch in the network.

If the switches in Figure 2.5 did not have SATs of at least 2,000 entries, the switches would not be able to maintain knowledge of all end users and as such may have to discard information about one user to learn information about another. If this happened, it is very likely that the switches would not have knowledge of end users' true locations when they received packets destined for those users. At such time, the switch would have to flood out those packets. This flooding would result in packets being delivered to ports that did not need to see them. This effect will not stop a switched network from functioning, but it does decrease the efficiency of the overall network.

The next element of capacity that should be evaluated in any switch is the switch's port capacity. Since switch ports will generally act as either the user access role or the network uplink role, any switch should be examined for port capacity in either role. A user access port is one that will provide connectivity to end users either directly or using a shared segment. A network uplink port is generally a higher-speed technology than the equivalent access ports on the same switch. Its role is to connect to other switches in the network core. Most switches will have a mixture of network and access ports, depending on their role in the LAN. It is also important that the switches allow for some level of expansion, if they are going to provide connectivity in an area of the network that will add users or whose existing users are expected to utilize more network capacity in the future. This expansion capability is usually best found in devices that are either entirely modular chassis-based switches, are stackable, or have modular uplink interfaces.

The final capacity-related component that requires examination in switch evaluation is the internal backplane capacity. The main reason switches are able to deliver packets at hundreds of thousands of packets per second it that they implement proprietary internal delivery mechanisms. Even though every vendor uses a different internal delivery mechanism, there should be no concern about interoperability as long as the external network interfaces are using standards-based network technologies. Since there are many different internal backplane schemes used by vendors of switches, it is important to understand what capacity that backplane has. The measurement should be given in bits per second indicating how much data can be delivered to the forwarding logic of the switch at any given time. Usually the switches will have gigabit per second backplanes for internal packet handling. Some switches confuse these issues by offering several backplanes for different technologies. When evaluating a switch for backplane capacity, first understand which backplane the packets of your desired technology will be using and then determine how many bits per second that backplane can deliver. As with forwarding capacity in packets per second, this number is generally found to be greater than any real-world traffic pattern can provide.

Table 2.4 provides a comparison of the capacity requirements of the various switches used in the three switched LAN areas.

TABLE 2.4 Capacity Comparison

Capacity Feature	Backbone Switch	IDF Switch	Workgroup Switch
Backplane capacity	Multigigabit per second with expandability	Up to 1+ gigabit per second capacity in most cases	Several hundred million bits per second capacity
Forwarding capacity pps	Very high level—(1 million pps +) and scalable to higher levels	High level—500,000 to 1 million pps or more	Several hundred thousand pps based on the number of ports
Port density	Large number of network uplink ports with trunking support on many groups simultaneously	Large number of network uplink ports with trunking supported to connect to the backbone switches	Large number of user access ports and one or more network uplink ports. Additional network uplinks and trunking may be required as load levels increase on access ports.
SAT table size	As large as the total number of users on the network	As large as the total number of users on the network	As large as the total number of users on the network

In most cases, the role of the switch will determine the required capacity of that device. It is always wise to deploy switches that have extra capacity than what is required today and allow for expandability in terms of forwarding capacity and port density. It is almost certain that the size of your switched network will expand in the future, and it is much simpler to increase capacity of existing deployed switches than to add new switches to an existing network.

Interswitch Connectivity and Aggregation of Bandwidth

In the previous section, the design issues related to evaluating the correct type of switch for the correct role in the network were examined. Once a proper set of switches has been selected, the process of connecting them to create a switched network must begin. This section examines the design rules related to the interconnection of switches to form the three major areas of a switched LAN. Each of the three areas will be examined for connectivity within the area and to the other areas of the network. The primary principle used in connecting the various areas of this system is to aggregate bandwidth towards the network core. The periphery switches should represent the lowest level of network performance; they should connect to the IDF switches that have higher capacity. The IDF switches then connect to the backbone switches, which represent the highest network capacity. Finally, the centralized resources attach to switches that exist at the same level as the IDF or even the backbone switches in terms of capacity. This hierarchy of capacity is shown in Figure 2.6.

Core Connectivity Design Rules

The core of a switched network is the most critical area of that system. It must be extremely reliable and must provide very high levels of throughput. It provides connectivity to the periphery areas and to the centralized resources areas. Within the core there are two major connections. The first is the connection between the designated backbone switches. These switches provide a central aggregation point for all IDF switches and represent the center of the network's traffic patterns. Almost all data will pass through these switches. The connection

Figure 2.6

Types of switches
and relative
capacity.

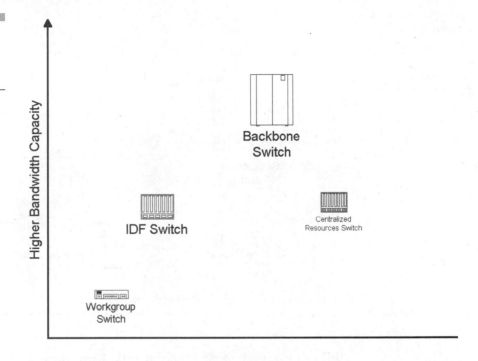

between these backbone switches requires the highest level of bandwidth available.

The physical layer technology choices for connection include 100Base-T/F; FDDI; gigabit Ethernet; ATM OC3, 12, and 48 links; and any other available high-speed technology. Full-duplex support in FDDI and fast Ethernet is also very desirable, if not mandatory. In order to maximize the capacity between backbone switches, vendor-specific trunking technologies will almost always be required. Since the cost of these types of network technologies is very high, it is critical that large backbone switches be utilized to maximize port count and minimize the number of separate switches that will be used as backbone switches. Figure 2.7 compares the use of one large backbone switch with the use of several smaller backbone switches.

In Figure 2.7, the upper backbone switch is larger in size and able to provide 18 interfaces to other switches. The lower set of switches represents backbone switches with less port density. Three of these switches are needed to provide the same amount of interswitch connectivity as the single, larger backbone switch. What is more significant is that the three lower switches also require connectivity to the other two backbone switches. This connectivity may be a trunk group of 100-megabit

Figure 2.7

Advantage of a
high-capacity
backbone switch.

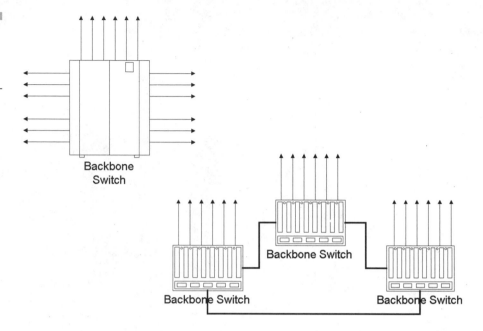

Figure 2.7

Advantage of a
high-capacity
backbone switch.

links or even a gigabit Ethernet link. Regardless of what technology is chosen, those interconnections are expensive and reduce the switch's port density available for IDF switch connections. By using the single, larger switch, these external links were not needed and more IDF to backbone connectivity became available. While the cost of an enterprise class backbone switch is not small, the ultimate cost of having to deploy many smaller chassis and then provide interswitch connections will usually be far more expensive than the deployment of fewer larger switches.

The second core connectivity configuration that is required is the connections between the backbone switches and the IDF switches. These connections will require high capacity and must allow for scalability should the bandwidth demands of the end users through the IDF switch increase. The preferred choice of technology is one full-duplex 100-megabit port or a trunked group of 100-megabit LAN ports. The number of uplinks should be chosen depending on how many end users are supported via the IDF switch. Figure 2.8 shows some common examples of IDF to backbone connectivity.

The first option uses 100Base-FX in full-duplex mode. This allows several kilometers distance using fiber-optic cable between the switches. As

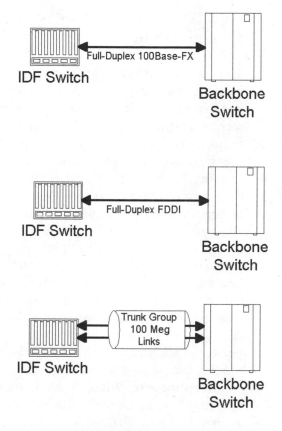

Figure 2.8
IDF to backbone
connection options.

a full-duplex link, the connection provides 100 megabits in both directions simultaneously. The second option utilizes full-duplex FDDI. Since FDDI full duplex is a nonstandard option, the switches on either side must generally be from the same vendor's product line. This option allows over 20 kilometers between the switches, using single-mode fiber if necessary. The final option extends the other two options by utilizing a port trunking mechanism between the switches. Since port trunking is also vendor specific, the switches at either end must generally be from the same vendor. This option allows scalability beyond a single 100-megabit full duplex. In most cases, connections using a single high-capacity link to an IDF switch will be used initially. As the network scales in size, network baselining will reveal where additional capacity is needed. At that point, the third option of port trunking may be implemented to scale the capacity where it is needed.

Centralized Resources Connectivity Design Rules

The centralized resources area of your switched network contains the resources globally used on your network. The type of resource will vary but generally includes large servers, Internet firewalls, routers, name servers, mainframes, and even supercomputers. These types of devices are usually located in central computer rooms with proper environmental protections such as air conditioning and uninterruptible power systems. When connecting these devices to the core of the network, the design rule is simply to provide network links that match the capacity of the resources. Since most of these types of devices can accommodate 100-megabit interfaces, the switches and the links to the core must be able to handle a great deal of network traffic.

There are two connections of interest in this area. The first is the connection from the common resource (server, firewall) to its switch, and the second is the connection from the switch to the core. It should be noted that it is possible to directly connect these resources to the core of the network if the backbone switches have available interfaces and capacity. In such a case, only the connection from the common resource to its switch would be needed.

The connection linking the common resources to their switches consists of a variety of technologies that are dependent on the interfaces present in servers, firewalls, routers, and so on. The technologies used could range from full-duplex 10 megabit Ethernet to gigabit Ethernet server links. The rule, however, is that the type of connectivity provided to a common resource should reflect the level of traffic it participates in. Some servers that provide only interactive login or terminal emulation require limited bandwidth and could possibly utilize a standard Ethernet connection. Servers that provide file transfer, such as Novell servers and UNIX hosts providing NFS services, could potentially require huge amounts of network bandwidth. The best rule to follow is that, given the relationship shown in Figure 2.6 between different types of switches and their bandwidth capacity, servers should always have one level higher network capacity than the clients they service. If the average client for an order-entry server is a shared access Ethernet low-end user, then the server may be suitably placed on a full-duplex 10-megabit Ethernet link. However, in the case of a client with a dedicated 10-megabit Ethernet connection NFS mounting a large shared database, its server would usually be best placed on a 100-megabit dedicated switch port.

Evaluate the type of client using the common resource and try to provide that resource network connectivity one level faster.

The second connection of interest in this area is the connection between the switches that the servers, firewalls, and so on attach to and the network core. As was stated earlier, the common resource could connect directly to a backbone switch if ports are available on that switch. If the resources are connected to a local switch, which then connects to the core, that switch must provide significant bandwidth to the core. A minimum connection into the core for this type of switch would be a full-duplex 100-megabit link. More appropriate would be a set of multiple trunked links back to the core. Using proper baselining techniques, the design could begin with a single full-duplex link. If the baselining showed that link was close to saturation, then port trunking could be implemented to handle additional load. The links between the core and the centralized resources area switches are one of the most likely places for network congestion.

The last design rule for the centralized resources area deals with the resources themselves. Routed networks had one interesting effect on the servers, firewalls, and other common resources. The routers could not forward traffic at extremely high load levels, and as such they introduced a bottleneck in the traffic pattern on the LAN. With the advent of switching, it is usually true that the switches remove that network infrastructure–related bottleneck. Now, very high traffic rates can traverse the network between devices. As such, the new bottleneck in almost all switched LANs is the communications capacity of the common resources, such as servers and firewalls. It is critical that each server in the LAN be evaluated for its own capacity. If that server is the focal point for a large amount of network traffic, the server must have internal capacity to handle such load. The deployment of a switched infrastructure should be coupled with upgrades to your various common servers. These upgrades include faster network interfaces, processors, and internal bus structures. If you deploy the wrong combination on a server, there may be negligible performance improvements, since the server is easily saturated. An example of this type of error is the deployment of an FDDI network interface into an Intel 486–based Novell server based on ISA bus technology. That combination of a slow processor, a slow internal bus, and a fast network connection will most certainly result in very poor performance. A better combination would have been a Pentium Pro–based server with PCI bus and FDDI or 100Base-T network interface. In this case the processor, internal bus, and network connection are evenly matched and the result should be very high network performance.

Periphery Area Connectivity Design Rules

The periphery areas of a switched LAN will generally have the most diverse set of connectivity devices. These will include workgroup switches using various LAN technologies and shared access hubs of many types. In designing the periphery areas of the network, the design rules are relatively simple. First, determine what kind of user connectivity is required and then, based on the bandwidth those users will have available, choose the proper uplink technology to the core.

There are two choices of end-user connectivity in switched LANs: shared access and dedicated. Shared access connectivity involves creation of shared segments containing a small number of end users. This concept is known as MicroLAN segmentation. By giving small groups of users a common segment, they should be able to share the segment bandwidth much more efficiently than that same amount of bandwidth used by large groups of users. A typical shared MicroLAN will have between 12 and 24 end users. These end users should have similar configurations and network requirements. Examples of users suitable for MicroLAN segmentation are typical administrative users involved in such tasks as order entry and word processing, and e-mail users.

The second option for end-user connectivity is dedicated switch port connectivity. In this model, the end user is directly connected to a switch port. This provides the end user with all of the bandwidth for that segment. This connectivity model is usually more expensive to deploy but does provide significant increases in the overall performance of the end system. Network users implementing bandwidth-intensive applications such as multimedia, imaging, and Computer-Aided Design (CAD) are more suited for this mode of connectivity.

Figure 2.9 illustrates these two models of end-user connectivity. The upper model shows several users attached to an Ethernet segment that then attaches to a switch port. This model is very useful for connections of low-end devices or in situations where the existing network contains significant amounts of shared access hubs. The lower model shows dedicated per port user switch connections. This method of connection is preferred in situations where devices require more network bandwidth.

Figure 2.9

MicroLAN versus dedicated user connections.

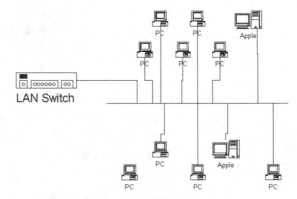

Shared MicroLAN Segment

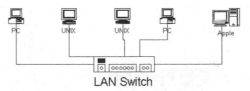

Dedicated Switch Connections

In most new installations, the dedicated connection model is the desired method of connection, even though it is generally more expensive to implement. Most networks today find some balance between these two end-user connection models when actually implementing a switched LAN.

Once the user connectivity has been decided for a periphery area of the network, the connection to the core must be planned. The type of connection to a core switch is based entirely on the potential bandwidth generated by the end users in that area. If the periphery area consists of 20 10-megabit Ethernet MicroLANs, the maximum bandwidth the users on those MicroLANs could generate is only 200 megabits per second. In reality, given the behavior of shared Ethernet, it is unlikely that even 100 megabits per second will ever be seen within those combined Micro-LANs. With this understanding, a single fast Ethernet uplink from the switch connecting those MicroLANs should be adequate for this design. If more capacity is required, options include adding additional uplinks in a trunk group or using full-duplex support on the existing uplink.

In situations where large numbers of dedicated switch port user connections exist, the uplink capacity of the workgroup switches may need to be significantly greater—for example, a workgroup switch with 96 10-megabit Ethernet user connections will definitely require more than one uplink. Since the end users could generate up to 960 megabits per second of bandwidth, the switch should have comparable uplink capacity. For this example, a trunk group of two or more full-duplex FDDI or fast Ethernet links would be appropriate.

In the periphery areas of the switched network, the design rules are summarized in two statements.

1. Determine end-user connectivity to be either dedicated or Micro-LAN, based on the expected required network load that user will generate.

2. Based on the combined capacity the end users in any area will generate, determine the uplink capacity to provide a comparable amount of throughput.

Case Studies

To conclude this chapter on design rules of switched networks, this last section will examine the design of some sample networks. Using the principles outlined above, the designs should result in scalable, high-performance networks.

Case Study 1: Small Switched LAN

A small switched LAN is to be designed to accommodate 300 (200 Micro-LAN and 100 dedicated) end users sharing five Novell servers, one Internet firewall, and three UNIX-based servers. The network will exist completely internal to one three-story building. The process of design for this network is as follows.

Step 1: Centralized Resources Area and Network Core Area Design Each of the nine server devices requires dedicated switched connectivity. To achieve this a medium-sized modular switch will be deployed. This switch will have 24 fast Ethernet interfaces. Each of the servers will be connected to a fast Ethernet interface. It is very desirable that the servers be equipped with fast Ethernet network interface cards. Note that the severs are not required to utilize fast Ethernet interface cards, since most fast Ethernet switch ports will operate as either 10- or 100-megabit Ethernet interfaces.

The remaining fast Ethernet interfaces of the switch containing the servers will act as the core connections for the uplinks from the periphery areas. By using this single switch as a core of the switched LAN, we are able to take advantage of its internal backplane capacity. This results in the servers connecting at 100 megabits per second, the periphery areas uplinking at the same rate, and the core operating at possibly gigabit per second rates.

Step 2: Periphery Area Design   To support the 300 end users in this system, a combination of dedicated and MicroLAN connectivity is required. To provide the required 100 ports of dedicated 10 megabit Ethernet, we will implement five 24-port workgroup switches. Each switch should also have one or two fast Ethernet uplinks. The five switches provide 120 Ethernet ports, of which nine will connect to MicroLANs and 100 will connect to end users. The uplinks will connect to the core switch using full-duplex support. Extensive traffic monitoring should be done on these uplinks. If the link is seen to operate at very high capacity, a second link should be implemented as part of a port trunk. We will utilize nine Ethernet stackable repeaters, each with 24 interfaces. This will provide 216 ports for connectivity. Two hundred of those interfaces will connect to end users, while nine will connect to 10-megabit ports of workgroup switches. The final design is shown in Figure 2.10.

The final design includes a layered structure with the end users either being connected on MicroLANs or to dedicated switch ports. Those user connections are then aggregated through 100 megabit per second uplinks to a core switch with an internal switching capacity of millions of packets per second. The centralized resources are connected to the core switch via 100-megabit links. This design provides a good bandwidth distribution between the clients and the servers of this network. Once the system is in place, the necessary baselining and monitoring functions need to be deployed. Those functions will be used to determine if this design contains any bandwidth bottlenecks that need to be corrected.

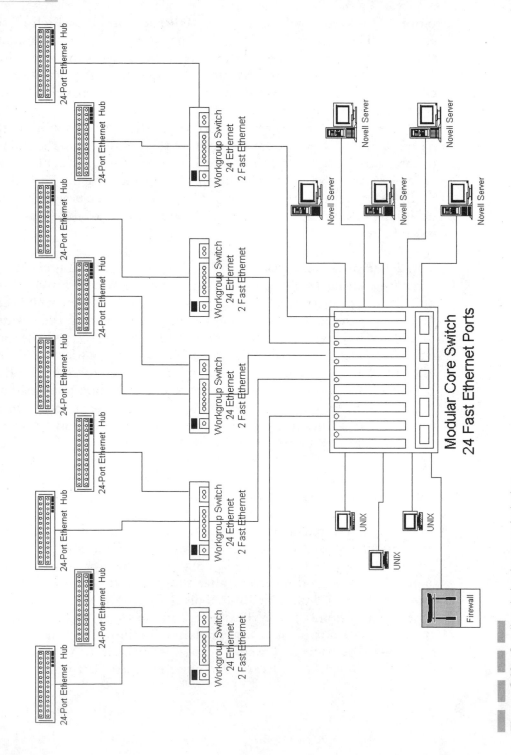

Figure 2.10 Small switched network design.

Case Study 2: Medium-Sized Switched LAN Design

This case study will design a switched LAN that spans two buildings. Each building will contain about 500 end users and a series of servers and other common resources.

Step 1: Building 1—Core and Centralized Resources Areas Design Building 1 contains 500 end users, of which 300 are to be attached to MicroLANs and 200 are to receive dedicated switch ports. Within the building are five Novell servers and ten UNIX servers providing NFS services. This building also contains the Internet router/network address translator for this organization. The core area of this building will consist of one backbone switch providing 30 fast Ethernet interfaces. This switch should have a multigigabit internal forwarding rate based on the large number of 100-megabit interfaces required. Attached to this backbone switch will be the 15 servers and the router. Additional ports will be used to connect the links to the periphery area switches. Each server will be given a 100-megabit interface to the backbone switch and as such should be capable of delivering and receiving that much data. This may require that the servers be upgraded in some cases.

Step 2: Building 1—Periphery Area Design The periphery areas of this building include 500 end users, of which 300 require MicroLAN connections and 200 require dedicated connectivity. To provide this level of connectivity we will deploy 13 Ethernet repeaters with 24 shared ports each. That will provide 321 ports of shared connectivity. We will then deploy nine 24-port Ethernet workgroup switches to provide 216 dedicated Ethernet ports. We will connect the shared segments to the workgroup switches and then uplink the workgroup switches to the backbone switch using 100-megabit links. Full-duplex and port trunking are available if required.

Step 3: Building 2—Core and Centralized Resources Areas Design Building 2 houses 500 end users and 20 server-type devices, including one mainframe. The users are all to be given dedicated switch ports. To build the core of this building, a single large backbone switch will be deployed. This switch will have about 40 fast Ethernet interfaces. The internal capacity of this switch should be in the multigigabit per second range to support so many interfaces. Each of the server resources will be given a dedicated 100-megabit Ethernet switch port. It may be necessary to provide one FDDI interface to the supercomputer, since that is its preferred technology.

Step 4: Building 2—Periphery Area Design   The periphery areas of building 2 consist of 500 end users, each requiring a dedicated switch port. To accommodate that number of users, two options exist. The first option is to deploy one or two large modular switches. The second option is to deploy 21 smaller 24-port Ethernet workgroup switches. Both options are valid, but for this design we have chosen the second option, since the end users are located over a large area and having multiple smaller switches provides more flexibility in switch placement and cable routing. Had the users been located in a more localized area, the larger switches would have been more appropriate.

Each of the workgroup switches provides 24 dedicated 10-megabit Ethernet ports providing a total of 504 ports. The switches will each uplink to the backbone switch using fast Ethernet interfaces. Full-duplex and port trunking are available options if more capacity is required after baselining the system.

Step 5: Building 1 to Building 2 Connection   To connect the two buildings, a trunk group of four to six full-duplex fast Ethernet interfaces will be used. Other options could include the use of a gigabit Ethernet link between chassis, if it is available, or the use of trunked FDDI connections if long distance is needed. The trunk group should be deployed with only a few links initially, since both buildings contain servers. Once the system is operational, the traffic levels and patterns through the trunked interbuilding links should be closely monitored. If the links are saturated, adding more links should alleviate the issues. Additionally, if the majority of traffic from either building is destined to a server resource in the other building, serious consideration should be given to relocating that server to the building housing the majority of its clients. If this is not possible, the increased number of trunk links should address the issues. The final design of this system is shown in Figure 2.11.

The final design provides a very good aggregation of bandwidth across the switched LAN. The clients are attached on shared or dedicated 10-megabit interfaces. The switches the clients attach to are linked to the core using 100-megabit interfaces. The core is built of two backbone switches that have multigigabit per second bandwidth capacity. The

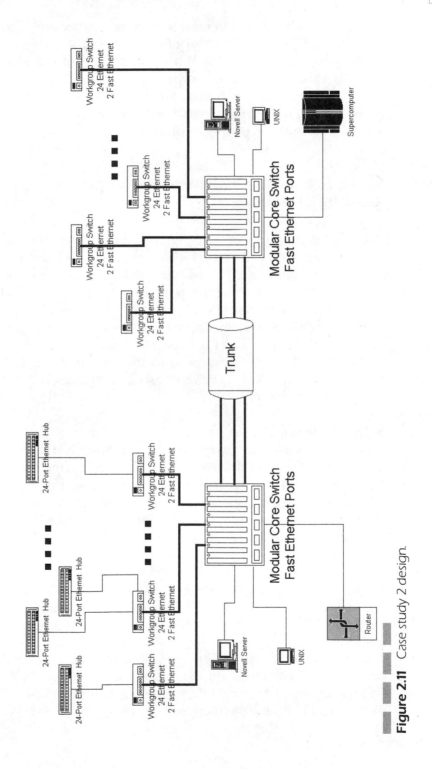

Figure 2.11 Case study 2 design.

servers and other common resources attach to the core using 100-mega-bit interfaces. This design provides a good initial configuration for a 1,000 user switched network. With proper baselining and analysis, the areas of this network that receive the most traffic can be identified. Once the bottlenecks are found, this design allows for relatively easy expansion using either more trunk links in the core or full-duplex and port trunking at the periphery uplinks.

Case Study 3: Design of a Large Switched Network

This case study examines the design of a large switched network consisting of about 3,000 end users and several centralized resources areas. All user connections are to be dedicated switch ports. It is very important that a network of this size not be built without proper analysis of the protocols and broadcast rates expected on the network. This case study will only focus on the physical construction of such a network and as such is only one portion of the complete network design plan.

The overall network is a campus of five buildings. Each building houses between 500 and 1,000 end users. The design calls for one large switch-based network.

Step 1: Buildings 1 and 2 Design   Buildings 1 and 2 each contain 500 end users and no local server resources. They are connected to building 3 using fiber-optic cables. For these buildings, a large number of dedicated switch ports is required. Since the buildings are only three stories high and all users can be cabled to a single central wiring closet, we have opted to install two large modular switches. Each switch can support over 300 Ethernet ports and several fast Ethernet uplinks. Figure 2.12 shows this building's network configuration.

Step 2: Buildings 4 and 5 Design   Buildings 4 and 5 contain about 500 end users each. They also contain several servers and other common resources. Unlike buildings 1 and 2, these buildings cannot utilize large centralized switches, since they are much larger in geographical area and their users are more distributed. To address their needs, we have chosen to utilize a model similar to that used in case study 2. Each building will contain one backbone switch, which will uplink to building 3. Within the building, the users will be connected to workgroup switch-

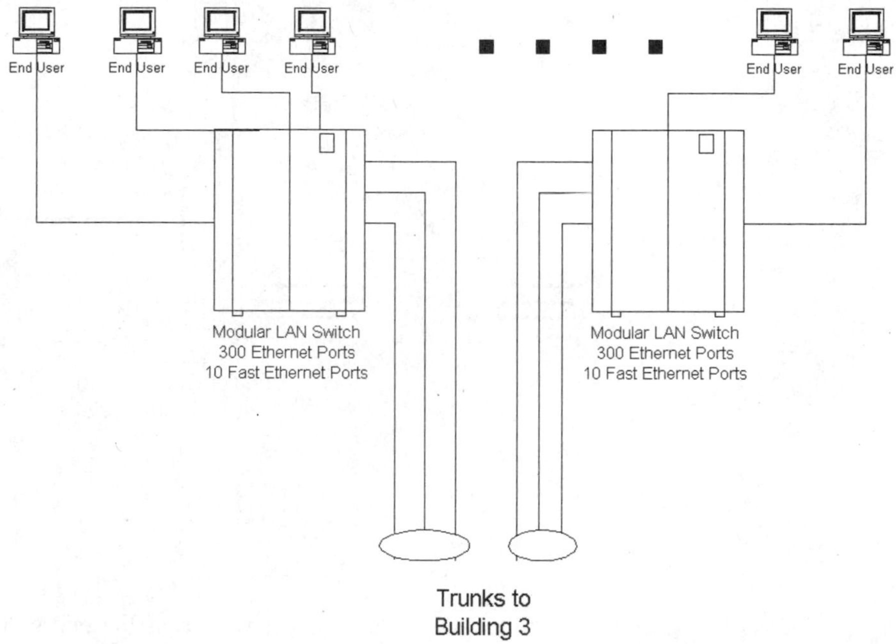

Figure 2.12

Case study 3—
buildings 1 and 2
configuration.

es, which will be collapsed into the local backbone switch. Common resources such as servers and firewalls will be connected to the buildings' local backbone switch. This model would result in a switch configuration similar to that shown in Figure 2.13.

Step 3: Building 3 Design   Building 3 is the core of this campus. This building contains over 1,000 end users and several clusters of servers and other centralized resources. All users require dedicated switch ports. This building is the focal point of all other buildings in this campus and as such must provide very high network bandwidth capacity in its core. For this building, six modular large backbone class switches will be utilized. Two will be the core backbone, connected using gigabit Ethernet links. Three of the six large switches will provide the local Ethernet connections to the end users in building 3. These three switches will connect to the core switches using trunk groups of fast Ethernet. The remaining switch will connect to the core using a gigabit Ethernet link and will provide connectivity to the centralized servers and resources in building 3. For redundancy, a fast Ethernet link to the core from this switch may be used, even though the spanning tree algorithm should place it in standby. Connections to the other buildings will be located in the two

Figure 2.13

Case study 3—
buildings 4 and 5
design.

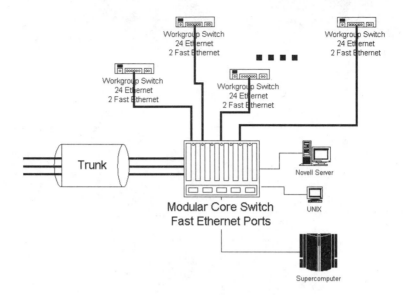

core switches using trunk groups of fast Ethernet. The final building 3 design is shown in Figure 2.14.

The complete switched network design for this 3,000 user network should provide a good aggregation of bandwidth towards the core of the network in building 3. Proper baselining and monitoring should expose any congestion points in this design, and additional links or resource relocation should be able to solve such congestion. The physical network of this case study should provide enough scalability to increase the size of this network in the future if needed. Once again, it is important to note that even though the physical design is sound, the logical protocol-related issues of such a large switched network need to be examined to fully design this network. The remaining chapters in this book focus on the design issues of switched LANs beyond the physical implementation discussed in this chapter.

Summary

The design of a switched LAN involves the process of first identifying the role each switch will play in the final network, then finding a switch with the needed features to fill each role, and, finally, connecting those switches together. This chapter provided some guidance in un-

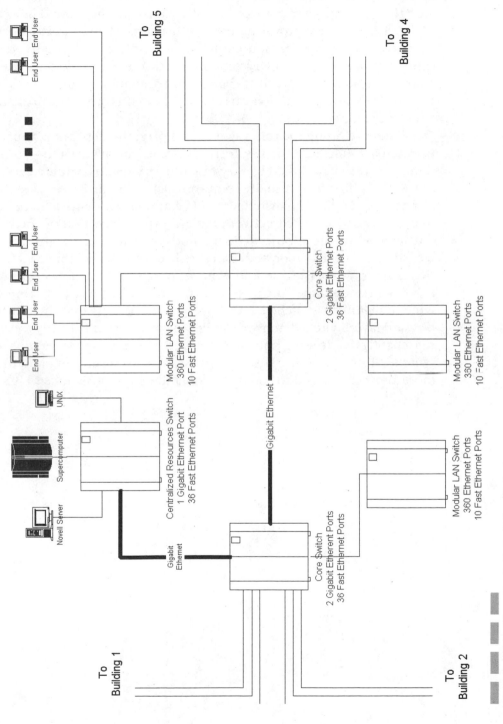

Figure 2.14 Case study 3—building 3 design.

derstanding the various roles switches play in a large network. It was seen that switches exist in three logical areas of any network. They can act in the periphery providing user connections, they can exist in the core acting as the aggregation point for user traffic, and, finally, they can act as interfaces into large common centralized resources such as servers and firewalls. In each of these roles, the switch is required to provide a certain level of bandwidth capacity, as well as other features such as traffic analysis.

By understanding the role a switch will play, the network planner is better able to identify the key features needed in that switch—for instance, a core switch should be very fast and very reliable, while a periphery switch does not usually require such a high level of either characteristic. Once the switches to fill each role are identified, the last step in physical switched network design is the connection of the various switches to one another. The methods of switch interconnectivity were discussed and demonstrated in the three case studies that conclude this chapter. While the case studies may not reflect your network exactly, they provide some guidance into the areas that must be examined when designing a switched LAN. Using this chapter's examination of physical layer switched network design in conjunction with the following chapters addressing the protocol and management operation of switched LANs, a network planner or system administrator should be more aware of the end-to-end operation and design of switched LANs.

CHAPTER 3

Scaling Issues of Flat-Switched Networks

The single biggest question a system administrator faces when building a switched local area network is, "How large can I make this network?" The question is based on past industry perception that bridged networks could only scale to limited sizes. In reality, most of the issues with bridged networks that limited their size are not often seen in today's switching systems. However, there is no blanket answer that can be given as to how big any one particular network can be. This chapter deals with understanding the issues involved in scaling a switched LAN. Techniques will also be presented to allow the system administrator to baseline the network characteristics before and after expanding the size of a switched area of the network. By understanding the factors limiting the absolute size of a switched network and how to monitor those factors, the resultant network will be built based on what the network requires, not some arbitrary de facto size limit.

Switched LAN Limitations

Ten years ago, when a system administrator designed a network using bridges and repeaters, there were certain issues and concerns. These issues included broadcast rates, broadcast storms, misbehaved applications, backbone utilization, the 80/20 rule,[1] and spanning tree failures. Some of these issues existed as functions of how bridges operated, but some were based on assumptions that misbehaved applications, defective bridges, and faulty network interface cards would exist on the network. Because of these assumptions, there was a general feeling that bridged networks should be limited in size and segmented using layer three routers. The primary role of those routers in the LAN was not to enhance performance or connectivity but to create small isolated bridged networks so that any of the possible failures mentioned above would be contained to a subarea of the overall network. Ten years ago, this step may have been necessary, but today few of these issues are relevant.

---

1. The 80/20 rule is a de facto design rule in segmented networks. It states that 80 percent of the traffic generated in one segment should be between users on that segment (or local). The remaining 20 percent of the traffic generated on that segment should be expected to be to or from devices not on that segment and as such should be required to leave this segment and cross the backbone of the network.

Spanning Tree Failures

In Chapter 1, the spanning tree algorithm was introduced. This algorithm provides a loop-free, single-path topology for bridged and switched networks. Its operation is required if any physical loop exists in the switched LAN. When the spanning tree algorithm was being developed and was considered a new standard, there were potential flaws in particular vendor implementations. It was not unheard of for a bridged network to fail due to spanning tree failures (due to buggy software on the bridges) if a physical loop existed. The failure would exhibit itself as an exponentially increasing broadcast rate as the broadcasts looped and replicated indefinitely in the bridged network. Ten years ago, this type of failure may have happened once in a while; today, however, it rarely happens. Vendors have mature spanning tree implementation, and it is generally accepted that spanning tree always works. This particular issue is no longer a limiting factor in the size of switched networks, due to the expected stability of the spanning tree algorithm.

80/20 Rule

The 80/20 rule was considered a design rule for segmented networks. Figure 3.1 shows the logic behind the 80/20 rule.

This rule was based on the limitation of the forwarding capacity of bridges in the past. While today's LAN switches may have forwarding logic similar to traditional bridges, they are completely different devices in terms of forwarding capacity. It is expected that a LAN switch today will provide near wire speed[2] performance. In addition to the current LAN switches being able to forward at wire speed, the placement of user resources is significantly different in today's networks. Current design practices place servers in centralized rather than distributed locations. This results in the clients having no local server and, as such, all of the client's traffic must be forwarded by the switch. A more extreme, but also more common, example can be seen in the use of individual switch ports for users. If the user is directly connected to a switch port, there

---

2. Wire speed: This is the term used to describe a packet forwarding rate of a particular device being equal to the maximum theoretical operational speed of a particular LAN technology—for example, 10 megabit Ethernet has a wire speed rate of 14,880 packets per second using 64-byte packets. A wire speed switch would then be considered able to forward 14,880 64-byte packets per second.

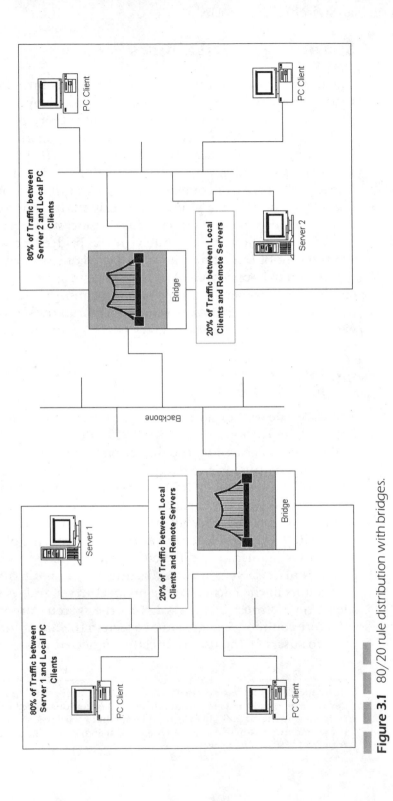

Figure 3.1 80/20 rule distribution with bridges.

can be no local resources, and, as such, all traffic to or from the user must pass through the switch. This situation could be called the 0/100 rule (0 percent local, 100 percent switched). Because of the increased switching capacity and the use of centralized servers and per port switching, it is safe to say that in switched local area networks, the 80/20 rule is obsolete.

Backbone Utilization

Bridged networks designed and implemented in the past had a limited set of technologies to choose from. 802.3 Ethernet (10 megabit) and 802.5 Token Ring (4 or 16 megabit) were the two primary LAN technologies available. These technologies were significantly faster than serial connections and older LAN architectures such as ARCnet but nevertheless imposed limitations on network design based on their maximum bandwidth. Most local area networks define some central segment as the "backbone." This term refers to the fact that most other segments will radiate from this segment, and, as such, most or all of the cross-segment traffic will cross this backbone. Figure 3.2 illustrates this concept.

The limiting factor for bridged network size was based on the performance the backbone could provide. If the backbone was an Ethernet 10 megabit segment, and most traffic (at least 20 percent based on the 80/20 rule) would cross this backbone, the design was limited to just five attached Ethernet segments radiating from the backbone. Five segments are chosen based on the mathematics of designing a nonoversubscribed network.

(5 segments * 10 megabits per segment theoretical maximum) * 20% = 10 megabits backbone capacity required

This formula assumes the worst case of maximum theoretical utilization on each segment and rigid compliance to the 80/20 rule. Most real networks could have a few more than five segments collapsed into a single 10-megabit Ethernet backbone but not a great many more.

The advent of new technologies such as Fiber Distributed Data Interface (FDDI), Asynchronous Transfer Mode (ATM), and 100Base-TX and 100Base-FX fast Ethernet, allowed backbones to scale to support a larger number of user segments. These technologies, however, did not remove all limitations, because the 100+-megabit technologies were also being utilized for user connectivity. If all the users are on 100-megabit ports

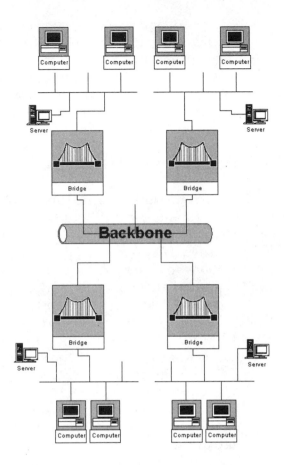

and the backbone is also 100 megabit, the scalability issue seen at 10 megabits is revisited using different numbers.

The final technology that allows switched networks today to overcome backbone limitations is switching itself. The internal capacity of large LAN switches today is typically measured in the 1,000+ megabits per second (or gigabits) range. This means that the switch can be the backbone of a network and provide enough capacity to support large numbers of 10- and 100-megabit segments without significant oversubscription. A conventional switched network design is illustrated in Figure 3.3. This type of design allows switched networks to scale far beyond the initial limitations of 10-megabit bridged networks.

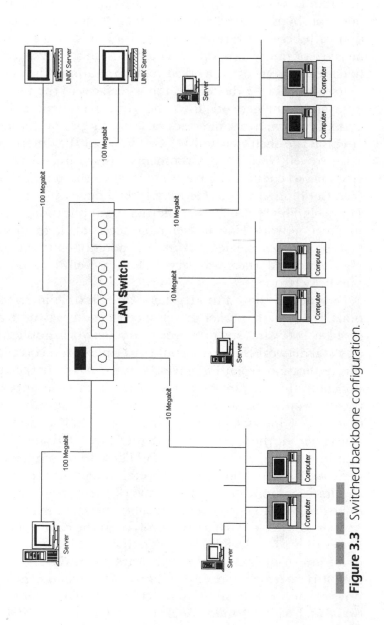

Figure 3.3 Switched backbone configuration.

Misbehaved Applications

Anyone who has ever written a software application or even a simple C program understands that all software can and usually does have some faults or "bugs." Since the network infrastructure acts as a communication path between various software applications, it is possible that misbehaved or faulty applications could exist in a networked environment. In the early years of networked communications, the applications were written to provide the service and interfaces to the user, as well as the interface to the network. It was not unusual to have a dedicated driver that locked a network interface card to a single application. An example of this is the Shell Gen and WS Gen'd Novell IPX interfaces used in the early Novell NetWare environments. These direct drivers provided an interface to connect the NetWare shell to the physical network interface. In doing so they effectively locked out any other applications or protocols. This type of design allowed the applications close access to the physical network. Having such close access made them simple and fast but also exposed the network to their potential software bugs. If the application failed, there was very little to prevent its failure from affecting the network.

In order to allow a more generic and flexible interface for applications, the generic packet driver specification was developed. This defined a software layer between the network applications and the physical network. This layer could multiplex protocols and could isolate the application from the networking hardware. If the application did not communicate directly to the network card, the application's failure usually would not cause network failure. The current implementations of network interfacing are defined in several software architectures. These include the Open Data Link Interface (ODI) and the Network Device Interface Specification (NDIS). These two architectures define generic interfaces, allowing complete independence of the software applications from the specific network hardware. They allow software to be designed to operate over a generic network with no direct knowledge or access to the hardware involved in the communication. This isolation allows for flexible software design and makes application failure irrelevant to the networking hardware. In an NDIS- or ODI-based system, it is extremely rare for application failure to negatively affect the physical network. In addition to NDIS and ODI, other software abstractions, such as the Window Sockets Interface, or WINSOCK, versions 1.1 and 2.0, are isolating the applications even further away from the actual

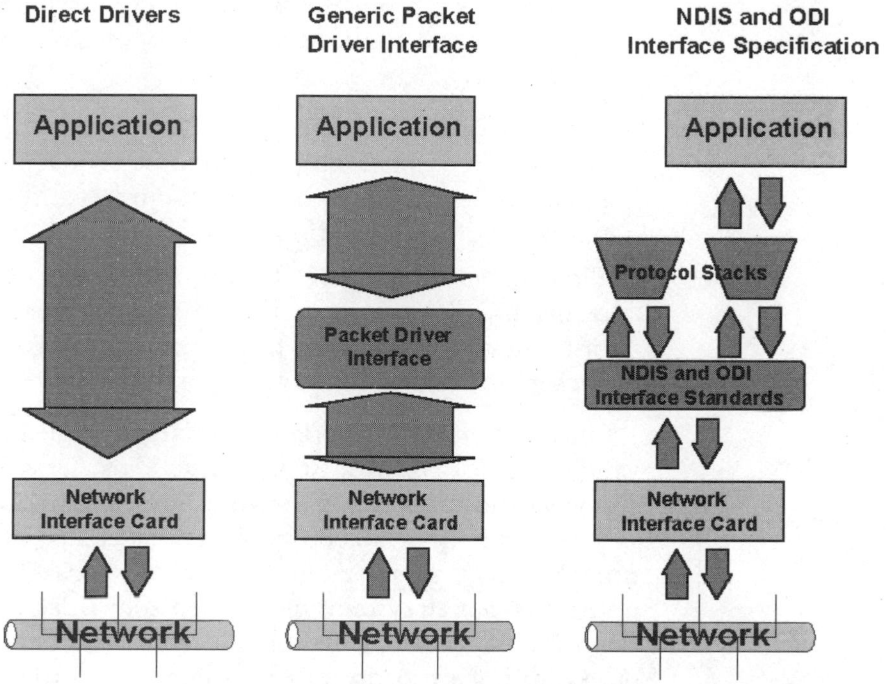

Figure 3.4

Network interface methods.

Direct Drivers	Generic Packet Driver Interface	NDIS and ODI Interface Specification

network hardware. Figure 3.4 illustrates the relationship of the various interface methods.

In the past, concern about failing applications may have forced a system administrator to limit the bridged network size. Today, the fact that more robust software interfaces exist makes this concern unnecessary. It is important to note that software failures could remotely still occur, and, as such, network thresholding and alarm limits at repeater and switch ports should always be utilized as a form of absolute protection. Chapter 8 deals with configuration and operation of these alarm limits.

Broadcast Storms and Rates

As described above, most of the issues limiting bridged and switched network size are not relevant in networks designed with today's computer and switching technology. There is one issue, however, that is extremely relevant in designing a large-scale switched network, just as it was in designing a bridged system. This issue is broadcast rate. Before broadcast rates can be discussed, a differentiation between the natural broadcast rate and a failure condition known as a broadcast storm must be made.

Broadcast Rate: Boadcast rate is the natural level of nonunicast traffic, measured in packets per second, seen on a network segment. This rate includes the necessary advertisements and requests needed for normal protocol operation.

Broadcast Storm: Broadcast storm is an error condition in which excessive broadcasts are generated due to network failure. This broadcast rate, measured in packets per second, consists of unnecessary packets with no valid network-related purpose.

Since a switched network is essentially a single broadcast domain, any valid nonunicast (broadcast or multicast) packet will be forwarded to all segments and users of the network. Since the nonunicast packet has no specific destination, all end systems must accept and examine each nonunicast packet. Some systems have the capacity to only accept certain multicasts, but all systems must accept a broadcast packet, since it is destined for all users (destination address is 0xFFFFFFFFFFFF). The action of examining a broadcast or multicast is a simple matter of processing an interrupt signal from the network interface card, reading a buffer, determining the relevance of the packet, and either passing it to a waiting protocol or dropping the packet. This entire process may take a few hundred or thousand cycles of the CPU. Since most systems operate at rates of tens or hundreds of millions of cycles per second (120 MHz = 120 million clock cycles per second), this broadcast and multicast processing is usually less significant to the CPU than moving your mouse (the mouse is also interrupt driven and follows a process similar to the reception of a packet). The normal broadcast rates of a network are usually so low that they have no real impact on the operation of an end system.

The broadcast rate of a network has rarely been the limiting factor in deciding how large a broadcast domain one should design. The real limiting factor has usually been the fear of an excessive broadcast rate caused by a network failure. Broadcast storms have traditionally been caused by two situations: failure of the spanning tree and faulty network interface cards. As discussed above, it is extremely rare to have a spanning tree failure today, since the protocol and its implementations are mature and stable. Also, as discussed above, misbehaved applications and faulty network cards are very rare given today's software and hardware architectures. If one is truly concerned about broadcast storms related to end-system failures, the use of alarm limits and thresholding should provide a suitable level of protection for the network against such a failure. Simple alarm limits would allow the local repeater or switch to disable the port to which the failing (broadcast generating) adapter is attached should some excessive broadcast rate be seen. This topic is more completely covered in Chapter 8.

Most networks have a natural broadcast rate dependent on the protocols and services being utilized. Table 3.1 lists some common protocols and the required broadcasts those protocols naturally generate.

TABLE 3.1

Some Common Necessary Nonunicast Packets

Broadcast Packet	Related Protocol	Natural Rate
Address Resolution Protocol Requests (ARP Request)	Internet Protocol	1 each time a new local IP device is contacted and no cache entry exists
AppleTalk ARP (AARP)	AppleTalk	10+ messages on power-up to determine an address
AppleTalk Name Binding Protocol (NBP)	AppleTalk	1 or more multicasts generated by either the requesting node or a router proxy when a device or zone is selected from the chooser
AppleTalk Routing Table Maintenance Protocol (RTMP)	AppleTalk	1 or more messages every 10 seconds for each Appletalk router on the switched network
Bridge Protocol Data Units (BPDU)	802.1D Spanning Tree Algorithm	1 every 2 seconds for each bridge directly attached to a segment
NetBIOS Name Advertisements	NetBIOS over LLC2, Internet Protocol, or IPX	1 every advertisement period depending on the type of NetBIOS interface being used—typically 1 every 60 seconds for each advertising NetBIOS device

TABLE 3.1

(continued)

Broadcast Packet	Related Protocol	Natural Rate
Novell Get Nearest Server and RIP Request Messages	Novell NetWare IPX	Between 2 and 40 messages over 30 seconds when a Novell client first enters the network—these represent the attempt to find a nearest and preferred server
Routing Information Protocol (RIP)	Novell NetWare IPX	1 every 60 seconds for every 50 IPX network numbers
	Internet Protocol	Each router advertises its routing table every 30 seconds
Service Advertisement Protocol	Novell NetWare IPX	1 every 60 seconds for each service-providing node (file servers, print servers)

It is important to recognize that the broadcasts and multicasts listed in Table 3.1 cannot usually be eliminated if the network is to operate. They are necessary messages in normal operation of an Internet Protocol, NetWare, AppleTalk, or NetBIOS network. If a network eliminated Service Advertisement Protocol, the Novell servers could not see each other and the clients could never find a nearest server. If the Address Resolution Protocol (ARP) were eliminated from an IP network, static mapping of the IP to MAC addresses would be required for any Internet Protocol communication, and if RTMP were eliminated in an AppleTalk network, no routing between networks could occur. In Chapters 4, 5, and 6 these protocols will be more closely examined and methods of reducing and optimizing the broadcasts will be discussed.

Once it is clear that broadcasts and multicasts are a necessary component of networking, the next task is to recognize what is normal operational behavior and what is an invalid condition or broadcast storm. There is no simple absolute threshold that could describe when excessive broadcasts are occurring for all networks—for example, a 1,000 user switched network may have an average broadcast rate of 30–40 nonunicast packets per second, while a ten user segment may have one broadcast every five seconds. On that ten user segment 40 broadcasts in one second would be 200 times the normal broadcast rate for that segment.

That is potentially an undesirable broadcast rate, but for the 1,000 user network that would simply be the normal broadcast rate. To fully understand what constitutes an acceptable and an unacceptable broadcast rate several elements of broadcasting must be examined.

1. What is the impact of broadcast and multicast packets on end systems? At what rate does a noticeable impact of CPU performance occur?

2. What is the average broadcast and multicast rate of the switched network? Is this rate below the level determined to affect the end systems of the network?

3. What is the peak broadcast and multicast rate of the switched network? Is this peak event acceptable given the determined rate at which noticeable impact of end-system performance occurs?

The rest of this chapter will focus on the process of determining the impact of broadcasts on typical end systems, and on methods for baselining the broadcast rates and peaks to make an educated decision as to whether the switched network is operating at an acceptable broadcast rate. By understanding the actual broadcast rate of a switched network, an informed decision can be made as to the expansion of the switch domain. Additional sections will address the long-term baselining of the network broadcast and multicast rates to make sure that, as the network size expands, the broadcast rate is always at a manageable level.

Broadcast Impact

The actual impact of nonunicast traffic on a typical end system is generally exaggerated. Given all of the discussion about broadcast storms, it would not be unreasonable to believe that most networks are being adversely impacted by broadcasts. In fact, the general image of switched networks is that if they grow beyond several hundred nodes, the impact of broadcasts will be so noticeable and severe that the network will be unusable. This image is too general at best and a blatant fallacy in most cases. How can the impact of broadcasts on a network be described without actually knowing what the real rate of broadcasts and multicasts generated on that network is and what that rate means to the typical end system used in that network? To make a general statement that switched networks experience broadcast-related end-system impact at some arbitrary number of nodes is a far too simplistic and general statement. Each network is unique in terms of the protocols used, the end systems attached, and the users' demands. Because of this, each network must be evaluated independently to determine if the broadcast rate is impacting that network and its end systems. Without this type of individual analysis, an informed decision cannot be made as to the growth of that switching system. This section will address the first question in network broadcast evaluation: What is the impact of broadcast and multicast packets on end systems—at what rate does a noticeable impact of CPU performance occur?

Following sections will address the measurement of a switched network's broadcast rate for comparison, as well as the techniques of long-term monitoring.

In order to answer this question, several pieces of information are necessary. What is a typical end system in terms of CPU, memory, network access, and so on? What is meant by noticeable effect on the end system? The only real way to understand what the effect of a particular broadcast and multicast rate will be on your typical end-users' systems is to test the effect yourself. In the following text, test results will be displayed to provide some indication of what effect broadcast and multicast packet rate has on CPU availability. If your system does not match one of the predefined ones, or you would like to confirm these tests, the following methodology was used.

Configuration used:

Attach a network analyzer and the device being tested to a dedicated isolated shared Ethernet or Token Ring, as shown in Figure 3.5.

Testing process:

1. Configure the end system to log broadcast and multicast packet counts and CPU utilization using whatever operating system tools that system provides. Examples of common tools include Windows 95 System Monitor, NT System Monitor, Sun Microsystems Performance Meter tool in Open Windows, and so on.

2. Generate broadcasts at incrementally higher rates starting with one pps through 1,000 or more pps. Make sure the tested end system provides a CPU resource indication at each level.

3. Generate a multicast rate at incrementally higher values from one pps to 1,000 or more pps.

Figure 3.5

Test setup for end-system broadcast analysis.

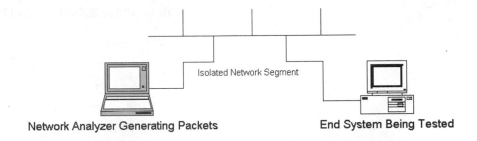

Isolated Network Segment

Network Analyzer Generating Packets   End System Being Tested

4. Chart the resultant values with CPU utilization as the y-axis and packet rate as the x-axis.

5. Generate broadcasts at the highest rate tested. Go to the tested machine and run typical applications. Make note of any obvious indications of the system's load. These include slower response of the mouse or hard disk access.

6. Repeat step 5 at several lower levels, noting any obvious indications that the system is under load. It is very possible that even at high levels, no system degradation will be seen.

Using this process, the results shown in Figure 3.6 for some typical end systems were seen.

It is obvious that the effect of broadcasts on typical end systems is inconsequential at normal traffic rates. From this example testing, it was seen that a Pentium 90 desktop may spend at most 6 percent of its CPU capacity dealing with a broadcast rate of almost 500 packets per second. A P5-133 laptop is similarly impacted, and a low-end Sparc LX workstation is impacted at a slightly higher rate. It is important to note that at these rates, no visible impact was seen in the application performance of any of the systems. It is also significant to note that when a similar number of multicast packets were sent to the three systems, the PCs behaved similarly, while the Sparc LX was not impacted at all due to its Ethernet controller being able to filter unwanted multicast packets (such as AppleTalk and NetBEUI).

The conclusion made from this testing is that only at extremely high broadcast and multicast levels are typical end systems affected. Given the increases in computing technology capacity and performance, the effect of broadcast-related processing will become less and less significant. It is also important to conclude that more advanced end systems such as workstations are generally unaffected by multicast traffic related to protocols they do not use.

Figure 3.6

Broadcast analysis
results.

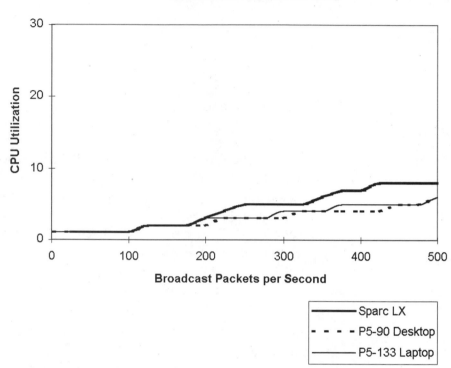

Figure 3.6

Broadcast analysis
results.

Broadcast Analysis

Once the effect of broadcasts and multicasts on the end systems of the
network has been gauged, the system administrator is now able to evaluate the broadcast and multicast rate of the switched LAN. This information can be used to determine if the actual rate is at a level that would
affect the end systems. In general there are two situations that require a
measurement of nonunicast traffic on the switched LAN. The first is
when the switched LAN is being initially implemented or expanded. The
second is when long-term monitoring and baselining is being configured
for the switched network. The subject of long-term baselining is covered
in depth in Chapter 8 and will not be discussed here.

   The initial deployment or expansion of the switched LAN requires
broadcast analysis to assure the design results in a network with acceptable broadcast and multicast rates. In most designs, LAN switches are de-

ployed to expand the size of existing segments and increase their capacity. This process of expansion will usually involve combining several independent segments isolated by router interfaces. Prior to combining, each of these segments had a specific broadcast rate. The concern that must be addressed is simply what the resultant combined segment will have for broadcast and multicast traffic levels. It is important to predict this level prior to combining the segments, since it is possible that one of the segments has applications or protocols that have very high broadcast and multicast rates. If no analysis is performed and the segments are combined, all of the resultant network will be exposed to this excessive nonunicast rate. Figure 3.7 describes a situation that without analysis yielded a switched network with unacceptable nonunicast traffic rates.

In Figure 3.7, analysis of the broadcast rates of each segment prior to combining the segments using switching would have revealed a reasonably high multicast rate on one of the segments. That rate could be attributed to the video software on the segment. Given this analysis, it would be recommended that that segment's operation be examined more closely to determine if the multicast rate could be reduced or if other protocols could be utilized. While that analysis is being performed, the remaining three segments could be combined using LAN switching.

Broadcast Analysis Process

The actual process of analyzing routed segments to determine if they can be combined effectively into one switched LAN is relatively simple using existing RMON tools or network analyzers. The basic goal is to examine each routed segment and determine its broadcast and multicast rates and users. The individual segment statistics are combined to generate a predicted broadcast and multicast behavior for the resultant switched LAN. The overall plan is shown in Figure 3.8, using the results from Figure 3.6. The network under consideration to be migrated to a switched infrastructure, rather than the existing router-based connectivity, is shown in Figure 3.9.

The structure of this network consists of six independent Ethernet segments. Two routers are used for connectivity. WAN access is provided by the second router and an older FDDI ring is used between the

Figure 3.7
Dangers of
combining
segments without
analysis.

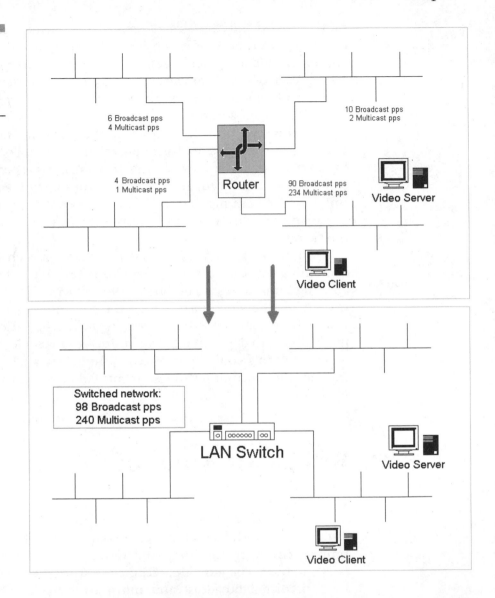

routers. The system administrator has determined that the performance demands of the users are beyond the existing routers' capabilities. Additionally, the use of an FDDI backbone in this all-Ethernet environment adds to the overall complexity of the network.

The proposed solution for this network, shown in Figure 3.9, involves introducing a LAN switch in place of router 1 and the FDDI ring. This switch will allow connections to the four segments previously attached

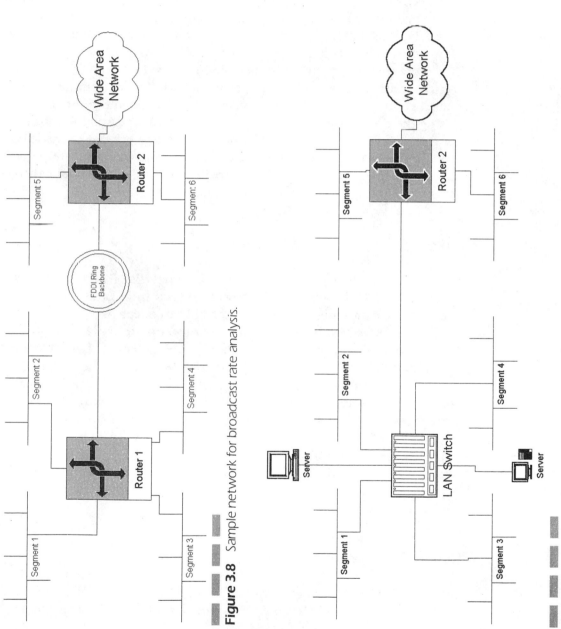

Figure 3.8 Sample network for broadcast rate analysis.

Figure 3.9 Proposed switched network.

to router 1 and will also allow additional dedicated connections for file server and high-end users. The protocols in use are able to accept the change of router location, as discussed in Chapters 4, 5, and 6. Router 2 will remain attached to this network for WAN access and to provide connectivity for some basic firewalling for segments 5 and 6. Router 2 will be connected to the new LAN switch using an Ethernet connection. If higher-speed access is required at this router, other options include fast Ethernet and full-duplex operation.

Before this design can be implemented, an evaluation must be made of the existing network traffic characteristics to determine if this switched network will have an acceptable broadcast and multicast rate. Using the process outlined in the following steps, a reasonable estimate of the overall nonunicast behavior of the new network can be made before implementing the changes. If the predictions demonstrate potential problems related to excessive broadcast rates, those issues can be examined and corrected prior to implementation.

Step 1: Segment Analysis

The first step in this process is a complete analysis of each of the segments. Using RMON probes in existing shared hubs or as stand-alone devices, the data shown in Table 3.2 should be collected.

In the network shown in Figure 3.8, a total of four RMON probes would be needed to examine the behavior of segments 1–4. A LAN analyzer could also be utilized to examine the behavior of the FDDI ring, but in our process that step will not be necessary, since a good estimate of router traffic can be made based on the HostTopN data related to the interfaces of router 1. Once the RMON probes are configured, they should be allowed to collect data for at least a week for the long-term statistics. The short-term history and HostTopN data can be extracted daily or just once at the end of the process. Daily collection would provide better data, but it is expected that the daily traffic patterns will not differ significantly.

Step 2: Data Collection

Once the RMON probes have had sufficient time to collect the required data, that information needs to be extracted and correlated. For

TABLE 3.2

Required
Segment
Analysis Data

Statistic	Description
Long-term history Duration: 1 week Interval: 1 hour	Each segment should have a long-term RMON history or statistics log generated showing the Ethernet history. This history should provide a historical trend of the broadcast rate, multicast rate, and error rate. At least one week's worth of statistics should be gathered to be assured that any typical LAN event, such as weekly backups, is seen.
Short-term history Duration: 8 hours Interval: 1–5 minutes	Each segment should be examined in closer detail for a typical workday to determine the times and quantities of broadcast and multicast rates. This smaller interval gives a better perspective regarding the peaks of nonunicast traffic.
Long-term HostTopN Broadcast out Multicast out	Identification of the top broadcast and multicast generators on each segment is needed to understand what will be contributing to the broadcast/multicast rate of the switched LAN. This is also needed to identify the overall router-related nonunicast traffic rate. Since router 1 will not be present and only a single router interface from router 2 will be attached to the switched network, it is necessary to exclude router 1's traffic when predicting the expected behavior.

the network shown in Figure 3.8, the data should be combined to form Tables 3.3 and 3.4.

The average rate values are found by simple spreadsheet analysis of the RMON history data. Import the RMON data into a common spreadsheet such as Microsoft Excel. Sum the broadcast packets column and divide that result by the total time collected in seconds. Repeat that process for the multicast packet counters. Determination of the peak rates can be obtained by close examination of the short-term RMON history. Simply find the sample with the greatest value, divide that value by the time of the sample in seconds, and a good approximation of the peak value is gained. If more accurate peak values are required, a shorter interval for the short-term history can be used, or an alarm limit can be set at a value below the expected peak. When this alarm limit is crossed, it is normal for the RMON probe to send a TRAP message including the actual value seen that crossed the alarm limit. Since the alarm limit can be set to watch over a very short interval (1–10 seconds is not uncommon), this can provide very accurate measurements of peak values.

TABLE 3.3 Average and Peak Broadcast and Multicast Rates

Statistic	Segment 1	Segment 2	Segment 3	Segment 4
Average broadcast rate in pps				
Average multicast rate in pps				
Peak broadcast rate in pps				
Peak multicast rate in pps				

TABLE 3.4 HostTopN Broadcast and Multicast Generating Stations

Statistic	Segment 1	pps	Segment 2	pps	Segment 3	pps	Segment 4	pps
First broadcast out								
Second broadcast out								
Third broadcast out								
Fourth broadcast out								
Fifth broadcast out								
First multicast out								
Second multicast out								

TABLE 3.4 HostTopN Broadcast and Multicast Generating Stations (continued)

Statistic	Segment 1	pps	Segment 2	pps	Segment 3	pps	Segment 4	pps
Third multicast out								
Fourth multicast out								
Fifth multicast out								

The data in Table 3.4 are obtained directly from the HostTopN groups on the RMON probe. It is recommended that the top five broadcast out and multicast out stations be tracked. The understanding of which stations are contributing to the overall broadcast and multicast rates is needed for two tasks. The first task is to identify the router's contribution so that it may be deducted from the average values in Table 3.3. The second task this information allows is the identification of stations generating excessive nonunicast traffic on any segment. This identification is critical in determining if the network should be built using switches.

Step 3: Switched Network Behavior Projections

Once the data defined in steps 1 and 2 have been collected, it will be necessary to develop an accurate prediction of the expected nonunicast behavior of the proposed switched network. The main reason for this step is to identify situations where the expected broadcast and multicast rates of the new switched area will be considered excessive. If, during this process, an excessive nonunicast rate is found, further analysis and possible broadcast reduction must take place before implementing the switched network.

The process of determining the expected nonunicast behavior of the new switched network involves three specific conclusions. Each of the three will be discussed in the following text.

1. What will the average broadcast and multicast rate of the new switched network be?

   To determine this value, the contribution of the router on each segment must be identified. To do this examine the host group results in step 2 and find the router's MAC address for broadcast and multicast out rate. The router will almost certainly have one of the highest rates on every segment. Once these data are known, the average rates for each of the segments are combined, less the router contribution to the segment, to develop an estimated value of the

TABLE 3.5

Data Required to Calculate Expected Average Nonunicast Rate of New Switched Network

Data Statistic	Data Value
Segment 1 broadcast average	
Segment 2 broadcast average	
Segment 3 broadcast average	
Segment 4 broadcast average	
Segment 5 broadcast average	
Segment 1 multicast average	
Segment 2 multicast average	
Segment 3 multicast average	
Segment 4 multicast average	
Segment 5 multicast average	
Segment 1 router broadcast rate	
Segment 2 router broadcast rate	
Segment 3 router broadcast rate	
Segment 4 router broadcast rate	
Segment 5 router broadcast rate	
Segment 1 router multicast rate	
Segment 2 router multicast rate	
Segment 3 router multicast rate	
Segment 4 router multicast rate	
Segment 5 router multicast rate	

TABLE 3.6 Calculations for Broadcast and Multicast Rate Totals

Segment	Broadcast Rate		Router Contribution		True Segment Broadcast Rate
1		−		=	
2		−		=	
3		−		=	
4		−		=	
5		−		=	
			Add all segment rates		
			Total broadcast rate	=	
Segment	Multicast Rate		Router Contribution		True Segment Multicast Rate
1		−		=	
2		−		=	
3		−		=	
4		−		=	
5		−		=	
			Add all segment rates		
			Total multicast rate	=	

switched network nonunicast rate. The last step in calculating an accurate average is to add the broadcast and multicast rates of the router interface with the highest value to the calculated segment rate total. This step is necessary because the router will still have one connection into the switched network. By using the existing interface with the highest rate, we provide a worst-case estimate. Table 3.5 lists the values needed for this calculation for the sample network shown in Figure 3.8, and Table 3.6 shows the actual calculation of the switched network's expected nonunicast rate.

Final result formula:

Expected_Broadcast_Rate = (Total broadcast rate) + (broadcast rate of most active router interface)

Expected_Multicast_Rate = (Total multicast rate) + (multicast rate of most active router interface)

If the expected broadcast and multicast rates of the switched network are of an acceptable level, it is generally viewed as safe to begin the actual implementation of the switched network once the peak values have been examined. If the rates are seen as excessive, then network analyzers must be used to determine what protocols and services are producing the excessive broadcasts and multicasts. If those protocols can be removed or modified to reduce the overall rate, the switched network can then be implemented.

2. What is the expected peak value of broadcast and multicast traffic on the switched network?

The peak value of nonunicast traffic represents the highest value expected on the switched network. Peak values, unlike average values, are not usually limiting factors in switched network design. It is necessary to understand what the peak values are going to be to be able to configure alarm limits and recognize potential failure situations. To predict the peak value expected in the resultant switched network, simply find the highest individual segment peak value from step 2. That peak value can be predicted to be the peak for the new switched network. The rationale for this choice is based on the fact that the peak represents a unique event. It is extremely unlikely that several individual peaks will occur at the same time; thus, a more accurate model of behavior is the assumption that all of the individual segment peaks will occur at different times on the new network. Given that model, the highest peak on the individual segments translates into the expected peak value of the new switched network.

3. Who are the expected top generators of broadcast and multicast traffic on the new switched network?

The top broadcast and multicast generating stations on the new network provide very important monitoring information. When the network is implemented using the new switched design, the single biggest statistic requiring monitoring is the broadcast and multicast rate. If that rate changes significantly, that may indicate a potential failure or protocol change in the network, such as the addition of a new router or server. By understanding which stations are expected to be the source of the majority of broadcast and multicast traffic on the switched network, new stations seen as sources of significant nonunicast traffic will be easily identified. When the existing network is analyzed to determine the expected broadcast behavior, examination of the top broadcast and multicast generating sources is easily done. By developing a list of the top five or ten sources of nonunicast traffic in the routed network, the system administrator has some understanding of which stations should also be the top five or ten sources of nonunicast traffic once the network is switched. Simply looking for changes in this list will provide some indication that the operation of the network is changing. Chapter 10 provides more detail of the proactive monitoring of switched networks.

To determine the expected top sources of broadcast and multicast traffic, the results of the HostTopN data in step 2 are used. Since the switched network will only have one router interface remaining, the other router interfaces are not included in this process. Using Table 3.4, exclude all router interfaces except the one remaining interface. Then identify the top five or ten source addresses for broadcast and multicast out statistics. Those addresses should be kept as reference for use in monitoring the behavior of the new switched network.

Example of Broadcast and Multicast Analysis

Given the process defined above for broadcast and multicast analysis, a sample network evaluation will be performed. The complete broadcast and multicast analysis process will be followed and expected network behavior will be defined.

Overview of the Network

Figure 3.10 represents the network being evaluated. This network is currently a series of individual segments bounded by router interfaces. Increased bandwidth requirements and a desire to simplify this network have resulted in the network manager examining a larger switched network as a replacement for a portion of the current routed network.

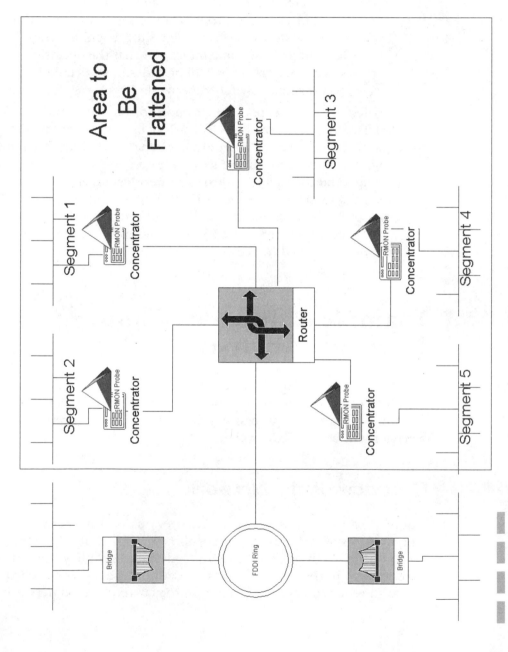

Figure 3.10 Network diagram for broadcast/multicast analysis.

RMON Probe Configuration and Segment Analysis   Each RMON probe shall be configured using the following parameters. Duration can be changed on all time-related statistics to match expected time to recover the data.

RMON statistics:

ENABLE this group

Configure one statistics group for each segment

RMON history:

ENABLE this group

Configure one history with four-hour duration, one-minute interval

Configure one history with seven-day duration, one-hour interval (Note that some RMON probes may not have enough memory to support these history time frames. If that is the case, reduce the duration or increase the interval.)

RMON host:

ENABLE this group

Configure one host group for each segment

RMON HostTopN (within the host group)

Configure one HostTopN for broadcasts out for four hours

Configure one HostTopN for multicasts out for four hours

Configure one HostTopN for broadcasts out for seven days

Configure one HostTopN for multicasts out for seven days

The configuration above should be allowed to run for seven days to assure that full historical and HostTopN data have been collected.

Data Collection   After the data have been collected by the RMON probes, the data shown on page 104 (top) needs to be extracted and collected.

This chart should contain the results of analysis of the statistics and history groups of the RMON probe. To obtain the average rate, RMON history should be used. To obtain the peak, either a short-term RMON history or the RMON statistics view should be used. (See page 104, bottom.)

Traffic Data: Time Frame Used for Average ___ Seven Days					
	Segment 1	Segment 2	Segment 3	Segment 4	Segment 5
Broadcast average rate:	5 pps	4 pps	6 pps	10 pps	9 pps
Multicast average rate:	1 pps	2 pps	1 pps	3 pps	2 pps
Broadcast peak:	223 pps	147 pps	85 pps	245 pps	174 pps
Multicast peak:	18 pps	34 pps	20 pps	75 pps	45 pps

Source Data Table: Time Frame Used for HostTopN: ___ Seven Days										
	Segment 1	pps	Segment 2	pps	Segment 3	pps	Segment 4	pps	Segment 5	pps
1st broadcast out	cisco125603	2	cisco125633	2	cisco12ad34	1	ctron223ad1	3	cisco234212	2
2nd broadcast out	ctrona432da	1	ctron132422	<1	netgen238aa2	1	ciscoad3245	1	intel745623	1
3rd broadcast out	sun1643af	<1	sun1242311	<1	ctron13afed	<1	sun239476	<1	sun092374	<1
4th broadcast out	sgi453fd3	<1	0836485322	<1	netgen12af34	<1	ctron094635	<1	sgi7453afd	<1
5th broadcast out	002345af34	<1	hp239574	<1	ctron127463	<1	intel1234df	<1	smc983ad2	<1
1st multicast out	ctron102734	1	apple98743	1	cisco12ad34	1	cisco2234d1	1	cisco234212	1
2nd multicast out	cisco125603	1	cisco125633	1	000065123 4fd	<1	apple769543	1	apple234561	<1
3rd multicast out	apple867453	<1	xlgics238561	<1	ctron876453	<1	shiva23afd4	<1	xlgicsad3421	<1
4th multicast out	hp158473	<1	08001235de12	<1	009236453a	<1	appleaa74fe	<1	ctron238622	<1
5th multicast out	intel985487	<1	intel192783	<1	netgenf43de	<1	intel324522	<1	0823642311 1	<1

This chart should list the results of a HostTopN for broadcast and multicast out statistics.

Switched Network Behavior Projections   Once the RMON probe data for the seven days have been extracted, the projections about the recommended switched network's broadcast and multicast rates must be made. Figure 3.11 shows the proposed switched network design.

Using the data gathered from the RMON probes on the existing routed network, projected nonunicast traffic levels for the proposed switched network need to be developed. Using step 3 of the broadcast and multicast analysis process, a valid estimate of the network's nonunicast traffic can be seen, as shown in the following chart.

Data Statistic	Data Value
Segment 1 broadcast average	5
Segment 2 broadcast average	4
Segment 3 broadcast average	6
Segment 4 broadcast average	10
Segment 5 broadcast average	9
Segment 1 multicast average	1
Segment 2 multicast average	2
Segment 3 multicast average	1
Segment 4 multicast average	3
Segment 5 multicast average	2
Segment 1 router broadcast rate	2
Segment 2 router broadcast rate	2
Segment 3 router broadcast rate	1
Segment 4 router broadcast rate	1
Segment 5 router broadcast rate	2
Segment 1 router multicast rate	1
Segment 2 router multicast rate	1
Segment 3 router multicast rate	1
Segment 4 router multicast rate	1
Segment 5 router multicast rate	1

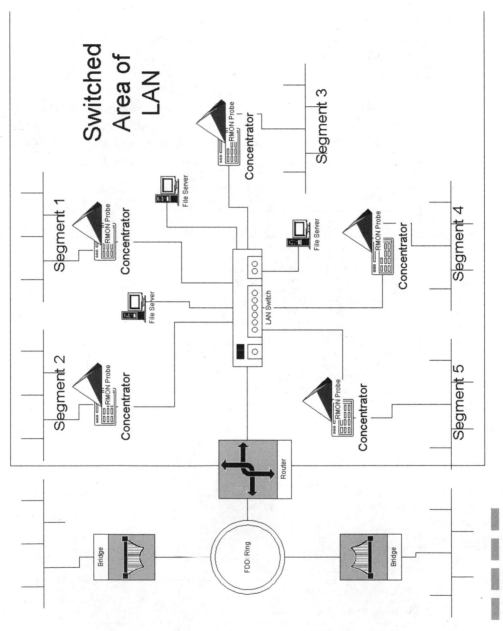

Figure 3.11 Proposed switched network design.

The following chart indicates the data required to calculate the expected average nonunicast rate of the new switched network.

Segment	Broadcast Rate		Router Contribution		True Segment Broadcast Rate
1	5	–	2	=	3
2	4	–	2	=	2
3	6	–	1	=	5
4	10	–	1	=	9
5	9	–	2	=	7
			Add all segment rates		
			Total broadcast rate	=	26
Segment	Multicast Rate		Router Contribution		True Segment Multicast Rate
1	1	–	1	=	1
2	2	–	1	=	1
3	1	–	1	=	1
4	3	–	1	=	2
5	2	–	1	=	1
			Add all segment rates		
			Total multicast rate	=	6

Final Result Formula

28 broadcasts/sec total = 26 broadcasts/sec from users + 2 broadcasts/sec from router interface

8 multicasts/sec total = 6 multicasts/sec from users + 2 multicasts/sec from router interface

Expected behavior analysis:

Statistics	Expected Value
Broadcast rate:	28
Multicast rate:	8
Broadcast peak:	245
Multicast peak:	75

User source data:

Top Five Broadcast Sources	Rate: pps	Top Five Multicast Sources	Rate: pps
ctron2234d1	3	apple985743	1
cisco234212	2	apple769543	1
ctrona432da	1	ctron102734	1
intel745623	1	cisco234212	1
netgen238aa2	1	0000651234fd	<1

It is predicted that this network will have an average broadcast rate of 28 packets per second and a multicast rate of eight packets per second. The peak values for broadcasts and multicasts should be approximately 245 pps and 75 pps, respectively. A known set of five top multicast and broadcast users is given, so that new users generating significant broadcast or multicast traffic will be identified. Overall, given this set of predictions, and knowing that the typical end systems of this network will not be affected by these rates, it is recommended that this network be moved to the switched configuration presented in Figure 3.9.

Summary

When answering the question, "How large can I make this network?" it is now obvious that the response is significantly different given today's switching technologies versus the legacy bridges of the past decade. Most of the limiting factors of older bridged designs are not relevant today, including failing adapter cards, spanning tree failure, the 80/20 rule, and misbehaved applications. Switch technologies have provided tremendously higher performance with manageable and intelligent network components. In general, the only real limiting factor of a switched network is the overall broadcast and multicast rates that end systems can tolerate. Given the analysis in this chapter, it is obvious that the typical end system of today's network is not impacted by broadcasts and multicasts unless they reach extremely high rates. It is also clear that most networks today operate at broadcast and multicast rates far below such a level. Given this understanding and the broadcast/multicast analysis process described in this chapter, the system administrator should be able to make informed conclusions regarding the scaling of domain size in the switched network. That informed understanding will be based on real data relating to the network and not some arbitrary suggestion for some limited user count. Each network is different in terms of protocols, end users, and activity. Because of this, each network requires its own analysis for answering the question, "How large can I make this network?"

Internet Protocol in Switched Networks

The implementation of a large switched network involves more than just the physical design and construction of a layer two system. It also involves the behavior of the layer three protocols used on the switched network. In the design of a switched network, routers are removed or relocated to the periphery of the network. These changes in the router placement alter the relationship some end users have to those routers. As such, if the router is moved, and the relationship between it and the end systems is no longer valid, the end systems must be adapted to understand the new flat network construction.

Most protocols can handle the relocation of routers without end-system reconfiguration. Certain protocols require some end-system changes. This chapter will discuss the operation of Internet Protocol in large switched networks. The following chapters will discuss additional protocols such as Novell IPX.

Internet Protocol Overview

Internet Protocol is possibly the most common network protocol used today. Its origins date back to the DARPA Internet, and its evolution has been ongoing for the past 20 years. In today's networks, it is by far the most flexible and efficient layer three protocol available. The actual protocol is defined by the Internet Engineering Task Force (IETF) as a series of standards. Because no specific vendor owns the rights to the protocol, it is an open standard. Within these standards, an architecture of layered protocols is defined to make up the Internet Protocol Suite. Figure 4.1 defines some of the various subprotocols that make up the Internet Protocol Suite.

It can be seen from Figure 4.1 that the term *Internet Protocol* can either refer to the entire protocol suite or to just the network layer protocol, which acts as the primary transport of this protocol suite. This section provides a brief overview of the Internet Protocol operation. Since the area of interest in a switched network is primarily just the layer three logic of this protocol, only that area will be examined in depth. If the reader is not familiar with Internet Protocol or requires more detailed discussions of the higher-layer operations of this protocol suite, there are many excellent books devoted solely to this protocol.

Figure 4.1

Internet Protocol
Suite.

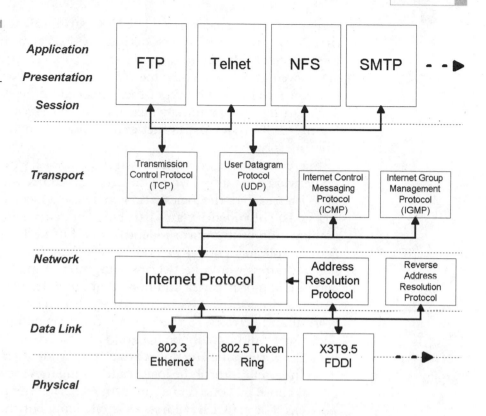

Application

Presentation

Session

FTP | Telnet | NFS | SMTP

Transport

Transmission Control Protocol (TCP) | User Datagram Protocol (UDP) | Internet Control Messaging Protocol (ICMP) | Internet Group Management Protocol (IGMP)

Network

Internet Protocol | Address Resolution Protocol | Reverse Address Resolution Protocol

Data Link

802.3 Ethernet | 802.5 Token Ring | X3T9.5 FDDI

Physical

Address Classes and Route Determination Operation

IP Addressing Overview

Internet Protocol is defined as a network layer protocol against the OSI model. At the network layer, this protocol is responsible for defining the packet formatting and the logical addressing structure for all communication between Internet Protocol nodes. The packet format consists of a predefined data unit with fields for such things as addresses, checksums, control information, and data. The logical addressing structure involves the defining of a mechanism to identify each IP node uniquely. The current version of IP (IP version 4) uses a 32-bit address consisting of two major parts. The first part is called the network identifier. This part of the address defines the logical grouping a particular user belongs to. By having a common network identifier, two IP devices are viewed as being in the same physical network (or on the same side of a router). The second part of the logical address is the node identifier. This part is used to uniquely identify the end user within the network. Figure 4.2 illustrates an abstract example of this network and node addressing format.

In examining the example shown in Figure 4.2, we can see that the total network consists of two logical areas called network 10 and network 11. Within each of the logical areas, there are nodes having unique identifiers. To fully identify any particular node in the total network, the combination of its network identifier and its node identifier is used—for example, to identify the node on the far left of Figure 4.2, the total logical address would be 10.1, meaning node 1 in network 10. It is this combination of network and node that fully defines the end users in a logical address space. We can see that while there is a node 1 in both network 10 and network 11, they are not the same node, because their total addresses would actually be 10.1 and 11.1, respectively. Since the total address is not the same, the nodes are uniquely identifiable.

In Internet Protocol the logical addressing uses the same concepts discussed above but in a different form to define the network and node portions. The actual IP address is 32 bits long, but the protocol defines five different types of network addresses, based on how many of the 32 total address bits define the network identifier. The normal representation of the IP address is in a form known as dotted decimal, with four decimal digits separated by periods. Each of the digits represents eight bits of the total 32. In this format, IP addresses can range from 0.0.0.0 through 255.255.255.255. The five different forms are known as address classes, or major network types. Each type allocates a different number of bits to define the logical network identifier and uses the remaining bits for nodes and subnets. Figure 4.3 breaks down the formats of the different classes of IP addresses.

These classes were created so that IP could support logical groupings of users that ranged in size from 254 nodes in the case of a class C network to over 16 million nodes in a single class A network. The actual IP network address numbers used for each class of network are shown in Table 4.1.

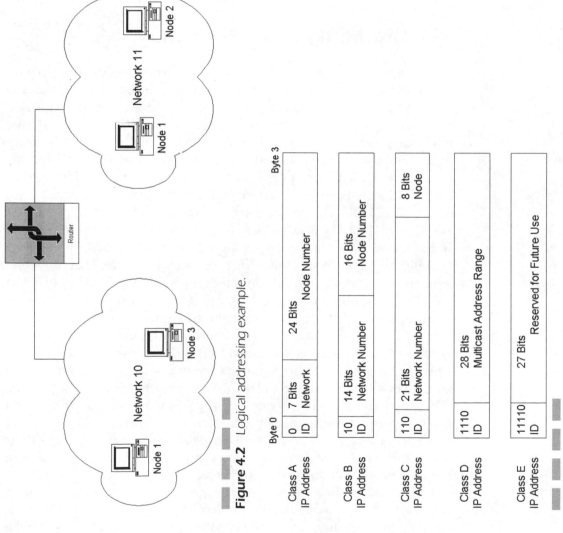

Figure 4.2 Logical addressing example.

Figure 4.3 IP address classes.

Address Class	Starting Address	Ending Address
Class A	1.0.0.0	126.255.255.255
Class B	128.0.0.0	191.255.255.255
Class C	192.0.0.0	223.255.255.255
Class D	224.0.0.0	239.255.255.255
Class E	240.0.0.0	255.255.255.255

TABLE 4.1

IP Network
Class Address
Ranges

Network Masks and Subnetting

The Internet Protocol addressing scheme described above allows for users to be grouped together in networks ranging in size based on the class of the address. In addition to the actual address given to an end user, that user is given a network mask. The purpose of the mask is to define how many bits of the 32 total are used to describe the network identifier. Each of the network address classes has what is called a natural default mask, which maps in the binary form to define the bits used to describe that network—for example, the natural mask of a class B address is 255.255.0.0. This mask, when converted to binary, is defined as 11111111.11111111.00000000.00000000. If that mask is compared to the total IP address of a user in a class B network, such as 172.16.2.3, the result is 172.16.0.0, based on the binary AND operation. The value 172.16.0.0 represents the network the user belongs to. This mask is primarily useful in the route determination process discussed in the next section.

In addition to natural masks for the three major network classes (A, B, and C), Internet Protocol was extended to support a concept known as subnetting. Subnetting was added to IP to handle the situation where a network required further segmentation of a single class A, B, or C major network. If we examine a class A network, the structure of just one class A network provides for one logical grouping of over 16 million end users. It is very unlikely that a single network would contain that many nodes in one physical layer two network. The owner of that address may require router interconnection via a wide area link to another site. It would make little sense to acquire a second class A network to handle the other end of the wide area link when there are plenty of addresses remaining in the class A already owned. Through the subnetting process, the administrator can use some of the node identifier bits to describe subnetworks within the major network number. In Figure 4.4, the

Figure 4.4

Subnetting a class A
network into 255
class B size subnets.

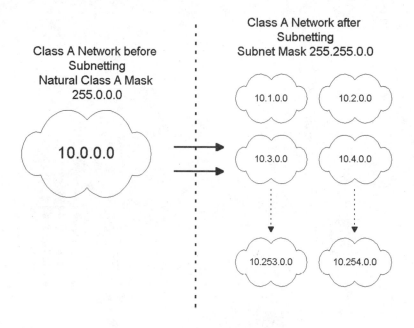

Class A Network before
Subnetting
Natural Class A Mask
255.0.0.0

10.0.0.0

Class A Network after
Subnetting
Subnet Mask 255.255.0.0

10.1.0.0   10.2.0.0

10.3.0.0   10.4.0.0

10.253.0.0   10.254.0.0

class A network 10.0.0.0 is subnetted into 255 class B size networks simply by extending the mask an additional eight bits.

The subnetting of the 10.0.0.0 network resulted in 255 subnetworks, each containing over 64,000 nodes. This mechanism is necessary to effectively utilize available IP addresses, since the alternative would be to utilize additional major networks.

In Figure 4.4, the subnetting of class A resulted in 255 large networks. It would be possible to further subnet class A by extending the mask—for example, extending the mask another eight bits would result in over 64,000 class C size networks. It is obvious that based on the network mask and subnet masking, the actual number of bits used to describe the logical network a user belongs to can change. With a natural mask of 255.0.0.0, a user in the 10.0.0.0 network is described as one user in one group of over 16 million addresses. With an eight-bit subnet mask of 255.255.0.0, that same user is now a member of one logical subnet of class A containing over 64,000 addresses. If the mask is pushed out to 16 bits of subnetting, resulting in 255.255.255.0, the user is a member of a small group of 245 nodes within the overall class A network. Figure 4.5 illustrates this concept.

Subnetting has provided a useful mechanism to effectively use a large, single address space to describe many smaller separate areas. Since

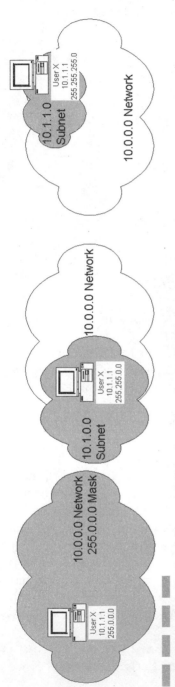

Figure 4.5 Some subnetting possibilities in a class A network.

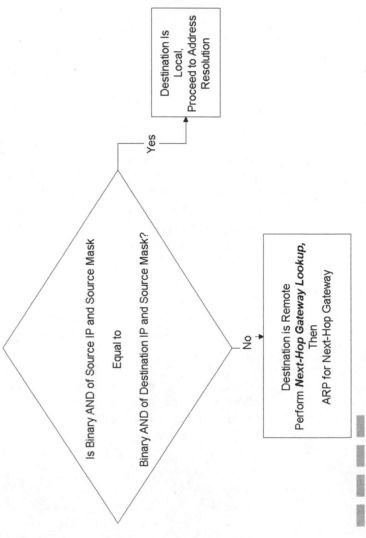

Figure 4.6 Route determination logic flow in Internet Protocol.

IP networks are in short supply given the growth of the global Internet, this ability to better utilize single major networks has allowed far more effective use of the Internet addresses defined in 32 bits.

Subnetting has also caused some unfortunate consequences. Because it is relatively easy to implement on most routers, many networks have oversubnetted their logical structure. Once the subnetting is put into place, the end users are bound to a particular subnet based on their IP address. If a class A network were subnetted to class C size subnets, each of those areas would be limited to just 254 devices. Given a standard end-system configuration in this environment, all other devices would be reachable only though the routers that logically connected the subnet to the rest of the IP networks. Five to ten years ago, limiting layer two bridged networks to 254 nodes might have made sense. Today, it is obvious that switched networks can support far greater node counts in one layer two system. Because of the subnetting that has been put in place over the years, even if the switched network could physically support thousands of nodes, the end-user configuration prevents use of the switching systems for direct communication to other subnets without the router. By subnetting the network in the past, the administrator may have unwittingly configured the network in such a way that it may be necessary to unconfigure the end-system subnetting in order to begin to utilize the switched network for user communication.

Route Determination

All IP hosts wishing to communicate must complete two processes successfully before any useful data can be exchanged. Those two steps are known as route determination and address resolution. All IP nodes will follow these two steps in the process of establishing any IP conversation.

Route determination is the process of recognizing a destination user as either local or remote. A local user is one determined to be directly attached to the same layer two network as the sending station. This determination is based on the users sharing the same subnet or network identifier in their IP addresses. A remote user is one determined not to be attached to the sending station's layer two network and as such is only reachable through a next-hop gateway (usually called a router). The information used to make this determination includes three parameters: the sending station's IP address, the destination station's IP address, and the sending station's network mask. Using these three parameters, the sending station will make a comparison between its IP address and its network mask using a Boolean AND operation.[1] It will then use the same Boolean AND operation to compare the destination station's IP address and the source user's mask. The results of a Boolean AND against an IP address and mask define which bits in the 32-bit address are defining the network identifier. If the results of these two comparisons are equal, the devices are considered local from the sending stations' perspective, because they share the same network identifier. If the results are not equal, the devices are considered remote, because their logical network identifier is different. This operation is shown in Figure 4.6 (page 118).

An example of this logic is shown in Figure 4.7. In this process, station 10.1.1.1 with a mask of 255.0.0.0 is attempting to determine if the device 10.4.128.1 is local or remote. The binary AND of the source IP and source mask yields a network number of 10.0.0.0. The binary AND of the destination IP and source mask yields 10.0.0.0. Since the result is equal, using the flow diagram in Figure 4.6, the destination is considered local. At this time the source station can begin the address resolution process directly for the destination station 10.4.128.1.

The analysis performed in Figure 4.7 resulted in a local destination, based on the network identifier being the same between the source IP address and the destination IP address. The sending station at this time truly believes that the destination station is located on the same layer two network and that no routers exist in between the two devices.

If Figure 4.7 were altered to use a network mask subnetted eight additional bits, the result of route determination would be significantly different. Figure 4.8 shows the result of that change in the route determination process. The source mask is now 255.255.0.0, reflecting the fact that the 10.0.0.0 class A network has been divided into class B size subnets, as seen in Figure 4.4. Now, when the route determination logic is applied to the source IP, destination IP, and source mask, the result is that the source user is in the 10.1.0.0 subnet, while the destination user is in the 10.4.0.0 subnet. This result tells the source user that the destination is not directly reachable at layer two. Since the destination is considered remote, the source user must now determine how to reach the destination by consulting its routing table.

---

1. A Boolean AND operation is used to compare two binary digits. Given that a binary digit can only be 0 or 1, the Boolean AND operation compares two binary digits as follows: 0 AND 0 = 0, 1 AND 0 = 0, 0 AND 1 = 0, 1 AND 1 = 1.

Figure 4.7

Local host route determination.

Source IP   *AND* Source Mask

10 . 1 . 1 . 1   00001010.00000001.00000001.00000001

255 . 0 . 0 . 0   11111111.00000000.00000000.00000000

──────────── Boolean AND ────────────

10 . 0 . 0 . 0   00001010.00000000.00000000.00000000

Destination IP   *AND* Source Mask

Equal Values Mean Destination Is Local

10 . 4 . 128 . 1   00001010.00000100.10000000.00000001

255 . 0 . 0 . 0   11111111.00000000.00000000.00000000

──────────── Boolean AND ────────────

10 . 0 . 0 . 0   00001010.00000000.00000000.00000000

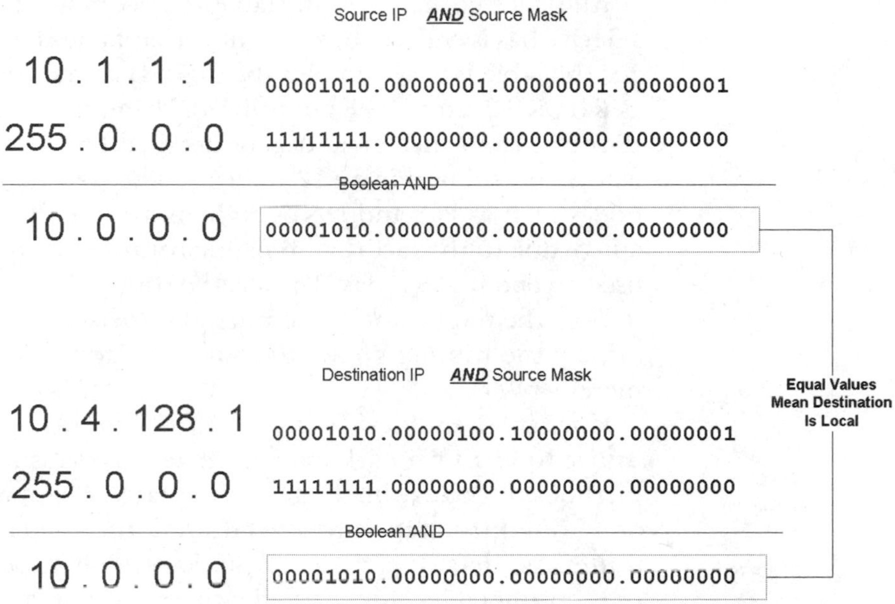

Figure 4.8

Remote host route determination.

Source IP   *AND* Source Mask

10 . 1 . 1 . 1   00001010.00000001.00000001.00000001

255.255.0 .0   11111111.11111111.00000000.00000000

──────────── Boolean AND ────────────

10 . 1 . 0 . 0   00001010.00000001.00000000.00000000

Destination IP   *AND* Source Mask

Not Equal Means Destination Is Remote

10 . 4 . 128 . 1   00001010.00000100.10000000.00000001

255 . 255 .0 .0   11111111.11111111.00000000.00000000

──────────── Boolean AND ────────────

10 . 4 . 0 . 0   00001010.00000100.00000000.00000000

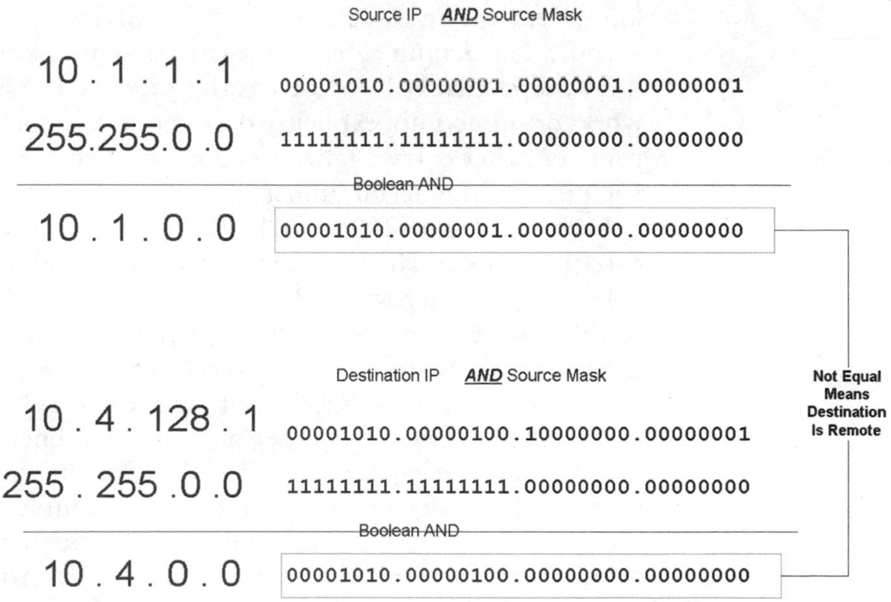

All IP devices have routing tables. The complexity of the routing table a device has is entirely based on how that table is populated. On IP routers, the table is very complex, because dynamic routing protocols such as RIP, RIP2, and OSPF are utilized. Using those routing protocols, an IP router can gain a great deal of detailed knowledge regarding all networks and subnets in an IP Internet. The routing tables found on end nodes such as PCs and UNIX stations are usually significantly less detailed, due to the fact that dynamic routing protocols are not typically used on end nodes today. To view the routing table on your PC or workstation, the most common command is "netstat –R." This command will display the routing knowledge your device has regarding reaching remote networks.

Since most end devices do not run the routing protocols IP routers utilize to learn network knowledge, end systems must have alternative methods of populating their routing table. The most common method of adding information to an end user's routing table is by using static routes and default gateways. A static route is a specific entry added to the routing table. This entry identifies the router to be used to reach a specific remote network or subnet. It may also indicate how many router hops that network is from the source device by defining what is known as a metric. A default gateway is defined as a special kind of static route. The default gateway provides an end user with the address of a local router that will be used as the gateway to reach any remote networks or subnets not explicitly defined in the routing table with a static route or other entry. Figure 4.9 demonstrates an example routing table for a user in the 10.1.0.0 subnet.

User X in Figure 4.9 has a relatively simple routing table consisting of three real entries. The first entry defines the local subnet 10.1.0.0 as reachable directly via its own address. The second entry is a static route to the 10.4.0.0 subnet using router 10.1.1.2 as the gateway. This entry would be used whenever user X wanted to reach a user with a 10.4.x.x IP address. The third entry defines a default gateway to router 10.1.1.1. This entry will be used to reach any other network or subnetwork in the Internet. The default gateway could be thought of as the end system recognizing that the router defined has a much more complete routing table, so in the event that the user's local routing table does not know how to reach a destination network, the determination of best route should be passed off to the default gateway. With just these three entries, the user has the ability to determine how to reach any IP destination.

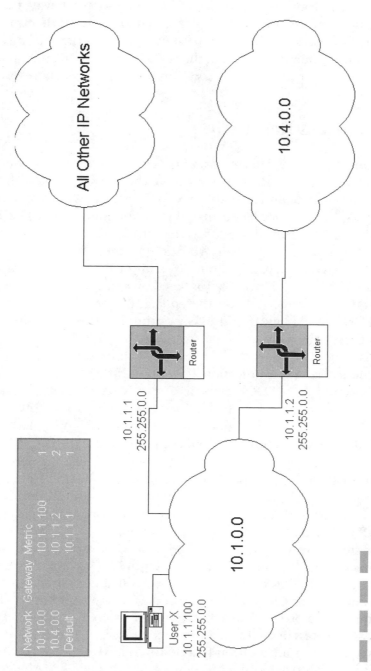

Figure 4.9 End-system routing table.

If the destination is considered remote, and the source device is able to use its routing table to determine a next-hop gateway, the address resolution process can now be performed. If the route determination process fails, because no next-hop gateway exists in the routing table and no default gateway is defined, the IP communication goes no further. The user will typically see a message indicating "network unreachable."

Address Resolution

Once the route determination process is complete, the source user will understand that the destination is either local or remote. If the destination is remote, an acceptable next-hop gateway will have been chosen by consulting the local routing table of the source user. The next process that must occur is the address resolution process. This process is used to determine the MAC layer address of either the local user or the next-hop gateway, depending on the result of route determination. The reason this process is necessary is based on a simple fact. The users and gateways are connected together physically by Ethernets, Token Rings, FDDIs, ATM Emulated LANs, or other layer two systems. Up until this process, the only addresses relating the source and destination users have been IP addresses. While the IP addresses do describe the end-to-end logical communication, they do us little good crossing an Ethernet, Token Ring, or FDDI segment. The only things that will allow communication to cross these technologies are their native MAC layer addressing, framing formats, and access method rules. We must use Ethernet rules to cross an Ethernet, and the same holds true for FDDI and Token Ring. It is the responsibility of the address resolution process to determine the proper mapping between the logical IP addresses and the necessary MAC layer addresses to complete this communication.

The address resolution process can either be static or dynamic at any IP end system. A static address resolution process requires that the end system have a predetermined table of MAC address to IP address bindings before IP communication is required. This table is usually referred to as an "ETHERS file." While a static configuration is possible, most end users opt for the dynamic method of address resolution. This method makes use of the Address Resolution Protocol, or ARP. The dynamic ARP process operates on an as-needed basis. When the source IP device requires communication to a destination IP address, the ARP protocol is invoked to determine the destination IP device's MAC address. The re-

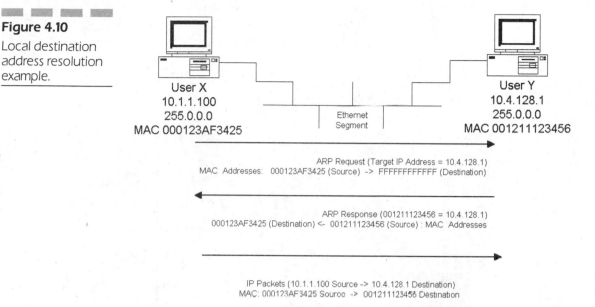

Figure 4.10

Local destination
address resolution
example.

User X
10.1.1.100
255.0.0.0
MAC 000123AF3425

Ethernet
Segment

User Y
10.4.128.1
255.0.0.0
MAC 001211123456

ARP Request (Target IP Address = 10.4.128.1)
MAC Addresses: 000123AF3425 (Source) -> FFFFFFFFFFFF (Destination)

ARP Response (001211123456 = 10.4.128.1)
000123AF3425 (Destination) <- 001211123456 (Source) : MAC Addresses

IP Packets (10.1.1.100 Source -> 10.4.128.1 Destination)
MAC: 000123AF3425 Source -> 001211123456 Destination

sults of the dynamic ARP process are cached in the source user's ARP cache and reused for some period of time to increase the efficiency of this process.

In a case where route determination resulted in a local destination when user X in Figure 4.10 attempted to communicate with user Y, the ARP process must be utilized to determine the MAC to IP bindings necessary to deliver packets across the Ethernet segment to user Y.

User X in Figure 4.9 determines that user Y is local, based on route determination yielding network 10.0.0.0 for both source and destination devices. User X then utilizes the ARP process to resolve the known IP address of Y to a MAC address, which will be utilized to build and deliver Ethernet packets across this segment to Y. The actual ARP process involves the transmission of a MAC layer broadcast packet to all nodes. Embedded in the data field of that ARP request packet is the IP address of the desired destination. Since this packet is a broadcast, it will reach all devices in the layer two network. Each device will examine the packet, but only the one whose IP address is embedded in the ARP request's "target IP address" field will understand this packet and respond. All other nodes will simply discard this request.

The ARP response from user Y is sent directly to user X as a unicast MAC layer packet. It includes the source and destination IP and MAC

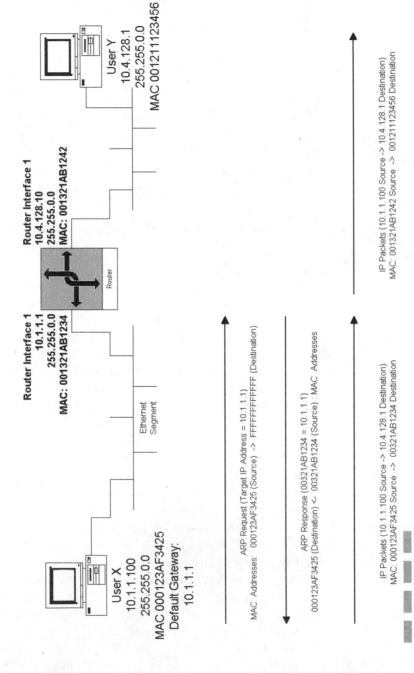

Figure 4.11 Remote host address resolution example.

addresses for this communication. Since user X required the MAC address of user Y before beginning IP communication, user X is now fully armed with both the logical IP and physical MAC addresses of Y. User X will also place the MAC to IP mapping for user Y into its ARP cache for future use.

In a case where the destination device is determined to be remote via the route determination process, the ARP process will happen just as it did in the local destination example, except that the ARP process will be used to find the MAC layer address of the next-hop gateway needed to reach the real IP destination. Figure 4.11 provides an example of a remote host ARP.

In this case, user X in Figure 4.11 determines that user Y is a remote destination, based on route determination yielding networks 10.1.0.0 and 10.4.0.0 for source and destination, respectively. User X then consults its routing table to determine a proper next-hop gateway to reach the 10.4.0.0 network. Only one entry exists in user X's routing table. That entry is a default gateway set to router 10.1.1.1. At this time the ARP process begins but is now responsible for finding the MAC layer address of the default gateway. The reason the default gateway's MAC address is required is based on the fact that the Ethernet communication from user X to reach user Y terminates at the router. Because of this, user X must be able to deliver Ethernet packets to the gateway router's MAC address instead of to user Y. The router, as with any other IP device, will respond to an ARP request with an ARP response providing its MAC layer address. Once the response is seen by user X, its ARP cache is populated with the router's MAC address. At this time, user X has all necessary information to begin sending IP packets to user Y.

The route determination process and address resolution process define the basic method of establishing IP host communication in any type of IP network. Since these processes must happen in order and be successful for any communication to occur, they provide a framework for understanding how IP host communication in a routed configuration will operate and how a flat-switched network will behave with respect to these two processes. If one understands this basic model of IP host communication, the implementation of a flat-switched IP network will be a simple matter of manipulating this process to accommodate the absence of next-hop gateways in the end-to-end path.

IP Configuration Options for Flat-Switched Networks

The implementation of a flat-switched IP network is dependent on one factor. That factor is whether or not the end systems believe that they can communicate directly without routers in the switched network area. The ideal IP configuration for switched networks is one where the end systems truly believe that all destinations are considered local in the route determination process. The process needed to reach that desired goal is simply that of reusing all the processes required to implement the routed infrastructure initially. When the router segmentation was initially done, end systems and routers were configured to understand each other's presence. That configuration involved setting the routing table of end systems to understand the various next-hop gateways it would require and configuring the routers to provide necessary services to those end systems. The process of flattening, or removing, that router segmentation is the process of undoing what was done to move to the oversegmented routed infrastructure in the first place.

In this section, four tools necessary to flatten most networks will be discussed. They include two end-system configuration options: default gateway set to itself and the use of the natural mask. Two router configurations will also be discussed: proxy ARP and secondary IP addresses. Using these four tools, a system administrator wishing to reduce the overall router segmentation and take advantage of larger switched areas should be able to complete that task for Internet Protocol.

Proxy ARP

Proxy ARP was developed as a method of making subnetting transparent to end systems. Internet Protocol initially did not allow for the subnetting of a major network. Networks were defined as either class A, B, or C size areas, and further segmentation or other sizes were not considered. It became obvious though that alternative size address spaces and segmentation of existing A, B, and C size networks would be required.

The ability to extend the network mask beyond the natural mask for a given network and in doing so create subnetworks was added to Internet Protocol with RFC 924. The unfortunate consequence of allowing subnetting was that not all IP implementations at that time could be updated to support the concept of a subnetted network mask. Proxy ARP allowed those nodes to exist in a subnetted environment through the assistance of routers.

Proxy ARP, as the name would suggest, is a variation of the ARP protocol on routers. The main change is that now the router will be able to respond on behalf of nodes reachable through the router. In a typical address resolution process, the destination end node or an explicitly known gateway is the station that responds to a source's ARP request. That process was seen in Figures 4.10 and 4.11. The source end system in Figure 4.10 ARPs directly for the local destination and receives a response directly from that station. The source end system in Figure 4.11 realizes that the destination is remote, based on its subnet mask in the route determination process, and then ARPs for the next-hop or default gateway specified in the user's routing table. In both cases the source ARPs for a known device and receives a response from that device.

Where proxy ARP becomes useful is in a situation such as the one shown in Figure 4.11, with one exception. This exception is that the source device cannot use a subnetted mask. In that case, user X would have a natural class A mask. This is illustrated in Figure 4.12.

In Figure 4.12, we see that user X has a natural class A mask of 255.0.0.0. When user X (10.1.1.100) tries to communicate with user Y (10.4.128.1), the route determination process results in Y being considered a local destination. The binary AND of the source IP and source mask yield 10.0.0.0, and the binary AND of the destination IP and source mask also yield 10.0.0.0. At that point, user X begins address resolution. For a local destination it should be remembered that the ARP request is looking for the MAC address of the actual destination station and not a next-hop gateway, as would be the case in a remote destination. User X will send an ARP request looking for the MAC address associated with user Y's IP address of 10.4.128.1. Without proxy ARP, the address resolution process would fail. The failure would be caused by the fact that the ARP request is a MAC layer broadcast, and routers do not forward MAC layer broadcasts. Without proxy, the ARP request would cross the first Ethernet segment and be discarded by the router, because the request is not for its IP address specifically.

With proxy ARP enabled on the router's local interface, the process would unfold differently, as shown in Figure 4.12. The ARP request would be sent by user X looking for user Y. Now, with proxy ARP enabled, the router would evaluate this ARP and determine if the target IP is reachable through this router via an interface different from the one the ARP was received on. If the router's routing tables verify that

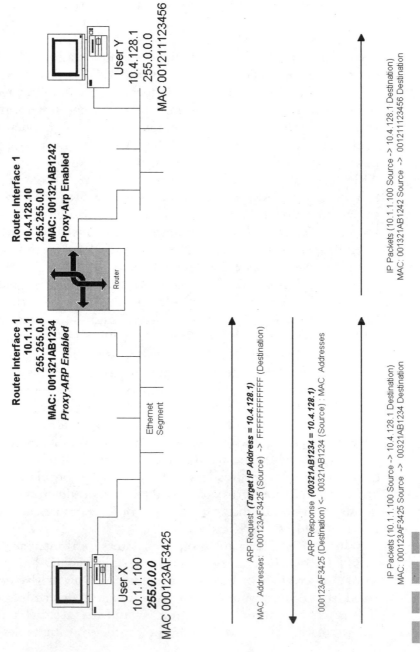

User X
10.1.1.100
255.0.0.0
MAC 000123AF3425

Router Interface 1
10.1.1.1
255.255.0.0
MAC: 001321AB1234
Proxy-ARP Enabled

Router

Ethernet
Segment

Router Interface 1
10.4.128.10
255.255.0.0
MAC: 001321AB1242
Proxy-Arp Enabled

User Y
10.4.128.1
255.0.0.0
MAC 001211123456

ARP Request *(Target IP Address = 10.4.128.1)*
MAC Addresses: 000123AF3425 (Source) -> FFFFFFFFFFFF (Destination)

ARP Response *(00321AB1234 = 10.4.128.1)*
000123AF3425 (Destination) <- 00321AB1234 (Source) : MAC Addresses

IP Packets (10.1.1.100 Source -> 10.4.128.1 Destination)
MAC: 000123AF3425 Source -> 00321AB1234 Destination

IP Packets (10.1.1.100 Source -> 10.4.128.1 Destination)
MAC: 001321AB1242 Source -> 001211123456 Destination

Figure 4.12 Proxy ARP function.

this router can reach the network on which user Y exists (10.4.0.0), the router will generate an ARP response on behalf of user Y. The ARP response will appear as if it came directly from user Y, but the target MAC address will be the router's local interface to user X. User X will receive this ARP response and truly think that user Y has just responded. It will then populate its ARP cache with the result and be unaware that a router has just proxied on behalf of the real destination. This process has effectively allowed user X to use its natural class A mask in a network that is physically subnetted into 254 class B size networks.

Proxy ARP was initially deployed to handle devices that could not support subnet masks. It is now available on most major routers as the default mode of operation on their interfaces. Its uses now have grown beyond this initial role. By using proxy ARP services, the system administrator of a routed network has the luxury of not configuring end systems in a subnetted environment with subnet masks. In more extreme cases, in which the entire IP network consists of only one class A, B, or C major network number, the system administrator can even leave the end systems configured without subnet mask and default gateways. This is possible with proxy ARP, for example, when the entire IP network of a company is one class B network subnetted to class C size areas. The end systems configured with natural class B masks of 255.255.0.0 will truly believe, based on route determination, that all devices with that class B network address are local. The proxy services of the routers performing the physical segmentation will allow any ARP for a subnet outside of the user's subnet to be responded to transparently. The end users will operate without knowledge of the physical segmentation. Since proxy ARP service on a router will respond for any nonlocal network, not just subnets, this tool will be a valuable router configuration option when building a large flat-switched network containing some routers on the edge of the switched network providing gateway services.

Secondary IP Addresses

The second configuration option useful in building large flat-switched IP networks is known as secondary addressing, or secondary IP addressing. When building a large flat-switched network, it is probable that the switched area will contain more nodes than one subnet or network can contain. It is also probable that routers will still be present on the edge of such a network. Their role will probably be reduced to providing wide area network connectivity and some firewall services. Since they will still be present, they must be configured to understand what networks or subnets are contained in the switched network. They need this information to make sure it is advertised to the rest of the IP Internet so that packets destined for one of the IP networks in the switched area can be routed properly.

Secondary addressing is simply the process of adding additional IP addresses and networks to a single router interface. If a switched network were built as shown in Figure 4.13, containing 1,000 devices, and the class B network 172.16.0.0 had been subnetted eight bits to a mask of 255.255.255.0, that single switched area could only be described using four of the subnets if we wish to keep our network mask consistent. Each of the two edge routers that connect to the switched area is configured with one primary and three secondary IP addresses. Since the routers have one address per local network, all local networks will be advertised using their routing protocols to all other routers on this network. This configuration also provides a pool of over 1,000 IP addresses for use in the switched area.

Some consideration should be taken when using secondary addresses regarding the routers' performance levels. While most current routers are able to support large numbers of secondary addresses on a single interface, doing so is an additional burden on a router. The interesting effect though is that since the switched network area, if properly implemented, will handle all direct communication between devices in the 172.16.10.0 through 172.16.13.0 networks, the router will actually have less forwarding responsibilities and can use those resources to handle the proper routing into and out of the switched area as defined by the secondary IP addresses. It can actually be said that implementing large switched areas has the effect of prolonging the usefulness of lower-end routers, since most of their former packet forwarding responsibility is now the burden of the much higher performing LAN switches.

Natural Mask

As discussed above, Internet Protocol addressing involves not only the 32-bit IP address but also a corresponding network mask indicating which of the 32 bits defines the network identifier. For each of the three useful major network types—A, B, and C—a default or natural mask is specified. That natural mask can be a very useful tool in implementing a flat IP network in situations where a single major network number has been subnetted. In traditional routed networks, the end systems are

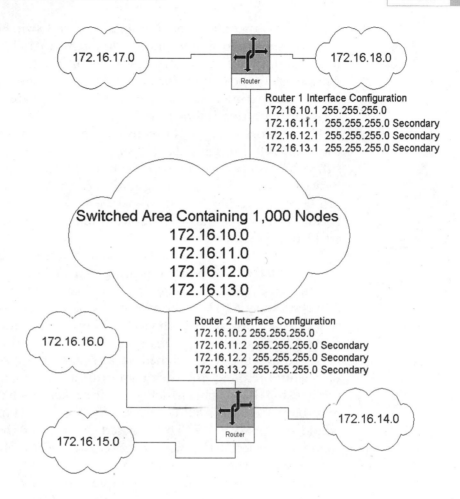

Figure 4.13

Secondary address configuration.

172.16.17.0

172.16.18.0

Router

Router 1 Interface Configuration
172.16.10.1 255.255.255.0
172.16.11.1 255.255.255.0 Secondary
172.16.12.1 255.255.255.0 Secondary
172.16.13.1 255.255.255.0 Secondary

Switched Area Containing 1,000 Nodes
172.16.10.0
172.16.11.0
172.16.12.0
172.16.13.0

172.16.16.0

Router 2 Interface Configuration
172.16.10.2 255.255.255.0
172.16.11.2 255.255.255.0 Secondary
172.16.12.2 255.255.255.0 Secondary
172.16.13.2 255.255.255.0 Secondary

172.16.15.0

Router

172.16.14.0

usually configured with a network mask matching that of the router interface they are attached to. This was necessary so that those devices could determine, via the route determination process, which destinations were local and which were on the other side of their gateways. Since the local network or subnet was determined by the network mask, the end system was required to have the same perspective as the router to assure that this understanding of local and remote destinations was consistent. Proxy ARP changed this configuration requirement in subnetted environments in that it allowed end systems to retain their natural class A, B, or C mask and still communicate through the attached routers.

As a tool for implementing flat IP networks, the natural mask, coupled with proxy ARP if routers are present, provides a simple configuration option to allow maximum use of the switched network. The recommended configuration of end systems in a flat network consisting of subnets of one major network is simply to configure their network mask to the natural form. In doing so, the devices will believe that all devices sharing their major network number are local destinations. This configuration is shown in Figure 4.14.

The network in Figure 4.14 consists of a switched network containing the 172.16.10.0 through 172.16.13.0 subnets. It also includes the 172.16.14.0 subnet and other major networks connected via a router to the switched network. Examining the configuration of the nodes in this network, it can be seen that they have their mask set to the natural class B 255.255.0.0 form. Their configuration is allowed, since the router has proxy ARP enabled.

If user X (172.16.10.10) wished to communicate with user Z (172.16.12.10), the route determination process using user X's 255.255.0.0 mask would result in user Z being a local destination. This would be based on the fact that the binary ANDs of the source IP and source mask and the destination IP and source mask both yield 172.16.0.0. Since the destination is considered local, user X would simply ARP directly for user Z. The two users are attached to a switched network, and the ARP would reach Z, who would respond, and their communication would then proceed directly using the switches to deliver their packets. Even though the router may have seen the ARP from user X, it is important to note that it would not proxy for Z. This is based on the fact that proxy only responds if the destination network is reachable through an interface other than where the request was seen.

As a second communication example, if user X wished to talk to user Y, the process would require the services of the router's proxy ARP function. Using the route determination logic for X (172.16.10.10) to Y (172.16.14.10) communication, the result would be that user Y is a local destination, because both devices share the network address 172.16.0.0 given X's 255.255.0.0 natural mask. User X would then ARP directly for user Y. This broadcast packet would reach all nodes in user X's switched area. User Y is not in that area so without some assistance from the router, the communication process would fail. That assistance comes in the form of proxy ARP. The router would receive the ARP broadcast for Y and evaluate it. If the network user Y exists in is reachable via an interface other than the one on which it is received, the router will respond to the ARP request on behalf of user Y. In this case, the 172.16.14.0 subnet is reachable on another interface, so the router sends an ARP response to user X with user Y's IP address but its own local MAC address. User X

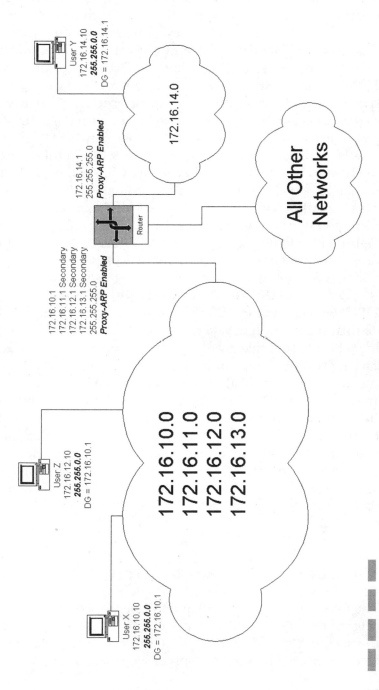

Figure 4.14 Natural mask configuration.

does not know that the router responded instead of user Y, but it does not care. Once the response is seen, user X will begin IP communication to user Y using the MAC layer address of the router as the layer two destination. This process demonstrated that, from user X's perspective, the entire 172.16.0.0 network is local, even though reality shows that some of that network is actually located on the other side of a router.

If the router were to be removed from its location between the 172.16.14.0 subnet and the rest of the network, the network's logical perspective would not change from the perspective of user X. This is due to the fact that when an end system has a natural mask it is unaware of any router segmentation of its local major network.

While the natural mask seems an ideal configuration for end systems in flat-switched networks, it has one significant limitation. The natural mask is only useful in flattening subnets of one class A, B, or C network. This limitation is illustrated in Figure 4.14, if user X attempts to communicate to a node in some other major network number such as 10.1.1.1. In Figure 4.14, the 10.0.0.0 class A network is reachable via the third interface of the router. When user X (172.16.10.10) performs route determination to reach user 10.1.1.1, the result is that the destination is remote. This is based on 172.16.10.10 AND 255.255.0.0 compared to 10.1.1.1 AND 255.255.0.0, resulting in 172.16.0.0 not being equal to 10.1.0.0. As a remote destination, a next-hop gateway must be used. Examining user X's routing table, we find that there is a default gateway of 172.16.10.1 available. The address resolution process is then used to ARP for the 172.16.10.1 router. The router will always respond to an ARP request for its address, and, as such, user X will have resolved its next-hop gateway to reach the 10.1.1.1 node. It is obvious that the natural mask has failed in this process by allowing user X to view the 10.1.1.1 node as local. Because of the fact that natural masks only flatten subnets of one major network, another technique is required to effectively implement flat-switched networks containing several class A, B, or C networks. That technique is a special static route technique, which allows the default gateway of an IP node to be itself.

Default Gateway Set to Itself

The fourth tool used in flattening IP networks is the technique of setting the default gateway of an IP node to itself. This may appear to be unusual, but in reality it is exactly the same process as the commonly accepted procedure used to support secondary IP networks. That process is the use of static routes with a metric of 0. Figure 4.15 shows such a situation. Users X and Y have the normal expected default gateway settings of a local router, but, since the local segment or switched area contains two class C networks, if the users attempt to communicate with each other having only a default gateway set to the router, they will actually treat each other as remote destinations and require that the router forward packets between them.

This is undesirable, since the two nodes exist on the same segment. Using the router is a completely inefficient configuration. A common addition of the routing tables of the two nodes would involve the addition of a static route to the other locally attached network. This static route would have the gateway address of the local interface and have a metric of 0, indicating that this is reachable directly. Essentially this static route tells the local device that the other class C network is reachable directly using the device's own local interface as the gateway to reach that network. Once the two users are given that static route, they will no longer attempt to utilize the router for communication, since they are now aware that direct communication is possible. This technique is utilized in many networks consisting of two or more major networks sharing one switched area or segment.

The default gateway set to itself is the logical extension of this concept. In Figure 4.15, the users' routing tables were modified to allow the end users to believe that one additional network was considered local. Setting the default gateway to the local interface's IP address effectively tells the end users that all remote destinations are to be considered directly attached. As such, the device will now ARP for any device regardless of its network and the results of route determination.

In switched networks that contain more than one major network, the use of a natural mask will not allow the end systems to understand how to communicate directly to the other local networks. It is in those cases that the concept of setting the default gateway to the host's local interface IP address is the only practical option to flatten the end systems. The most interesting feature of this technique, however, is that end nodes in routed networks can use this option also. If a node in a routed network configures its default gateway to its own IP address, the effect will be that the device will believe that all destinations are locally attached and thus will ARP for any destination.

If the routers attached to that user's segment are configured with proxy ARP, the routers will respond whenever the user ARPs for a nonlocal device. The end user will be unaware of the fact that the router's proxy ARP responded rather than the real destination. In Figure 4.16,

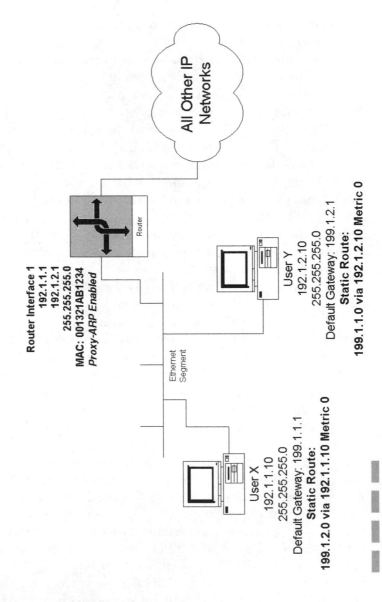

All Other IP Networks

Router

Router Interface 1
192.1.1.1
192.1.2.1
255.255.255.0
MAC: 001321AB1234
Proxy-ARP Enabled

Ethernet Segment

User Y
192.1.2.10
255.255.255.0
Default Gateway: 199.1.2.1
Static Route:
199.1.1.0 via 192.1.2.10 Metric 0

User X
192.1.1.10
255.255.255.0
Default Gateway: 199.1.1.1
Static Route:
199.1.2.0 via 192.1.1.10 Metric 0

Figure 4.15   Static route with a metric of 0.

user X has been configured with its own IP address as its default gateway. The top of the figure represents the actual physical construction of the network. The network is actually a highly subnetted class B network built using routers. This complex network, however, is transparent to the user, since its perspective treats all destinations as local, as shown in the bottom portion of the figure. The configuration shown in Figure 4.16 is perfectly valid, as long as proxy ARP is enabled on the routers attached to the segment containing the users with their IP address set as their default gateway. If your network is migrating towards a flatter environment using larger switched areas, the best recommendation that can be given is to configure your end nodes with a default gateway set to their local IP address. This configuration, when used with proxy ARP, will interoperate without difficulty with your routed network construction. Additionally, when you wish to flatten your network, the end nodes are already configured to be flat, based on their default gateway setting. If you change your end systems now to this configuration, the process of flattening your network will be as simple as removing the core routers, inserting switches, and adjusting the edge routers to reflect the changes. The end systems will never need to be reconfigured again, since they now support routed networks with proxy ARP and flat-switched networks.

The actual method of setting the default gateway to itself is the same as setting the default gateway to a router. That method, however, differs based on the IP software used. Most Microsoft stacks have graphical interfaces in their network control panel. Most UNIX machines have either graphical tools or make use of the route command to set the default gateway. A sample command may look like the following.

```
route add net default 172.16.10.10 0
```

One of the most useful tools for making this configuration of default gateway set to itself is found in the DHCP server in Microsoft's Windows Server NT 4.0 service pack 2. This update added the ability to set a registry flag called "SwitchedNetworkFlag." This flag, when set against a particular scope, allowed the DHCP server to automatically set the default gateway to the lease IP address. This topic is more fully discussed in Chapter 7.

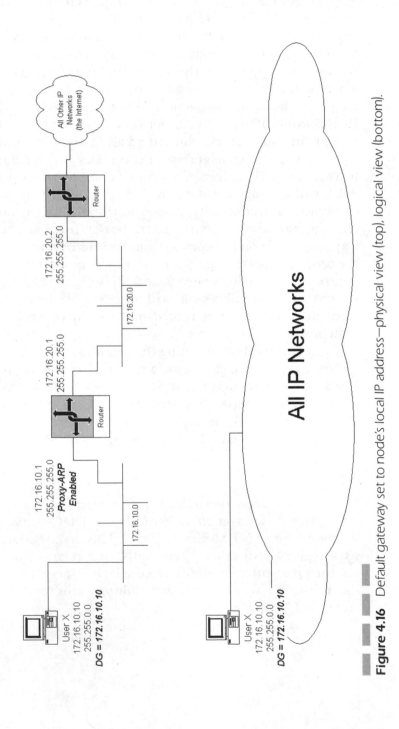

Figure 4.16 Default gateway set to node's local IP address—physical view (top), logical view (bottom).

Flat Internet Protocol Network Case Studies

Using the four tools described above, it is possible to remove the router segmentation of almost any existing IP network. It is also possible to build new, large flat-switched IP networks. This section will use these four tools in several case studies to demonstrate just how they are applied to create flat-switched IP networks. Each case study will start with a highly routed network and then recommend a migration plan to move this network configuration ultimately to a flat-switched network. If you are deploying a new switched network, refer to the final result of the scenario that reflects your addressing scheme as your starting point.

Scenario 1: Single Class A or B Network

The first scenario we will discuss involves an IP network consisting of a single class A or B network. This network is not directly attached to the Internet and contains only the single major network. This type of network is relatively common in corporate intranets that have chosen to utilize firewalls for Internet connectivity rather than layer three routers. In this network category, the flattening process begins in one of two ways, based on whether the end systems are taking advantage of proxy ARP. If they are, and as such are using a natural mask, the end systems require no changes to flatten this network. If the system administrator did not take advantage of the proxy ARP services and instead chose the complex mask and gateway configuration of all end systems, that process should be reversed as a first step. This option will be discussed in scenario 2.

Scenario 1, shown in Figure 4.17, assumes that the end users of this network have been configured with the natural class B network mask of 255.255.0.0. This would be common in networks that utilized proxy ARP at their routers.

This initial network configuration consists of a subnetted class B network. The routers are utilizing proxy ARP and the end systems take advantage of that feature by keeping their natural mask. In this configuration, the end systems believe, based on the route determination process, that all nodes in the 172.16 network are local. They are unaware of the routers. Figure 4.18 shows the first step in a migration to

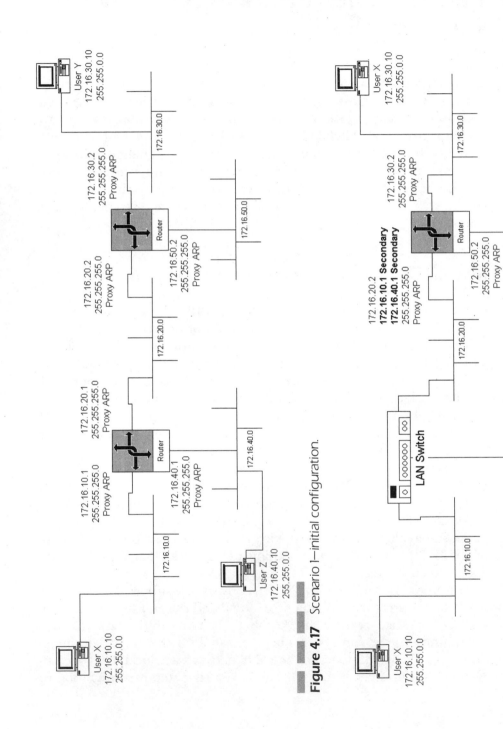

Figure 4.17 Scenario 1–initial configuration.

Figure 4.18 Scenario 1–step 1 in flattening.

flatten this network. This first step involves removal of one router in order to create a switched area containing three subnets (the 172.6.10.0, 172.16.20.0, and 17.16.40.0 subnets).

When the router is removed (Figure 4.18), the only change required is the addition of secondary IP addresses on the remaining routers. The end systems are not changed, based entirely on the fact that they utilize a natural mask and as such are unaware of the router in the first place. Its removal is not significant to them. This step may be repeated to ultimately absorb as many subnets as the switched network can contain. It can even be completed by removal of all LAN routers if the necessary broadcast analysis discussed in Chapter 3 is acceptable. Figure 4.19 illustrates this final result. It is important to note that a completely routerless network will usually not be possible in all networks, and therefore a network similar to that shown in Figure 4.18 will be the end result. Such a network will be primarily switched but still contain some routers on the edge for WAN connection and other services.

In scenario 1, the process was relatively simple and involved only changes at the routers. The end systems were not altered, because they were already relying on proxy ARP, which hid the router-based subnetting. This end-system configuration of a natural mask relying on proxy ARP may not be found in those networks where system administrators chose to explicitly configure the end system with extended masks as default gateways. If the end systems have, unfortunately, been configured in this way, the process of reversing the router-aware configuration must occur in order to take advantage of the switched network. If the network configuration for scenario 1 had begun with the end systems configured as shown in Figure 4.20, there are two possible paths to ultimately achieve the proper configuration on the end systems to best use the switched network.

The first method of moving this network to a switched network will involve changing the end-system configurations within the router-based subnets before switches are implemented. This process does involve a reconfiguration of the end systems. The recommended steps for completing this initial process are as follows.

1. Choose one subnet and enable proxy ARP on the local router interface. This will allow flattened and nonflattened devices to coexist in this subnet.

2. As time allows, go to the end systems and either configure their default gateway to be equal to their own IP address or set their mask to a natural mask. The first method is preferred, because it

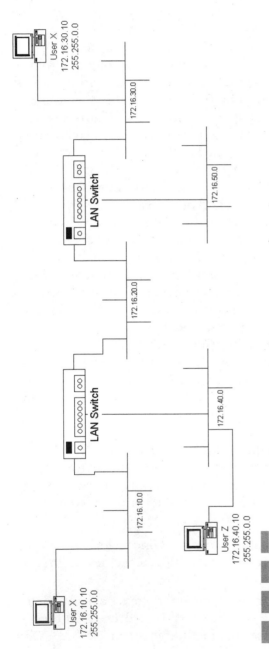

Figure 4.19 Scenario 1—final stage: completely switched class B network.

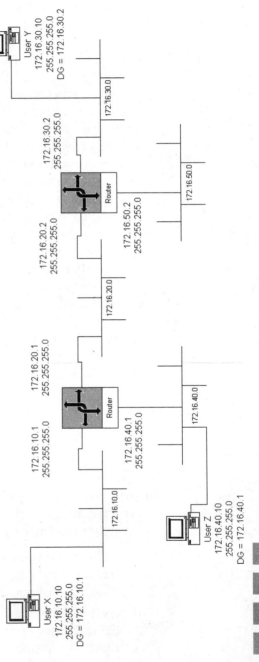

Figure 4.20 End systems configured with router knowledge.

will flatten the device in any IP network configuration. If your flat network consists of only one major network number, then a natural mask is acceptable.

3. Repeat the processes in steps 1 and 2 on other subnets.

4. Once at least two subnets are flattened, you may begin the process of removing the routers and adding switches. You are effectively now at scenario 1's initial point, shown in Figure 4.17.

This process can be done at your leisure. If a few end nodes cannot be flattened, that will not prevent this process. Those nodes should just be configured with a default gateway of a valid router interface remaining in the switched network. It is also significant to recognize that even without flattening, switches can be deployed within the subnets to increase their overall performance.

The second process for migrating the network in Figure 4.20 to an acceptable state in order to utilize a flat-switched network involves removal of most of the routers and then performing end-system reconfiguration. This method is recommended for networks that contain, as the majority of their traffic, other protocols that are simpler to flatten, such as IPX, SNA, and NetBEUI. The IP nodes will initially be dependent on the routers for communications to other nodes in the switched area, but reconfiguring them to be flat will correct that problem. The steps to complete this process are as follows.

1. Schedule downtime to perform the router changes. All end-system ARP caches will need to be cleared after this process is completed in order to resume communication.

2. Enable proxy ARP on any router interface that will remain in the switched network.

3. Remove one of the routers and configure the remaining router as shown in Figure 4.21. This configuration involves the relocation of the IP addresses of the removed router to the remaining router as secondary IPs.

This configuration will allow the 172.16.10.0, 172.16.20.0, and 172.16.40.0 subnets to exist in the same switched area. The users in that area do not have the ability to communicate directly, since they are still configured with the default gateway of a router and a subnet mask. If they try to communicate, they will actually send their IP packets to the router, which will then route them back into the switched network through the same interface. It is possible that the router will use a message called

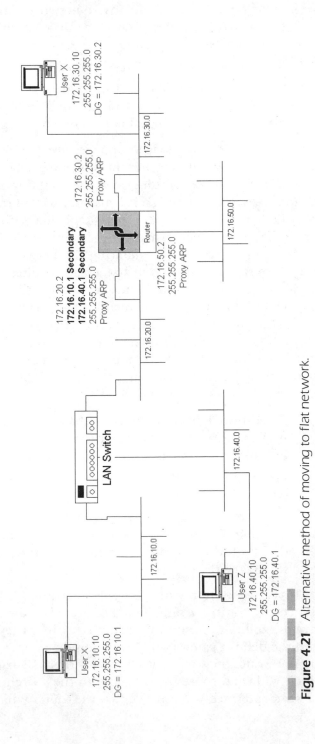

Figure 4.21 Alternative method of moving to flat network.

an ICMP redirect to tell the end systems to communicate directly, but that is not guaranteed behavior. This end-system configuration will not provide the optimal path for communication for the nonflattened devices, but, since our initial assumptions stated that IP was not the major protocol in these areas, the impact should not be severe.

4. Once the physical network is in place, follow the end-system configuration steps in the first method outlined above. As the end systems are flattened using either a natural mask or default gateway as themselves, the users will begin direct communication with anyone in the 19, 20, or 40 subnets.

These processes will provide a smooth migration to a flat-switched network in cases where the initial routed network consisted of only one class A or B network with subnetting. Please read Chapter 3 to make sure you complete a thorough broadcast analysis before any flattening process is undertaken.

Scenario 2: Single Class A or B Network with External Connections

In scenario 1, a single class A or B subnetted network was flattened using either simple or complex end-system configuration. That scenario assumed that the only IP addresses that would exist shared a single major network number. In cases where the majority of the network is a subnetted class A or B, and direct IP communication to other major networks is required, the following case study is examined. In this example, the 172.16.0.0 network is going to be moved to a larger flat-switched network. That network is directly connected to another, larger Internet, and, as such, nodes in the 172.16.0.0 network will need to communicate to other class A, B, or C networks via routers. This configuration is shown in Figure 4.22.

In this scenario, the end systems within the switched area will require a gateway. This requirement was not present in the first example, because the entire network was one major network. This fact allowed the natural mask to be used without any default gateway, since with a natural mask, all destinations in the major network are considered local, and, as such, the end node's routing tables are not consulted. With the presence of other major networks in this example, all nodes will not necessarily be considered local in route determination, and, as such, a valid

Figure 4.22

Single major
network with
connections to
other networks.

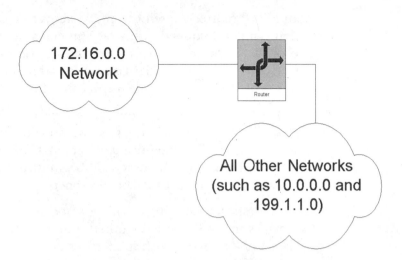

next-hop gateway will be required to allow communication to any remote destination.

For this example, the network illustrated in Figure 4.23 shows a portion of the 172.16.0.0 class B network before implementing switched connectivity. The actual physical network is a set of class C size subnets
separated by router interfaces. Attached to the 172.16.0.0 network are additional major networks, such as the 10.0.0.0 class A and 199.1.1.0 class C
networks. As this network is migrated to support a large switched area,
it is necessary that all IP devices continue to be able to communicate to
all networks.

The initial end-system configuration in this scenario will most likely
be as shown. The end systems will have an extended mask with a default
gateway set to the local router's interface. This is required to support
communication to the other IP networks. As an example, if user X
(172.16.10.10) wished to communicate with device Z (10.1.1.20) located on
the right-hand side of the far right router, the route determination
process would result in user Z being a remote destination. This result is
based on the binary AND of the source IP (172.16.10.10) with the source
mask (255.255.255.0) compared with the binary AND of the destination IP
(10.1.1.20) with the source mask (255.255.255.0). This comparison yields the
result that X is in the 172.16.10.0 network, while Z is in the 10.1.1.0 network. Since the result is not equal, this is a remote destination.

In order to reach a remote destination, the source's routing table must
be consulted. The only entry in X's routing table is the address of its default gateway (172.16.10.1). Since this gateway is known, the address reso-

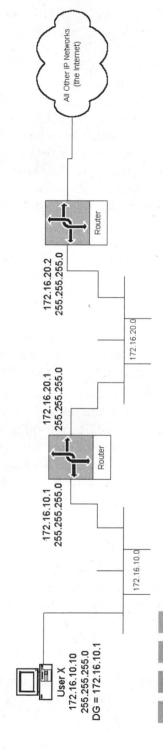

Figure 4.23 Single class A or B network with connectivity to other IP networks.

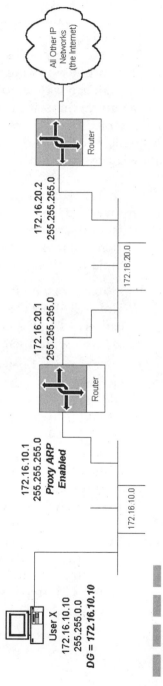

Figure 4.24 Default gateway set to itself in a routed network.

lution process at X can proceed, with X simply ARPing for the router's MAC address. X will then send its IP packets destined ultimately for Z to the router to be routed. Without that default gateway entry in X's routing table, the route determination would have failed, and the user at X would see the message "network unreachable."

There are two possible processes for flattening these end users and implementing switching in the 172.16.0.0 network. The first is to utilize the default gateway set to the user's own IP address. The second is to utilize a natural mask at the end user and set the default gateway to the IP address of the router connecting the flat area to the other IP networks. Both methods allow the 172.16.0.0 network to exist as one flat area while allowing communication to devices outside the 172.16.0.0 network.

Method 1: Utilizing the Default Gateway Set to Itself

In this method, the end users of this network will be modified to set their default gateway to their own IP address. As previously discussed, this action will make the hosts ARP for all devices. The actual procedure for completing this process is as follows.

1. Enable proxy ARP on all router interfaces in the 172.16.0.0 network. This will allow the routers to respond on behalf of remote destinations when the end systems are configured with the default gateway set to their own IP address.

2. Choose any subnet and go to the end systems and modify their default gateway to be set to themselves. The method of doing this will vary, based on the device's IP stack but usually is accomplished using either a graphical interface (network control panel in NT and 95) or using the route command. Some more obscure stacks can accomplish this task using an IP mask of 0.0.0.0 or a default gateway of the 127.0.0.1 local host address. Consult the vendor of the IP stack for exact details. You should reboot the end system after this is done to ensure that old ARP entries and routing table entries are purged. When the device reboots, it will now ARP for all IP destinations it wishes to communicate with. Since the routers are still present, it will rely on the proxy ARP functions of the router to ultimately reach any destination located through the router. This step is shown in Figure 4.24 (see page 149).

3. Repeat step 2 on each subnet.

4. As soon as two or more subnets have been configured as suggested, the router connecting them can be removed or realigned to

the periphery of the combined switched network. When that router is replaced with LAN switches, the remaining routers attached to the switched area must be configured to understand the logical IP structure. In order to accomplish this, those border routers must have secondary IP addresses for each of the subnets contained in the switched area. If the entire 172.16.0.0 network is contained in a switched area and no subnets exist as separate physical networks, then each router on the border can use the natural class B mask to describe the 172.160.0.0 network on that interface. Figure 4.25 illustrates the network configuration after this step is complete.

The router on the edge would respond to any ARP request for a device on its right-hand side. This behavior allows the device in the flat 172.16.0.0 area to be configured with a default gateway set to itself and still connect to devices outside of the switched area.

Method 2: Utilizing a Natural Mask and a Default Gateway of a Border Router   In this method, the default gateway set to itself will not be utilized. Instead, the end systems in the flat area will be configured with a natural mask and a default gateway set to a valid router on the border of the switched area. The natural mask will allow direct communication to all hosts in the switched network with a 172.16.0.0 address, and the default gateway will allow for communication to any device outside of the 172.16.0.0 network using the router as a gateway. This process is as follows.

1. Enable proxy ARP on all routers in the 172.16.0.0 network. This will allow the flattened devices to still communicate to other 172.16.0.0 devices before the routers are removed.

2. Decide which router or routers will remain attached to the border of the final switched network. These routers' IP addresses will be utilized as the default gateways of the IP end users in the switched network.

3. In each subnet, configure the end systems with a default gateway set to one of the routers that will remain on the border of the switched area when this process is complete. Set the device's network mask to its natural form of 255.255.0.0. The combination of these two steps will allow the device to ARP for any 172.16.0.0 device directly, while always using the router as a gateway for reachablitiy to any other IP network. Figure 4.26 shows the network configuration of this step.

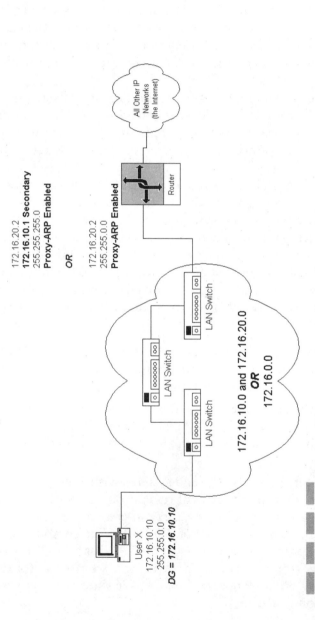

172.16.20.2
172.16.10.1 Secondary
255.255.255.0
Proxy-ARP Enabled

OR

172.16.20.2
255.255.0.0
Proxy-ARP Enabled

172.16.10.0 and 172.16.20.0
OR
172.16.0.0

LAN Switch

LAN Switch

LAN Switch

All Other IP
Networks
(the Internet)

Router

User X
172.16.10.10
255.255.0.0
DG = 172.16.10.10

Figure 4.25 Flattened class B network with connectivity to other networks.

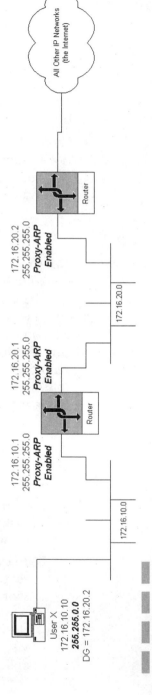

All Other IP Networks
(the Internet)

Router

172.16.20.2
255.255.255.0
*Proxy-ARP
Enabled*

172.16.20.0

172.16.20.1
255.255.255.0
*Proxy-ARP
Enabled*

Router

172.16.10.1
255.255.255.0
*Proxy-ARP
Enabled*

172.16.10.0

User X
172.16.10.10
255.255.0.0
DG = 172.16.20.2

Figure 4.26 End-system configuration for method 2, step 3.

4. Repeat the configuration of each subnet until at least two subnets are configured as described.

5. Combine the flattened subnets using LAN switches. In this process, the remaining routers on the periphery of the switched network must be configured with secondary addresses reflecting each of the subnets contained in the switched area. When this process is completed, the resulting network will contain the 172.16.0.0 IP network and be connected to the other IP networks using the remaining routers on the border. If a device in the switched area attempts to communicate to another node in the switched 172.16.0.0 network, the route determination process will result in a local destination and they will communicate directly. If that same node attempts to reach another IP network, the route determination process will result in a remote destination, and the end node will ARP for the router defined as its default gateway. When that router responds using proxy ARP, the device will then communicate to the remote destination using the router as its gateway. This final network configuration is shown in Figure 4.27.

This method made use of standard configurations of the default gateway and network mask. While this method is not as absolute a way of flattening a network as method 1, it is supported on all IP stacks. Depending on the method you feel most comfortable with, either method can be used to achieve the goal of a flat-switched IP network. It is also very important to recognize that the task of end-system reconfiguration in all of these methods can be done in your current routed network as long as the routers are using proxy ARP. Some of these configurations can even be made automatically, using tools such as DHCP (discussed in Chapter 7). While end-system reconfiguration may be required to take full advantage of a switched network containing multiple subnets or networks, that task can be done over time and implemented on a subnet-by-subnet basis.

Scenario 3: Multiple Major Network Numbers

Possibly the most difficult IP network configuration to flatten is one in which the flat network will ultimately contain several major network numbers. An example of this would be a flat network consisting of the

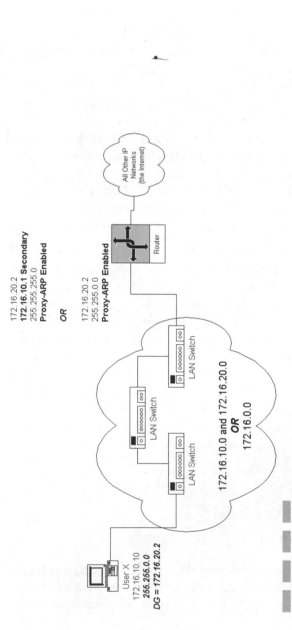

Figure 4.27 Final network configuration using method 2.

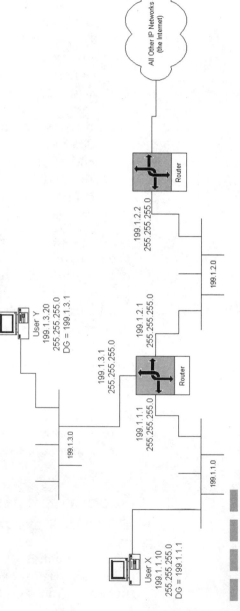

Figure 4.28 Routed network with several class C IP networks.

199.1.1.0 and 199.1.2.0 class C networks. This type of configuration is difficult to work with, because the network mask usually cannot be used to allow direct communication between these networks. The reason it is unusable is due to the fact that the natural mask of a class C network is 255.255.255.0. While it is always possible to make that mask subnetted by using some of the last eight bits to extend it, it is usually not possible to make the mask smaller than the natural size. It would be illegal on most IP devices to use a 255.255.0.0 mask for the 199.1.1.0 network, since this mask would be smaller than the natural mask. While some routers allow this as part of Classless InterDomain Routing (CIDR), end systems do not usually allow for this option. Without the ability to manipulate the mask, the methods of flattening end systems are reduced to one: The default gateway set to itself.

For this case study, we will assume that the network to be flattened is constructed of several separate class C networks. This type of IP configuration is found today in networks that desire Internet connectivity but have only recently applied for valid IP addresses. These newer networks are usually given a series of class C networks rather than a class B or class A network, simply because there are very few remaining class A or B networks available. If your network is constructed with a series of class C networks, it is still possible to take advantage of larger networks based on LAN switching with some end-system reconfiguration. An additional option is available through the use of RFC 1918 and firewalls; that option will be discussed in the following section.

The network to be flattened in this example is illustrated in Figure 4.28. It consists of several true class C networks connected via traditional routers. Since each class C network can only contain 255 end nodes, this network is forced to be highly segmented. The disadvantage of this segmentation is found in the fact that any communication between networks must traverse the router. The system administrator of this network has decided to move to a larger LAN-switched domain by relocating the routers to the periphery and adjusting the IP stacks of the end users.

In the network shown in Figure 4.28, communication between user X (199.1.1.10) and user Y (199.1.3.20) will traverse the router linking their segments. The route determination process for communication from X to Y results in Y being a remote destination, since X exists in the 199.1.1.0 network, while Y exists in the 199.1.3.0 network. User X would then consult its routing table and determine that the default gateway to reach remote devices is 199.1.1.1. X would then ARP for the router and, when it responded, would send the IP packets ultimately destined for user Y to the router's local interface. The process of ultimately flattening this network to allow all users to communicate directly without the router in the path is outlined as follows.

1. Within the existing router network, enable proxy ARP on all router interfaces. This will enable the router to respond on behalf of remote devices when the end users are flattened.

2. Inside each subnet, modify the default gateway of the end systems to be set to themselves. This is usually done in the network control panel on windows-based systems. On UNIX hosts the command route "add net default <local IP address> 0" or some similar syntax is used to set the default gateways to themselves. To make the change permanent, the initialization files of the UNIX host should be made to include this statement. Consult the particular UNIX system administrator's guide for exact details.

3. Once two subnets have been flattened in the process in step 2, remove the router connection between them and connect the subnets with LAN switches. A remaining router connection will be required to connect the switched subnets to the rest of the IP networks. On that router ensure that the interface has a secondary address for each IP network in the switched area. This step is shown in Figure 4.29.

4. Continue the process of flattening the subnets and replacing the router connection with LAN switching. As the process continues, the switched area will increase in size with each additional class C network. The resulting network will exist as a totally switched network with routers on the boundary connecting the switched area to the rest of the Internet.

While this process of flattening routed networks with multiple major networks contained internally will work, be advised that there is another option if your network is composed of more than a few distinct major networks. That option is to utilize a private class A or B size Internet based on RFC 1918 and, if connection to the real Internet is required, to utilize a proxy firewall or network address translator. The next section will discuss this option.

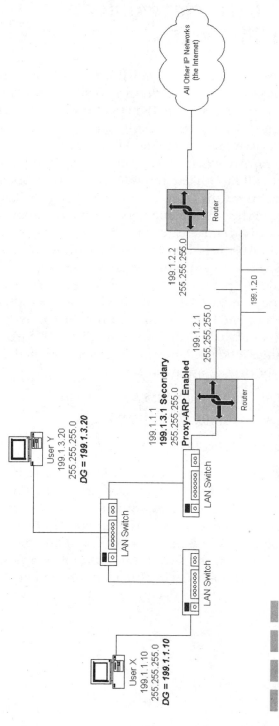

Figure 4.29 LAN switches used to flatten a portion of a multiple class C network.

RFC 1918 Networks with Firewalls

The massive growth of the global Internet has created one unfortunate consequence. The 32-bit addressing form of Internet Protocol is unable to provide enough unique IP networks to meet the demand of the user community. While there are still many available IP addresses, the majority of the networks not currently in use are of the class C size. Today, if a new company wishes to register a valid IP address to attach to the Internet, it will most likely receive a class C network address. If that company has more than 254 nodes, it will most likely get more class C networks rather than a true class B. From the above case studies, we can see that this trend creates an obvious problem when implementing switched LANs. It is much more difficult to build a large flat-switched network consisting of multiple class C networks.

In order to provide some other option for those users planning on large-scale switched LANs but having only valid class C networks for the Internet, the IETF has allowed for the construction of valid private internets of class A, B, or C size using RFC 1918 (formerly 1597). The address ranges allocated by the Internet Assigned Numbers Authority (IANA) for private use are as follows.

Class A: 10.0.0.0–10.255.255.255

Class B: 172.16.0.0–172.31.255.255

Class C: 192.168.0.0–192.168.255.255

These address ranges are officially allowed to be utilized in customer networks as long as direct connectivity to the Internet using routers is not present. These addresses would be utilized in cases where a customer was building a nonconnected IP network and wished to have the flexibility of a class A or B network but could not obtain a valid IP network of that size from the IANA. The concept of a nonconnected network and the options of achieving Internet connectivity from such a network are the focus of the following section.

Private Internets and Nonconnected Networks

A private internet or nonconnected network is defined as an IP network that does not have direct router-based connectivity to the global Internet. Such a network may exist for any number of reasons, but the most common reasons are as follows.

1. The company building the network has no requirement to connect to the Internet from its corporate network, since its internal connectivity is sufficient for its business operation.

2. The company requires Internet connectivity but desires a higher level of control over access to the Internet than traditional routers provide. In this case the customer has implemented an application layer firewall system to allow connectivity to the Internet for specific reasons.

3. The customer has been given a number of separate class C IP networks from the IANA to define its network. Rather than attempting to implement its corporate network using this difficult IP configuration, the customer opts for a simpler class A or B private internet and firewall or network address translator connectivity to the Internet.

When a company has a valid reason, such as those above, the choice of a private internet becomes very logical. The implementation of such a network involves renumbering the IP devices to use the new RFC 1918 addressing scheme and implementing any proxy firewall services that may be needed for Internet connectivity.

Proxy Firewalls

A proxy firewall is a device that has become the preferred method of connecting to the global Internet for most enterprises and governments over the past few years. This device can be viewed as a two-port gateway from the private internal internet to the global Internet. Its gateway services are not like those of a traditional router in that it forwards only application layer requests to the Internet and in doing so effectively terminates the network layer communication on either side. By only forwarding the application layer information, this type of device is able to apply much more control over what kind of communication should exit or enter the private network. Figure 4.30 shows the difference between the connectivity a router and a firewall provide to the Internet.

In Figure 4.30, we see that the traditional router is designed to forward or filter network layer packets. That results in the router generally being unconcerned with the actual payload of the packet. At layer three, services such as Telnet, FTP, e-mail, World Wide Web, and so on do not exist. They are all just IP communication between two devices. Routers have been enhanced over the past ten years to allow for filtering of layers four through seven information, but that is not what they were initially designed to do. Because higher-level analysis of traffic into and out of the Internet is usually desired, new devices known as firewalls are being implemented to provide connectivity to the Internet.

These firewalls, shown in Figure 4.30, operate as application layer interfaces between two networks. In this capacity, they are able to make detailed decisions about allowing or prohibiting communication between devices, based on what application or service is being used. While the router primarily controlled just the IP communication, the firewall controls what will be done inside the IP communication. By examining the application layer conversations, the firewall is able to make a more detailed access policy for your network. An example of such a policy is the firewall prohibiting World Wide Web access to a particular Internet destination, while allowing e-mail to be forwarded to the same site.

The role of a firewall in a private or nonconnected network is as a single end system. Since the firewall is the IP destination with which all internal nodes communicate, and its valid Internet address is the source of all communication into the Internet, the firewall acts as if it were just a single IP node in the private network and a single IP node on the global Internet. Figure 4.31 illustrates the traffic pattern involved in communication through a firewall.

Since the devices inside the private network talk to the internal IP address of the proxy firewall in order to ultimately reach external Internet-connected devices, the private internet's IP addressing scheme can be any form. In this example the RFC 1918 class A network is used. This choice allows for a great deal of flexibility in the design of the private internet. With the presence of the firewall, this private internet is still able to connect to the Internet. It is important to note that since the firewall is application based, not all IP applications can traverse this type of

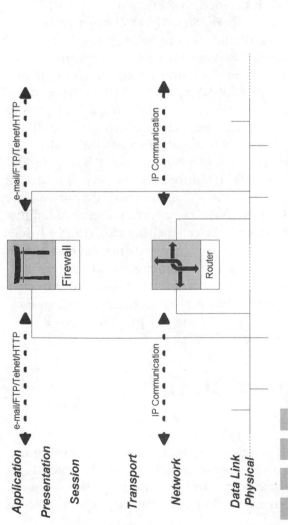

Figure 4.30 OSI layers of operation of traditional routers and application layer firewalls.

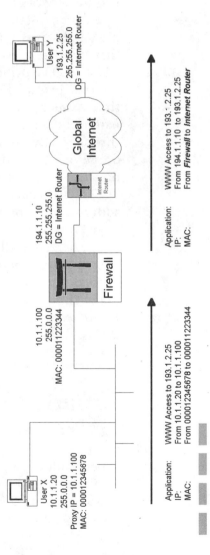

Figure 4.31 IP communication through a firewall.

device. Most normally used applications, such as Telnet, FTP, Web Access, and e-mail (SMTP), can be transmitted through the firewalls available today.

Network Address Translators

A second option for connecting a private internet to the global Internet is the network address translator, or NAT. This device operates in the same way as a traditional firewall or router in that it physically links the private network to the global Internet, but its function is very different. The basic function of a NAT is defined in RFC 1631. In this RFC, the NAT is defined as a device or service on a traditional router or firewall that translates private network IP addresses to valid global Internet IP addresses. The principle of operation is based on the concept that not all internal private IP devices will require Internet connectivity at one time. As such, the NAT can use a pool of valid global IP addresses to dynamically replace the private source IP addresses of packets passing through it. By doing this, the private network is able to use valid IP addresses while on the Internet and private IP addresses internal to the nonconnected network. The operation of a NAT is shown in Figure 4.32.

This function of swapping a valid IP address for the private source IP address allows for direct communication from internal IP devices to the global Internet. It is normal for the NAT function to be embedded in a router or a firewall as an additional service. In either case, the NAT does allow a private network to access the Internet with no real end-system changes. This NAT option can be used in conjunction with router filtering or firewall application-level security and access control to provide a secure seamless interface into the Internet while maintaining an RFC 1918–style IP addressing scheme internal to your private network.

Broadcast Reduction in IP Networks

When building a large-scale switched network, the major limiting factor in scaling the network is the overall broadcast rate. Chapter 3 discussed the methods of baselining and monitoring the network broadcast rate to ensure your network is operating at acceptable levels

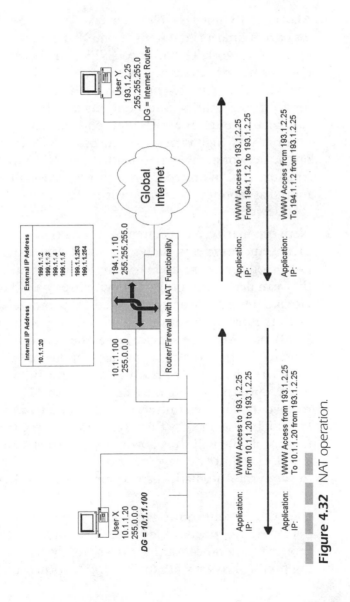

Figure 4.32 NAT operation.

of nonunicast traffic. In this section we will discuss some methods of reducing the overall broadcast and multicast rates on your network that are attributed to Internet protocol.

Internet Protocol is generally not very broadcast intensive. Most of its operations transport data with no nonunicast packets involved. Because of this nonbroadcast-intensive behavior, the majority of the suggested broadcast reduction techniques in the following list deal with improperly configured devices or protocols.

1. Manage NFS mounts—Network file system mounting is the process of mapping a file system of one IP device to another IP device over the network. The protocol, NFS, utilizes IP unicast packets to communicate between the two devices. NFS mounts assume that the other device is present. In cases where the other device is no longer present, the NFS applications can attempt to restore IP connectivity through the ARP protocol. This ARP broadcasting can occur at very high rates when the other NFS device is not present on the network. It is recommended that NFS mounts be managed to assure that mounted devices that leave the network are removed as mount points on the other devices running NFS against that device.

2. Network management systems—When the common network management systems, such as SunNET Manager, HP OpenView, Cabletron Spectrum, and IBM NetView/6000, discover a network, they can detect any pingable device present. When any such device is detected, the device is added to their database, and, in most cases, the management system will begin polling the device via SNMP or ICMP. If the device leaves the network, the management system will still attempt to contact that device using ARP requests. Since the device is not present, the ARPs will be repeated indefinitely until the polling is turned off or the database modified to remove that device. It is recommended that end systems such as PCs not be managed by these systems, since the typical end system most probably will shut down often in the future. If the end system docs require management, do so on a case-by-case basis—not through the automatic discover process of the management system.

3. Use OSPF as your routing protocol—Open Shortest Path First (OSPF) generally provides a less broadcast intensive method of layer three routing. Since routing tables are not broadcast in this routing protocol, as they are in Routing Information Protocol (RIP),

the total broadcasts generated by routers will be reduced significantly in large networks. It is not always possible to utilize OSPF easily, due to its complexity, but, if it is an option, it should be considered preferable to RIP.

4. Watch for unconfigured IP devices—IP devices that have not been configured with valid addresses will usually attempt to obtain an address using one of three automated mechanisms. They are DHCP (discussed fully in Chapter 7), Bootstrap Protocol (BOOTP), and Reverse Address Resolution Protocol (RARP). If servers are configured to allow these address resolution protocols to operate properly, then they are perfectly valid protocols on your network. Unfortunately, most IP devices will attempt to use one or more of these services to obtain an IP address, even if there is no server configured to support the protocol. Watch your network using a network analyzer or RMON probe for the presence of these broadcast protocols, and, if found, go to the source device and disable their IP stack or provide them with a valid IP address. The most common type of device exhibiting this behavior is unconfigured print servers.

5. Keep high bandwidth IP multicast applications off the switched LAN—The services of IP multicast using Internet Group Management Protocol (IGMP) are used for a variety of applications. Low-bandwidth applications such as network time updates are not usually an issue on switched networks. High-bandwidth applications using IP multicast, such as video conferencing or radio feeds, are not usually suitable for switched LANs without some additional method of control. Using virtual LANs (discussed in Chapter 9) and multicast filters (such as 802.1P) or multicast switching can control these types of applications, but these services are not found in most LAN switches and are usually proprietary. It is best to keep multicast applications behind existing routers until some method of controlling those services is decided upon for your LAN.

Additional sources of invalid broadcast traffic include misbehaved and custom applications. It is generally recommended that the procedures outlined in Chapter 8 be followed to baseline and monitor your network for increased broadcast and multicast activity. If such monitoring is done on a regular basis, broadcast and multicast applications can usually be identified and controlled or removed before they impact the overall network performance.

Troubleshooting Switched IP Networks

Once the switched network has been implemented and the IP configuration completed, the overall network performance and simplicity should be significantly greater. It is possible that connectivity issues may occur in this network just as in any other network. When communication fails to operate or fails to perform at the level you may expect, it is recommended that the procedures outlined in Chapter 8 be followed to troubleshoot the switched LAN before focusing on possible IP-related issues. If the Chapter 8 troubleshooting flow charts indicate that the failure is protocol related, then the following section should be used to address some of the more common IP-related issues in switched networks. All of these issues relate to misconfiguration of end systems or services rather than defective devices.

Passive RIP Nodes

Symptom: UNIX hosts are unable to communicate to all of the devices within the switched LAN. They do, however, have access to any network on the other side of the routers attached to the switched network.

Probable Cause: The UNIX hosts are still running the UNIX RIP routing daemon ROUTED to build their routing tables. Even though these hosts are not routers, they are listening to the periodic RIP updates from the attached routers. Because the routers operate using a mechanism known as simple split horizons for their routing table updates, only routes learned on other interfaces are advertised into the switched network. As such, the primary and secondary networks of router interfaces attached to the switched network are never advertised into the switched network. This lack of advertising results in the UNIX hosts having no route to the other IP networks inside the switched network. Figure 4.33 shows the normal routing updates from a router using simple split horizons attached to a large switched network.

Solutions: There are two possible solutions to this issue. The first is to disable the ROUTED process on the UNIX host and simply configure it with a natural mask or default gateway set to itself. This option permits direct communication inside the switched network and routed communication outside the switched network as long as proxy ARP is enabled on the attached routers. This is the preferred method of resolving this issue.

A second option can be implemented at the routers attached to the switched network. This option requires disabling simple split horizons on the router interfaces attached to the switched network. This will allow the routers to advertise their entire routing table, including the networks attached to the interface sending the routing updates. By doing this, the UNIX hosts will obtain a complete routing table, including the networks making up the switched area. This option is not preferred, since it increases the routing update size and can increase the network's susceptibility to conditions known as count to infinity. Split horizons was developed to address both issues. Please also note that disabling split horizons is not the same as enabling a feature known as poison reverse, which enhances the split horizons operation to better avoid count to infinity issues. For more details on split horizons, poison reverse, or RIP routing, please consult one of the many texts on those topics.

NIS

Symptom: Network information services are not available after flattening the network. The specific failure involves the inability of the YPBIND process to find an NIS server for its domain.

Probable Cause: The NIS process YPBIND is configured to automatically find any NIS server in its domain name by using an IP network broadcast. The destination address of such a broadcast is usually the network address—for example, a device with an IP address of 172.16.1.23 and a

Figure 4.33

Split horizons
routing updates
into a switched
network.

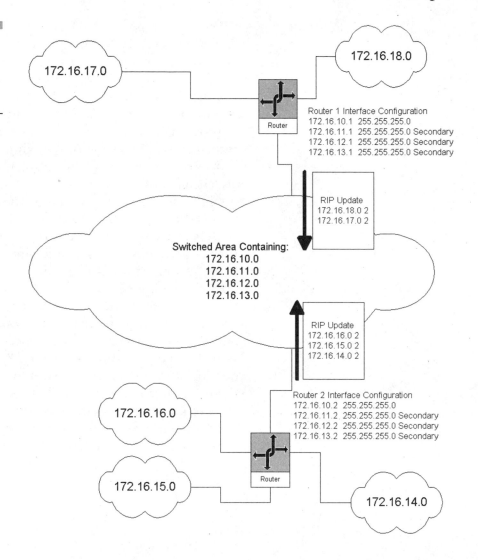

mask of 255.255.0.0 would send its YPBIND to the destination address 172.16.0.0 (or possibly 172.16.255.255)
when attempting to reach any NIS server local to it.
When the network is flattened, the routers that connect the various networks combined into one
switched area are no longer present. One of their roles
was to provide IP helper addresses or UDP redirectors.
These services allowed the local router to redirect sub-

net or network IP broadcasts to a particular server that was not actually local to the device. When the router is removed, this service may not be available, and, as such, if no local NIS server exists, the YPBIND process will fail.

Solutions:
There are two solutions to this issue: move an NIS server to the local network or enable IP helper addresses on the remaining routers to reach a remote NIS server. Either option is feasible, but the preferred method is to make sure that an NIS server (either a master or slave server) is in the switched network and has the same network address as the NIS clients. In the case of a switched network with several unique class C networks, a separate NIS server may be needed for each of the class C networks in the switched area requiring NIS service. Once the servers are present, they will respond to the YPBIND network broadcast and the process will complete.

ARP Caches

Symptom:
After flattening the network, some end systems are unable to reach other IP devices that are known to exist in the switched network. This failure only occurs after the routers have been relocated and generally does not affect all devices in the switched network.

Probable Cause:
The ARP cache of the end nodes at one or both sides of the conversation are still populated with a router's MAC address for the destination IP address. It is very probable that the end users in a proxy ARP environment have the IP address of other IP devices all mapped to the MAC address of the local router. When that router is removed and direct communication is allowed, the end users will still send IP packets to the router's MAC address for all communication they have resolved to their local ARP cache. It is also possible that the routers remaining in the switched network on its border may have invalid ARP cache entries after the

switched network is implemented. This invalid ARP mapping in either router or end system will cause IP communication to fail.

Solutions: Since the ARP cache is dynamic in most cases, it will eventually age out and the device will re-ARP for the IP destination. At such a time, the correct MAC to IP binding will be placed in the ARP cache and IP communication will occur. If you suspect this kind of issue, it is advisable that you check the ARP cache of the devices involved in the failing IP communication using the ARP –a command (available on almost all IP stacks). If a value exists in the ARP cache for the other device and you are unsure of its validity, delete it with the ARP –d <IP Address> command. The device will then be forced to re-ARP and the result should then be valid. This process may be required at both sides of the failing IP communication, since both ARP caches could be incorrect. A more reliable solution to this issues is to simply reboot all devices in the switched network when the physical infrastructure is changed though the flattening process. If this is done with scheduled downtime, the ARP caches are guaranteed to be accurate, barring a duplicate IP situation.

Network Unreachable

Symptom: When IP communication is attempted to another IP device, the message network unreachable is returned to the user interface by the IP stack. The communication fails and no ARP cache entry is seen for the destination.

Probable Cause: The network unreachable message is generated when route determination fails in the IP host communication process. Recall that the route determination is the process of using the source IP address, the destination IP address, and the source mask to determine if the two devices exist in the same IP network (local) or different networks separated by gateways (remote). If the destination is determined to be remote, the route determination process must consult its routing table to determine a next-hop gateway to reach the destination. If that lookup fails to find any next-hop gateway, the network is considered unreachable. This message is generated when the source device has either an improper mask in a flat network or a misconfigured routing table. Figure 4.34 shows the scenario of an incorrect mask and how it would affect host communication in the flat network 172.16.0.0.

Figure 4.34 shows the impact of an incorrect mask in a flat network of one major network. In this case, users X and Y are able to speak simply because they are in the same network, 172.16.0.0, based on their mask. Additionally, when user Z attempts to speak to user Y, user Z is successful, because they are both in the same network, 172.16.2.0, based on user Z's mask. The network unreachable message appears only when user Z attempts to contact user X. In this case, based on user Z's mask of 255.255.255.0, they are in different networks (172.16.1.0 and 172.16.2.0, respectively) and, as such, considered remote. At that point user Z consults its routing table, but there is no default gateway defined so the network is considered unreachable.

Solution: The solution to network unreachable messages is to correct the mask and/or routing tables of the hosts affected. The message is an indicator that the devices are not configured properly and, as such, are failing route determination. To correct the mask or routing table, determine the proper mask and gateway parameters, based on your addressing scheme, and reapply the correct configuration using the IP stack's configuration files or interfaces. It is recommended that both devices involved be examined to determine their masks and routing table configurations and to make sure that the issues are corrected. The IP tools used to view the mask and routing table are usually ifconfig –a and netstat –r, respectively.

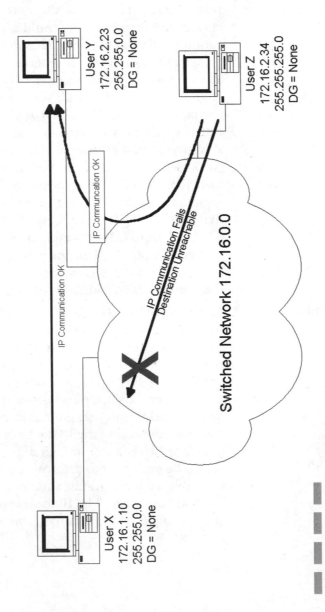

Figure 4.34 Destination unreachable scenario.

Mixed Flat and Nonflat End Nodes and ICMP Redirects

Symptom: User communication is slow and network analysis shows a large number of ICMP redirect messages being sent to users.

Probable Cause: It is very possible that a flat network may include devices that still wish to use the router to communicate to other logical IP networks, even if those networks are physically part of the same switched area. This condition can occur in cases where older IP stacks are present that cannot set their default gateway to themselves or where stacks are still configured with the IP address of the router as the gateway and continue to use an extended mask. In these cases, the devices will attempt to communicate through a router interface, which has the source and destination networks defined on it as primary or secondary IP addresses. In these cases, the routers are usually intelligent enough to tell the end nodes that they are not the best path, using the ICMP redirect message. If the users understand this message, they should adjust their routing table so as not to use the router for this particular conversation. If the users do not listen to this message, the router will route its packets back into the switched area to their destination but will continue to send one ICMP redirect message for each packet sent in this conversation. The cause is incorrect end-system mask or gateway configuration in all cases.

Solution: The solution is to adjust the IP stack of the end system receiving the ICMP redirect messages to understand that it can communicate directly to the other IP networks inside the switched network. This can be done using static routes, default gateway set to itself, or a natural mask. If the hosts cannot be reconfigured, there is no harm done other than slow performance in letting the router route back into the network. If such a case exists, where the end user cannot be adjusted, it is recommended that the router interface have ICMP redirects disabled to reduce the traffic from the router.

Summary

From the above discussions, the process of implementing an IP addressing scheme in a large switched network should be clear. The actual process of configuring IP to operate directly in a large switched LAN can be as easy as removing the routers and replacing them with switches in the case of a subnetted class A or B network already using proxy ARP. The implementation may be more complex in a network in which end systems have explicit knowledge of the routers. In such cases, that knowledge must be removed or altered to reflect the new switched network. This process is known as flattening and only involves four tools: natural mask, default gateway set to itself, proxy ARP, and secondary addressing. Once that process is complete and the infrastructure is rebuilt with LAN switches, the routers are eliminated or moved to the periphery of the network to provide wide area network connections and simple firewalling. At this point, the IP communication between users in the switched network is handled by the LAN switches, which provide much faster, lower latency, and scalable performance levels with a tremendous simplification of end-system administration in cases such as adds, moves, and changes. It is always possible to implement a switched network supporting IP as long as a proper choice of end-system and router configuration is made. Using this chapter and its case studies, you should have a much greater awareness of your options in implementing the most suitable switched LAN with IP.

CHAPTER 5

Novell NetWare in Flat-Switched LANs

Novell NetWare continues to be the dominant network operating system in LANs today. Because of this fact, it is necessary to understand its operation in switched networks to assure that any implementation of a large switched network does not impact Novell NetWare. Unlike Internet Protocol, which had a wide variety of configuration options to explore when implementing a switched network, Novell NetWare is significantly easier to deploy in a flat-switched network. This chapter will provide the necessary background information on the structure of NetWare and its protocols to fully understand its operation when used in a large switched LAN. Configuration case studies will be presented and optimization recommendations will be offered to maximize the overall efficiency of NetWare in your switched LAN.

Novell Architecture

Novell NetWare is described as a client/server architecture. As a client/server system, there are two primary components that make up a NetWare network: clients and servers. The server is described as the location of centralized resources and services. On the server files are stored, printers are accessible, and centralized resources such as e-mail are available. The client is described as the user of the server's resources and services. The client is where applications are executed and user interfaces exist, but those applications access their data and other services through communication to the server. This centralization of services provides for maximum control and management of these resources, while the distribution of processing to the clients (where the applications are actually run) allows for a maximization of computing capacity. The combination provides a very desirable type of network computing architecture.

It is not just the client/server architecture that has made Novell so popular over the past decade. It is also the fact that Novell has made a concerted effort to provide network computing without a great deal of added complexity. Implementation of NetWare on end systems is almost transparent. It usually involves the loading of a few programs, which allows clean hooks into the native operating system of the client (such as DOS). After these programs are enabled, the end user sees Novell NetWare as a logical extension of the local resource. This extension can look like additional drives or additional printers. In addition to the clean integration to the client's native operating system, Novell also enhances usability of this network operating system by defining network services by name rather than some cryptic logical address. While those cryptic addresses are still utilized, the NetWare operating system allows the user to be shielded from them through its own naming service. Most users can understand common names of services much better than logical network addresses. In general, these two features of NetWare—seamless integration and use of names—make Novell a very desirable network operating system and account for its continued popularity.

Novell NetWare has evolved through several major revisions. On networks today, NetWare servers of versions 2.x, 3.x, and 4.x are present. While the scalability and features are significantly different between these versions, their operation over the switched network is not. Because the protocols and messages sent for all the versions of NetWare are extremely similar, this chapter will address those general protocols and messages rather than the intricacies of the NetWare upper-layer services. If the reader desires a more detailed understanding of the services and systems making up Novell NetWare, there are countless texts on the subject.

The overall protocol suite of Novell NetWare is derived from the XNS protocol suites of Xerox. While based initially on XNS, NetWare is not XNS; it is its own protocol suite having its own service architecture. The overall architecture is shown in Figure 5.1. This architecture provides for network services that map roughly to the OSI model of communications.

Novell NetWare has a protocol suite similar to that of IP but significantly simpler. At the network layer, NetWare utilizes one main protocol: Internetwork Packet Exchange (IPX). This layer three protocol transports all of the other higher-layer protocols. Those protocols include NetWare core protocol for client/server communications, SPX for peer-to-peer applications, and RIP and SAP for maintaining the network topology. The following sections will explain the operation of these protocols in terms of switched network operation.

Protocol Operation

IPX

Internetwork Packet Exchange (IPX) is the main protocol utilized in NetWare networks for transporting packets. All other protocols used by NetWare-based services are transported by this protocol. Its primary

Figure 5.1

Novell NetWare
Protocol Suite.

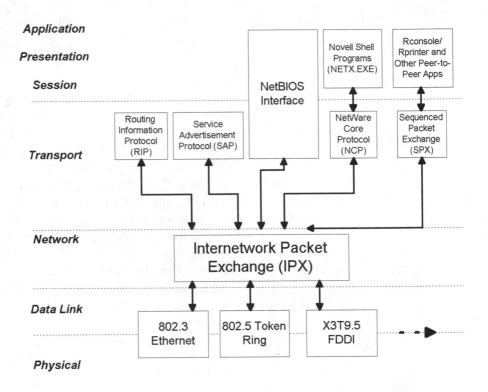

role is to assure formatting and delivery of upper-layer protocol information. As a network layer protocol, data formatting and the logical addressing and routing of packets are its responsibilities. Since IPX is the main protocol routers must deal with in NetWare communication, we will focus on it as the main protocol affected when routers are removed from a network to allow for a larger flat-switched network.

An IPX Protocol Data Unit (PDU) is the primary data unit used in NetWare; its structure is illustrated in Figure 5.2. This PDU is actually transported inside the data field of Ethernet, Token Ring, FDDI, and other layer two technology frames. The fields of the IPX PDU are used in the process of addressing and routing individual packets over a hierarchical network.

The initial fields in an IPX PDU provide several administrative services for this packet. The first field of the PDU is the 16-bit checksum. Novell opted not to utilize this field, since the lower-layer Ethernet, Token Ring, and FDDI networks have their own 32-bit checksums for the entire frame. Because this field is not utilized, the two bytes are set to 0xffff in all IPX PDUs. The second field indicates the length of the IPX

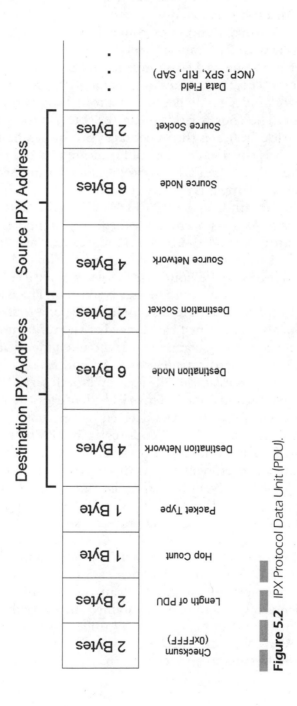

Figure 5.2 IPX Protocol Data Unit (PDU).

PDU in bytes. In the past, the IPX PDU was limited to 576 bytes. This limit has been extended to the maximum transmission unit of the physical medium negotiated between client and server. The third field indicates the total number of router hops this packet has traversed. IPX routing with RIP limits the total hop count to 16 hops. When this field is set to 16, the packet is discarded by the router that incremented the counter. This field makes sure that an IPX packet cannot be left on the network indefinitely because of a router loop or other invalid configuration. The fourth field in the IPX PDU is the packet type indicator. This field indicates the upper-layer protocol contained in the IPX data field. It is this field that would indicate to a receiving station that this packet is NetWare core protocol versus routing information protocol or some other upper-layer service.

The remainder of the IPX PDU defines the destination and source addressing. As a layer three protocol, IPX supports a logical addressing structure just as IP did. Its logical addressing format is based on the same network:node structure. The first of the three elements that define an IPX address is the four-byte network identifier. This field indicates what logical group the end user belongs to. These logical groups or networks are defined in terms of which side of a router the user is attached to but also are defined based on what type of logical link is utilized. The second addressing component is the node identifier. This six-byte field is either the hardware device's MAC address or a symbolic internal address, such as 000000000001, used by Novell servers to define their internal IPX protocol stack. This field identifies the end user as a unique entity within the network defined by the first field in the address. The final component of an IPX address is the IPX socket. This two-byte field is used to indicate the process involved in this communication: By having a socket identifier in the address tied to the particular process being used, a server can distinguish one session to a client from another. Following the IPX addressing in the PDU is the IPX data field, which will contain the upper-level protocols such as RIP, SAP, NCP, SPX, and so on.

Given this form of the IPX PDU and its addressing, a NetWare network can be built as a flat layer two system in which all devices share the same network identifier. It can also be built as a routed network in which groups of users are combined into networks based on different IPX network numbers. To fully understand the logical structure of a NetWare network based on addressing, it is necessary to examine the IPX addressing structure in depth.

IPX networks, as defined by the IPX network number, are logical structures that identify a logical grouping of users isolated by routing. This was also the case in Internet Protocol, but NetWare is very different regarding how those networks are actually defined on the physical network. There are two major differences in how NetWare defines networks versus IP. The first is that NetWare utilizes several different Logical Link Control (LLC) methods over a single physical medium. This allows for each LLC to represent a different logical network over the same physical segment. The second difference is that NetWare introduces the concept of internal and external networks. An internal network is the logical network internal to a server. Since all servers are inherently routers, NetWare defines that they will all contain an internal IPX network, which is used to link all external networks they may be connecting. It also serves as a method of uniquely identifying that server to the network. External networks are logical networks consisting of all nodes on a particular layer two LAN sharing a common LLC.

IPX Addressing Format   The IPX addressing format allows for over 4 billion networks based on its 32-bit size. Each IPX network is either an internal IPX network identifying a server or an external IPX network identifying a logical group of users in a layer two LAN sharing an LLC frame type. Figure 5.3 shows the physical placement of such internal and external IPX networks.

The server has the internal IPX network of 0x012AABB1. This value uniquely identifies the server to the NetWare network. The server also has connectivity to three external IPX networks: the 1, 2, and 62 IPX networks. What is most interesting in Figure 5.3 is that even though there

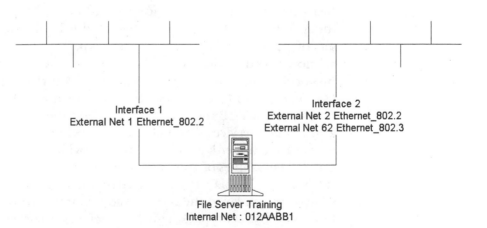

Figure 5.3

IPX internal and external networks.

Interface 1
External Net 1 Ethernet_802.2

Interface 2
External Net 2 Ethernet_802.2
External Net 62 Ethernet_802.3

File Server Training
Internal Net : 012AABB1

are three external networks, the server has only two physical interfaces. This is possible based on NetWare's ability to utilize several different logical link control types as separate networks over the same physical network. To fully understand this ability to have multiple external networks occupy the same physical medium, an understanding of the logical link control layer of the OSI model is needed.

Logical Link Control (LLC)

At layer two of the OSI model, the Medium Access Control (MAC) and the Logical Link Control (LLC) layers exist. The MAC defines the layer two addressing and access methods of the transmission medium (e.g., CSMA/CD in Ethernet). The MAC is always specific to a particular technology, such as Ethernet, Token Ring, FDDI, and so on. Since it is undesirable to build networking protocols and software that are specific to a particular LAN technology, there must be an isolating layer between the MAC and the network layer. If that layer can be generic enough to allow network layer protocols to operate based on its interface rather than the MAC's, and if it can operate over any MAC, there can be true separation between the network layer and the MAC layer. This would allow the particular protocol to operate over any underlying physical medium without direct knowledge of it. The obvious advantage is that the same protocol stack software could be deployed over a mixed Ethernet, Token Ring, or FDDI network.

The LLC layer is responsible for the separation of the MAC and network layers of the OSI model. Based on IEEE standards, the architecture that is responsible for this layer is the IEEE 802.2 standard. It defines a relatively complex set of services that allow for MAC and network layer independence. IEEE 802.2 goes beyond this basic role and defines three sets of services at the LLC layer. LLC type 1 defines connectionless, unacknowledged services for connecting the MAC layer to its upper-layer protocols. This LLC type is used by protocols that have services such as flow control and sequencing already implemented in higher-level protocols such as TCP and IPX. LLC type 2 defines connection-oriented, acknowledged services. This LLC type is used primarily for protocols that do not have upper-layer services that provide flow control and sequencing. Two examples of this type of protocol are NetBEUI and hierarchical SNA. This LLC type is actually a relatively complex protocol somewhat similar to the transmission control protocol of IP. The third LLC type is LLC type 3. This LLC defines a connectionless, acknowledged service. It is primarily utilized on IEEE 802.4 token bus networks running in customized networks for industrial applications. It provides for very reliable but simple data delivery. It is not usually found on LANs used for conventional purposes.

This IEEE 802.2 standard is the defined method of linking layer three network layer protocols to the layer two MAC services of Ethernet, Token Ring, FDDI, and so on. Even though this is the recommended method of LLC, it is not the only one. In fact, there are four different LLC methods defined and commonly utilized over Ethernet networks— FDDI utilizes three and Token Ring utilizes two. What is even more difficult to deal with is that the various methods are completely incompatible, and NetWare can utilize several LLCs simultaneously over a common LAN segment. Each of the LLCs will be discussed in the following sections for functionality to gain a better understanding of their operation on a NetWare network.

Novell Raw

The simplest LLC method utilized by NetWare is called Novell Raw or sometimes Ethernet 802.3. Only NetWare on Ethernet LANs utilizes this LLC method. Its development was based on the standardization of Ethernet as IEEE 802.3. When Ethernet was defined as an IEEE standard, rather than the older DEC Intel Xerox (DIX) Ethernet II architecture, NetWare opted to utilize the new MAC layer framing of the IEEE Ethernet. This new framing versus the older DIX Ethernet framing is shown in Figure 5.4. The notable changes involve renaming the preamble to the preamble and start frame delimiter and replacing the protocol type field with a length field. While the preamble renaming is just a change in terminology, the removal of the protocol type field is a conscious change to make this MAC layer architecture fully independent of the upper-layer protocols. With the protocol type present in this layer two frame, the separation of the network and MAC layers is not complete.

NetWare chose to utilize this IEEE 802.3 framing to carry IPX PDUs over Ethernet. This choice was in reality not an option based on IEEE 802.3, since the 802.3 standard defines only physical and MAC layer services and relies on IEEE 802.2 for LLC services. NetWare, for some reason, chose not to implement 802.2 but to utilize the 802.3 frame. Because of this choice, NetWare's implementation is known as Novell Raw and is considered to be proprietary. The actual behavior of this LLC is shown in Figure 5.5.

Figure 5.4

IEEE 802.3 versus
DIX Ethernet II
framing.

IEEE 802.3 Ethernet Frame

Preamble	SFD	Destination Address	Source Address	Length	Data Field	CRC

DEC Intel Xerox Ethernet II Frame

Preamble	Destination Address	Source Address	Protocol Type	Data Field	CRC

Figure 5.5 shows that user Z sends its IPX PDU by simply placing it into an IEEE 802.3 frame. The packet is addressed to user Y at the MAC layer and delivered over the segment. When the packet reaches user Y, it is received based on the MAC layer destination, and the IPX PDU is extracted by the software IPX drivers resident on user Y. This process appears to be proper and without any undesirable side effects. In this particular example, with all devices running just Novell Raw, the Novell Raw framing does work without any negative impact on the systems. Where the process breaks down is in environments where the attached systems are using more advanced network drivers, such as packet drivers, open data link interface, or Network Device Interface Specification (NDIS). These driver architectures allow for a single physical interface to support many protocols. In order to do so effectively, the incoming

Figure 5.5

Novell Raw LLC
operation.

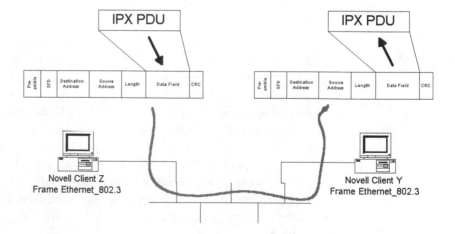

frames must somehow be recognized as one protocol or another. Upon examination of Novell Raw, we see there is no information contained in the non-PDU portion of the frame to identify it as IPX; because of that, stations using IPX with Novell Raw framing and other protocols will be unable to determine what is contained in the Novell Raw packets. This lack of intelligent multiplexing and demultiplexing makes this LLC unsuitable for multiprotocol environments. Additionally, 802.5 Token Ring does not support any Novell Raw framing, and FDDI only supports raw framing in proprietary hardware and software.

Ethernet II

To address the issue of multiprotocol networks, the early versions of Ethernet utilized a specific MAC layer field called the protocol type. This two-byte field in the MAC layer Ethernet frame defined explicitly what protocol was contained in the data field of the packet. By doing this, the receiver of an Ethernet frame could easily determine which of the upper-layer protocols this PDU was destined for. The operation of Ethernet II is shown in Figure 5.6.

Figure 5.6

Ethernet II LLC
Operation.

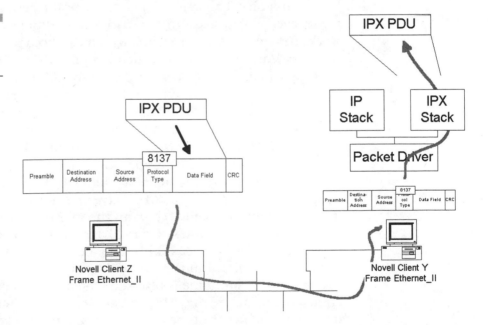

This method of indicating where the PDU is in the MAC layer type field does allow end systems to utilize multiple protocols in an efficient manner. NetWare does support this mode of operation for its LLC, but there are some compelling reasons why this method should not be utilized. The first reason is that this method is dependent on the protocol type field. While that field is available on Ethernet, Token Ring and FDDI do not support it in their MAC layer services. As such, this method of LLC cannot traverse a switched network consisting of several technologies without translation. The second reason why this LLC is not desirable is based on the fact that a better, more interoperable LLC is available for NetWare. That LLC is known as IEEE 802.2.

IEEE 802.2

As discussed earlier, the IEEE 802.2 standard is the recommended method of implementing the logical link control layer of the OSI model in LANs. The primary reason this standard is preferred is that, as a separate standard, it is completely interoperable with all common MAC layer technologies. This interoperability allows PDUs contained in this type of LLC to move freely from Ethernet to Token Ring to FDDI without LLC translation. This can result in significant performance improvements over systems requiring translation. Additionally, since this LLC works for any MAC layer technology, it can become the standard LLC for a NetWare network and, as such, simplify the end-system and server configurations. Since NetWare utilizes only LLC 1, we will focus on that LLC type for this discussion. If the reader desires more detailed information regarding the IEEE 802.2 standard and other LLC types, the best reference is the IEEE 802.2 standard itself.

The IEEE 802.2 LLC operates much as Ethernet II did in terms of multiprotocol networks. It utilizes additional fields in the frame to indicate information about the contents of the PDU. Unlike Ethernet II, 802.2 does not utilize fields in the MAC layer portion of the frame. Instead, it creates a subframe, which contains the 802.2 fields, and places this subframe in the MAC frame's data field. Figure 5.7 shows the relationship between the PDU, the 802.2 subframe, and the MAC layer frame.

The PDU is placed in the data field of the 802.2 subframe and then the entire 802.2 subframe is placed in the data field of the MAC layer frame. The format of the 802.2 subframe consists of four fields. The control field indicates the type of LLC message this packet is related to. In LLC type 1 the control field is one byte in size and can indicate one of

Figure 5.7

802.2 subframe
relationship.

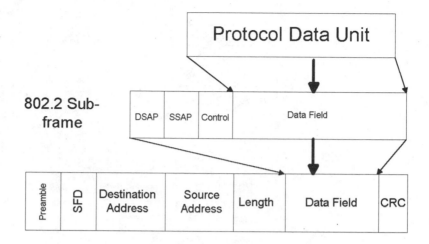

three message functions (XID, UI, or TEST). The only message typically used in NetWare is the UI, or Unnumbered Information. LLC types 2 and 3 have many other messages and the possibility of a two-byte control field. These will not be discussed, since NetWare does not utilize them. The Destination Service Access Point (DSAP) and Source Service Access Point (SSAP) define one-byte values indicating the destination and source services or protocols the PDU is utilizing. In most cases, the SAPs reflect the protocol being used, but, since there is a source and a destination SAP present, they can be used much like IP or IPX sockets that define the process or subprotocols. The actual value to be used in the SAP is a dynamic one-byte value. Unlike Ethernet II, whose type fields were based on fixed registered type codes, the 802.2 SAPs are only significant between the two devices communicating and as such can be reused. There are some well-known SAPs that certain protocols use, but these are only accepted common values, not fixed values. IPX, for instance, uses the well-known SAP of E0, but as long as both communicating devices agree on a common value for the IPX service, any valid number could be used.

The operation of 802.2 is shown in Figure 5.8. In this figure we see that the subframe is built by the source station and used by the destination station to determine what protocol or service is contained in the PDU. In this case, the source station builds an 802.2 subframe from SSAP E0 to DSAP E0 indicating IPX-to-IPX communication. It then places the PDU in the 802.2 data field and delivers the packet to user Y. User Y is able to determine if this is a NetBEUI or IPX PDU by examining the DSAP of E0. The most important part of this entire process is that the only field

Figure 5.8
802.2 LLC
operation.

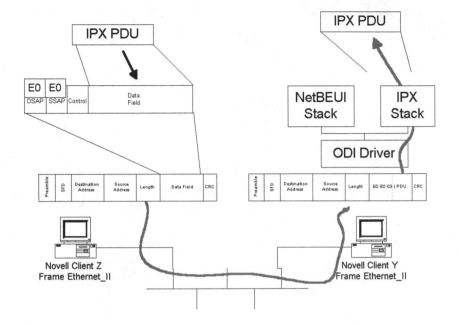

required in the MAC layer frame to perform this intelligent multiplexing and demultiplexing is the data field. Since this is the case, this process will operate over any MAC layer system capable of delivering data.

Subnetwork Access Protocol (SNAP)

IEEE 802.2 LLC is the preferred method of LLC for NetWare networks. This recommendation comes from all major vendors of networking hardware, based on the fact that 802.2 provides a common LLC for all MAC layer LAN technologies. One additional LLC exists and must be discussed to fully understand all options for LLC services in a LAN. That option is known as SNAP, or Subnetwork Access Protocol. One of the drawbacks of the 802.2 LLC method is that it does not use the protocol type field. Instead, it utilizes the one-byte SSAP and DSAPs to indicate PDU payload. While some protocols can adapt to use the SAPs rather than the type codes, some cannot. The primary examples of protocols that were implemented on Ethernets using DIX Ethernet II encapsulation are Internet Protocol and the early DECnet suite of protocols. These protocol suites are tied to their protocol types mainly because they include several network layer protocols and use a single protocol stack to support all of them. In order to distinguish among the various protocols used in the protocol suites, the type codes are used. If the protocol suite changes LLC to support 802.2, it would need to change how the basic layer three protocols are identified in its internal protocol stacks. An example of this change would be in IP. IP has three major layer three protocols: ARP (type 806), RARP (type 8035), and IP (type 0800). To support 802.2, SAPs would need to be chosen for all three protocols and the associated drivers rewritten to understand the SAP identifiers rather than the types. This would not be easy and would result in an incompatibility with all IP stacks currently running Ethernet II.

SNAP attempts to work through this issue by simply extending the 802.2 subframe with two additional fields, known together as the protocol discriminator. The first field is the Organizationally Unique Identifier, or OUI. It is a two-byte field that serves two roles. If set to 0x000000, this field indicates that the second field, the type field, contains protocol types derived from Ethernet II. If it is set to the vendor's three-byte IEEE vendor ID (e.g., 0x00001D for Cabletron Systems), the type field is defined as indicating a vendor-specific protocol identifier. The actual format of a SNAP packet in relation to the PDU and MAC layer frame is shown in Figure 5.9. SNAP is identified within the 802.2 subframe by using the reserved DSAP and SSAP of 0xAA and 0xAA.

The main reason SNAP exists is to allow older protocols that have a basis in Ethernet II to operate over other MAC layer technologies without significant changes. This is accomplished by allowing Ethernet II

Figure 5.9
SNAP LLC
encapsulation.

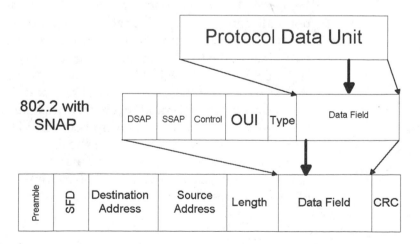

protocol types to be transported over any technology by simply moving the type field to a location inside the data field. Without SNAP, protocols such as IP would require significant changes to operate over a Token Ring or FDDI network. SNAP is not relevant to IPX in most cases, due to the fact that IPX operates very well using basic 802.2. There is no real reason to utilize SNAP when 802.2 can be used. To use SNAP would be to deliberately add five bytes of overhead to every IPX packet sent, while realizing no benefit.

LLC Type and IPX Networks

Logical Link Control (LLC) describes the method of encapsulating the IPX PDU into a MAC layer frame. This is significant in terms of IPX network addressing in that NetWare allows several LLC methods to operate over a single layer two LAN. Each of the LLCs is treated as an independent IPX external network through which it must be routed. In Figure 5.3, the server was connected to two physical networks. The left-hand segment had one logical IPX network using Ethernet 802.2 framing, while the right-hand interface connected to a segment containing two IPX external networks. Network 62 utilized Novell Raw, while network 2 utilized Ethernet 802.2 framing. This configuration is supported in NetWare, because the file server is able to support multiple logical interfaces (called "boards") and route between them. An example of a more complex network configuration exemplifying this concept is shown in Figure 5.10.

Figure 5.10 shows two servers connected on a single segment. One supports all four frame types, while the other supports only 802.2 and SNAP. The lower portion of the figure shows what their logical connectivity is described as. Even though they are on a single segment, they are really defining four logical IPX external networks. Networks 2 and 4 are shared by the servers, while networks 1 and 3 are reachable through server 1 only. Server 2 could reach networks 1 and 3 but only by routing through server 1. This relationship between LLC methods and external networks is vital in understanding the logical model of a NetWare network in a switched environment. Since the switched network will attempt to minimize the overall use of routing, minimizing the number of logical frame types is a requirement.

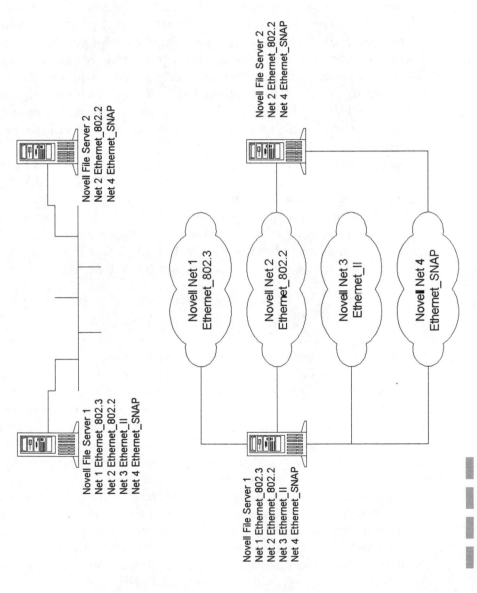

Figure 5.10 LLC relationship to IPX external networks.

RIP

Routing Information Protocol (RIP) is the protocol responsible for routing processes on a NetWare LAN. RIP in IPX is similar to IP RIP in form and process, but the two are not compatible simply based on the addressing format and the metrics utilized. RIP serves two purposes in NetWare. The first is to build and maintain routing tables in all routers on the NetWare LAN. This task is accomplished by periodic distribution of routing tables. Every 60 seconds each NetWare router (or server acting as a router) will broadcast its routing table using split horizons (discussed in Chapter 4) to all adjacent IPX networks. This means that in the case of Figure 5.10, server 1 would send four updates from its one physical interface. This process is relatively simple and will not be discussed in detail.

The second process RIP is involved in includes the NetWare clients. Unlike IP, NetWare clients do not have a routing table. Instead, they are allowed to ask the local routers for reachability information as they need it. The message used is called "get local target." This participation in the routing protocol greatly simplifies the operation and configuration of the end systems in a NetWare LAN. This process will be discussed in a later section, where the login process of a NetWare client is examined.

SAP

Service Advertisement Protocol (SAP) is responsible for the naming service in Novell NetWare. One of the most significant features of NetWare is the fact that services are known by name, not address. By allowing services to be viewed and accessed by name rather than cryptic address, the system becomes significantly simpler to operate from an end-user perspective. Additionally, since SAP operates automatically in NetWare, the administrative burden needed to make it function is also minimal compared to IP name services such as DNS.

SAP operates in all NetWare devices. Servers initiate SAP by advertising their service name or names. Routers and servers acting as routers then propagate the advertised names to all other servers and routers on the network. Once the advertisements are seen, servers and routers will build a Service Information Table (SIT) listing all services on the NetWare network. The SIT will be readvertised every 60 seconds in SAP response packets. Each SAP response can advertise seven services, so there may be a large number of SAPs in a sizable NetWare network. In fact, on most large networks, IPX SAPs are the single largest source of broadcasts present. The clients in a NetWare network also utilize SAP. When clients initialize, they will send a SAP request called "get nearest server." This message is asking the local network for the name of any server on the network. Once that name is returned, the client can then send a get local target RIP message and obtain a route to the server. Once that is accomplished, the client can attach to that server and then have access to the NetWare bindery or directory service to find all services on the NetWare network. This message will be examined in a later section, where the login process is examined.

NCP

NetWare Core Protocol (NCP) is the protocol all client/server communication utilizes. NCP operates over IPX just as RIP and SAP do. Its role is to transfer commands and data between server and client. NCP is unicast based and relies on RIP and SAP to resolve any addressing and routing issues. In general, NCP is of little consequence in a discussion of implementing switched networks, since it simply follows what IPX chooses to do at layer three.

Login Process

To summarize the NetWare protocol operation, a discussion of the process used by NetWare clients to attach to their servers is appropriate. Since NetWare clients are very simple devices, most of their network and addressing knowledge is obtained during the login process. In a routed network, the routers and Novell servers will participate in the client login process. In a switched network, these devices will still participate in the login, but the network construction will be different enough to require some special considerations. This section will discuss the basic login process of a NetWare client and then subsequent sections will examine the issues of NetWare in flat-switched networks.

The Novell client is essentially a plug-and-play device. This means that there is very little configuration needed on a NetWare client to allow it to access the network. This lack of configuration is very appealing to most system administrators, since they save considerable expense and time by not being required to perform complex customized configurations on each end system. In general, the default client configurations obtained by just loading the necessary drivers will allow for network access. Only in networks that contain unusual configurations of frame types or features is any real customized client configuration necessary.

Novell servers are significantly more complex than the clients in terms of configuration, but since there are relatively few servers in relation to the number of clients, the configuration burden is minimal. The server must be configured with proper external and internal network numbers and frame types. User accounts must be set up and permissions granted. Once these tasks are completed, the server can join the NetWare network. Other, more complex services such as e-mail and print services can also be configured on the server but are not required for basic file service support.

Once the server is configured with the proper external and internal networks and frame type(s), the client can attempt to log into the network. This login process is done using a combination of IPX SAP, IPX RIP, and IPX NCP. While the login process involves several protocols, it is relatively simple and is almost always done in the same manner, regardless of what operating system the client is using. The steps involved in the login process are as follows.

Step 1: Get Nearest Server Request   All Novell clients enter the network with absolutely no network knowledge. They do not know their IPX network number, and they do not know the addresses of any servers or routers—they are only aware of the frame type they have been configured to use and their node address (their MAC address). Since the client has no knowledge, it must use the service of SAP to determine some entry point into the NetWare network. To do this, the client generates a SAP request called "get nearest server." This broadcast message is sent to the local layer two network the client is attached to using the client's frame type. When a server on that LAN or a router attached to the LAN sees this message, it will respond with a message called "give nearest server" containing the IPX address of a server that is considered nearest to the client. The actual criterion for being nearest depends on the router or server. All local servers will respond, if configured to do so, with their own address, and routers will respond with a server considered close based on their routing tables. The first response will usually be used. Once the server or router responds with the unicast give nearest server, the client has knowledge of the IPX address of the nearest server. The actual server given does not matter, since the NetWare network is completely accessible once any server is contacted, based on the SAP protocol distributing the server information table to all servers.

Step 2: Get Local Target   Once the NetWare client has received the IPX address of the nearest server, the client must determine how to get to the server. Since the nearest server may be on the other side of a routed network, the client must utilize the RIP protocol to determine a best route to the server. Sending a get local target request to the routers on the network does this route determination. The RIP request is broadcast to the local LAN containing the IPX address of the nearest server. If that server is present on the local LAN, the server will respond with a RIP response (or give local target) message indicating the IPX and MAC addresses used to get to the server. If the server is on the other side of a routed network, the routers who have routes to that server will all respond with RIP response messages offering themselves as gateways. The first response will usually be utilized to begin the communication to the server. At this time, the client knows the IPX and MAC addresses of the server it wishes to communicate with and can begin the use of NCP to actually attach to the server.

This process of getting a nearest server and using RIP to find a route to it is very important in NetWare, since it allows the clients to enter the network essentially as unconfigured devices yet still reach any device on the NetWare network. The clients do not require static addressing, routing tables, or ARP caches as IP clients do. Additionally, almost all network clients, regardless of operating system or hardware, use this process in the same manner. That fact makes this process very easy to troubleshoot. The only addition to this process is if the client specifies the name of a preferred server. If that is done, the first steps do not change. A nearest server is always found first. The only change is that now the client will issue a second RIP request for the preferred server after it has attached to the nearest server and queried the SIT for the IPX address of the preferred server. The entire process is shown in Figure 5.11.

Flat IPX Networks

Implementing IPX on a flat layer two switched network is relatively simple. Since the login process discussed previously operates the same way whether a local server or a router is providing the nearest server ad-

Figure 5.11

NetWare client login process.

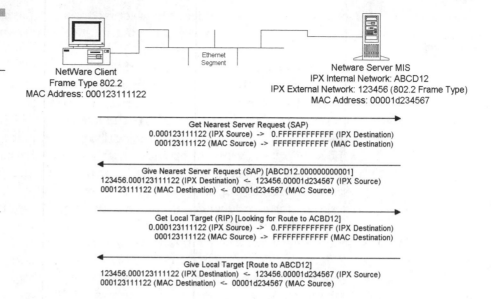

NetWare Client
Frame Type 802.2
MAC Address: 000123111122

Netware Server MIS
IPX Internal Network: ABCD12
IPX External Network: 123456 (802.2 Frame Type)
MAC Address: 00001d234567

Ethernet
Segment

Get Nearest Server Request (SAP)
0.000123111122 (IPX Source) -> 0.FFFFFFFFFFFF (IPX Destination)
000123111122 (MAC Source) -> FFFFFFFFFFFF (MAC Destination)

Give Nearest Server Request (SAP) [ABCD12.000000000001]
123456.000123111122 (IPX Destination) <- 123456.00001d234567 (IPX Source)
000123111122 (MAC Destination) <- 00001d234567 (MAC Source)

Get Local Target (RIP) [Looking for Route to ACBD12]
0.000123111122 (IPX Source) -> 0.FFFFFFFFFFFF (IPX Destination)
000123111122 (MAC Source) -> FFFFFFFFFFFF (MAC Destination)

Give Local Target [Route to ABCD12]
123456.000123111122 (IPX Destination) <- 123456.00001d234567 (IPX Source)
000123111122 (MAC Destination) <- 00001d234567 (MAC Source)

dress and routing information, the clients are unaware of the presence of routers in the LAN. If they are not present or relocated, the clients are generally unaffected. Because the clients are generally not involved in the logical network changes needed to build larger switched networks with less router segmentation, the process of doing so is usually much simpler than with IP.

There are two major issues involved in flattening the structure of an IPX network. The first is maintaining the logical network addressing of the external IPX networks. Since the IPX networks are based on frame type and router location, the flattening of the NetWare network will require adjustments in the external network numbers as routers are removed. The second issue in flattening an IPX network involves the actual LLC frame types. Since routers and servers acting as routers can route between external networks with different frame types, the changes in these routing services may require changes in the frame types used. These two issues must be addressed, since the IPX network must be flattened if the process is to be successful. The following sections will address both issues.

External Network Addressing

An IPX network is built as a group of logically separate networks identified by their external network number. Each of these external networks is separated from other external networks either by physically being on different sides of a router or by having an LLC frame type different from other external networks on the same segment. Each IPX external network can contain an almost limitless number of end devices, since the logical layer three IPX addresses provide 48 bits of space to identify any node. This 48-bit node address usually corresponds to the device's unique layer two MAC address. Since a single IPX external network should be able to handle all the nodes of any company's network, the need for router segmentation as a method of adding more nodes is not present in IPX as it was in IP class B and C networks. With this fact in mind, it should be obvious to the reader that construction of large IPX switched networks is definitely supported by its addressing structure.

In many networks built over the past decade, unnecessary router-based segmentation has been implemented. Previous chapters discussed the initial role of those routers and the rationale for building such a network. Today, as also discussed previously, the need for such granular router-based segmentation is no longer evident. In order to implement a larger flat-switched IPX network, the primary change that will be made in the NetWare network is modification of the external IPX network numbers on the servers and remaining routers. If you wish to successfully implement a flat-switched network, the first rule you must adhere to is as follows.

> *IPX Flat Network Rule 1*: All servers and routers attached to the flat-switched network must share a common IPX external network number for common frame types.

Even though there may be no routing inside the flat-switched network, that part of the network must be identifiable to all devices inside and outside of it in a common manner. By sharing a common external network number, the devices in the flat area and the routers connecting the flat area to the rest of the routed network understand the flat network in the same way. If this rule is not followed, the connectivity to and from servers in the flat area will most likely fail and the servers will continuously log routing errors.

Figure 5.12

External network
number changes in
flattening—initial
configuration.

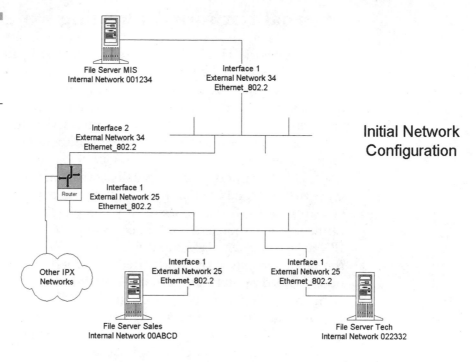

File Server MIS
Internal Network 001234

Interface 1
External Network 34
Ethernet_802.2

Interface 2
External Network 34
Ethernet_802.2

**Initial Network
Configuration**

Router

Interface 1
External Network 25
Ethernet_802.2

Other IPX
Networks

Interface 1
External Network 25
Ethernet_802.2

Interface 1
External Network 25
Ethernet_802.2

File Server Sales
Internal Network 00ABCD

File Server Tech
Internal Network 022332

Figure 5.13

External network
number changes in
flattening—final
configuration.

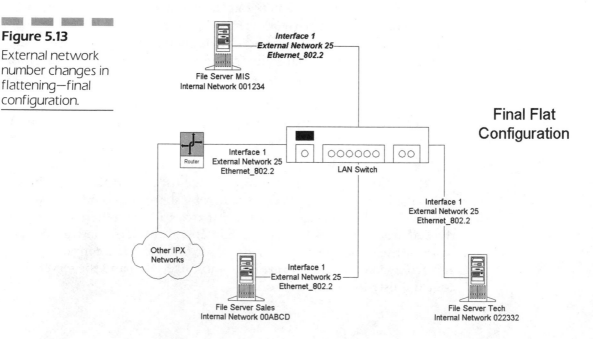

File Server MIS
Internal Network 001234

*Interface 1
External Network 25
Ethernet_802.2*

**Final Flat
Configuration**

Router

Interface 1
External Network 25
Ethernet_802.2

LAN Switch

Interface 1
External Network 25
Ethernet_802.2

Other IPX
Networks

Interface 1
External Network 25
Ethernet_802.2

File Server Sales
Internal Network 00ABCD

Interface 1
External Network 25
Ethernet_802.2

File Server Tech
Internal Network 022332

Figures 5.12 and 5.13 describe the changes that must be made in a small IPX network that is migrated to a flat-switched LAN. Figure 5.12 shows the network before the flattening is performed, while Figure 5.13 shows the changed server and router configuration required to successfully implement the flat space. The only real changes are the removal of one router interface and the external network number change at server MIS to make all servers agree that this IPX external network is number 25 for 802.2 LLC. The actual changes in external network numbers are done in the server configuration files, such as AUTOEXEC.NCF, and in the router configuration. It is recommended to do this change during scheduled network downtime, since these changes will require all IPX nodes to reestablish their understanding of the IPX external network space.

Frame Type Issues

The second issue in flattening IPX networks deals with the LLC frame types used. Earlier in the chapter, the four options for frame types on Ethernet networks were examined. All of these options can be utilized over the same network segment if desired. In order to communicate between the various frame types, there must be some routing done either by a router or a server acting as a router. When flattening the network, the router used to connect frame types may be removed or reconfigured. Because of this possibility, consideration must be taken regarding which frame types should be present after flattening and how they are to be connected. The second and third rules of flattening networks describe these considerations.

> *IPX Flat Network Rule 2:* Always minimize the number of LLC frame types present in a flat network. The optimal LLC frame type for a Novell network is 802.2.

> *IPX Flat Network Rule 3:* If more than one LLC frame type must exist in a flat IPX network, utilize routing on a minimum number of servers or routers to connect the external networks using different frame types. Do not load all frame types on all servers.

These rules state that the optimal network configuration for a flat IPX network involves only a single LLC frame type, with the preferred option being 802.2. If multiple frame types must exist in the flat area due to older devices being present, routing between the two frame types should only be done on a few devices. The rationale for this rule is that by routing on only one or two external routers, the servers are free of that responsibility and should be able to better act in the role of file servers. If multiple frame types were to be loaded on all the servers, they would by default be routers and be forced to support a much more complex role in the network. By minimizing their role, their performance is optimized. Figures 5.14 and 5.15 describe a possible evolution from a routed IPX network involving several frame types to an optimized IPX flat network containing primarily 802.2 but also supporting a few legacy Novell Raw devices.

In Figure 5.14, the network consists of two layer two LANs connected by a router. In each LAN, both Ethernet 802.3 and Ethernet 802.2 frame types are in use. The router and the servers are configured for both frame types. In order to increase performance by utilizing LAN switching, the router is moved to the periphery and the core of the LAN is implemented using a LAN switch. With this physical change, several logical changes must occur. The external network numbers for the two frame types are made consistent with IPX network 2, defining the Ethernet 802.2 framing, and IPX network 62, defining the Ethernet 802.3 framing. The end systems using Ethernet 802.3 are converted if possible to Ethernet 802.2. Limiting them to only one frame type, Ethernet 802.2, optimizes the servers. The remaining router interface is configured with both frame types to support routing between the few Ethernet 802.3 devices, such as the print server, and the majority Ethernet 802.2 network. If the print server had been able to support Ethernet 802.2, the router could have been configured with only Ethernet 802.2, further simplifying the configuration. In this case, the file servers are optimized for file service, and any routing is done on the router.

Ideal Configuration

In a flat IPX network, the ideal configuration of the network devices is as outlined in Table 5.1.

If the 802.2 frame type is universally used and file servers use only one frame type, the IPX network should be able to scale to a very large size by using switches as their infrastructure. It is important that proper broadcast analysis and baselining be done on this network, as discussed in Chapter 3, to ultimately determine how large this network can grow.

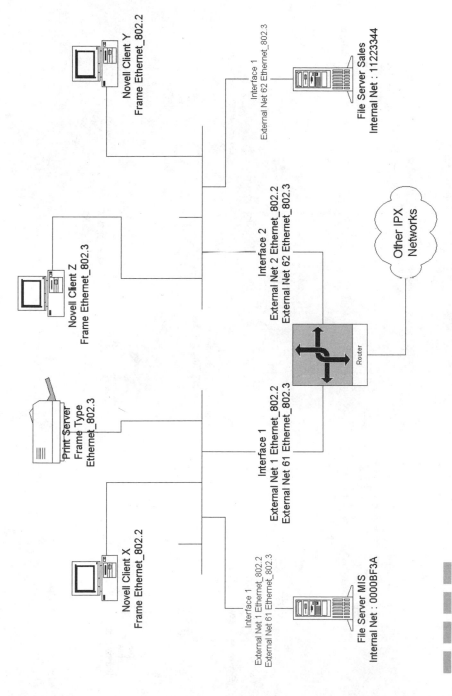

Figure 5.14 Frame type issues in flattening IPX networks—initial configuration.

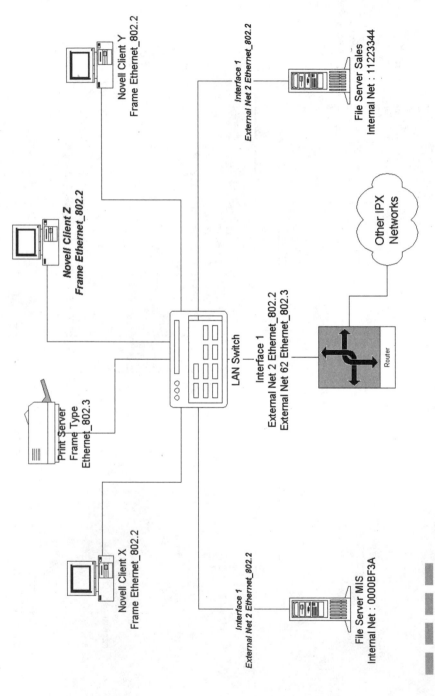

Figure 5.15 Frame type issues in flattening IPX networks—final configuration.

TABLE 5.1

Ideal IPX Flat Network Configuration

Device	Configuration
Legacy devices	Any legacy devices, such as old print servers or clients that cannot be upgraded, may require support for Ethernet 802.3. If these devices are present, they can exist but will rely on one or more routers to reach the rest of the network. It is vital that these devices be eventually upgraded to support 802.2 if an optimal network is to be created.
Clients	All Novell clients should be configured to support 802.2 LLC framing. Use Windows NT, Windows 95, or any DOS ODI drivers, if this is possible. If the client's Novell drivers do not support 802.2, the client should be upgraded.
Routers	If any legacy devices exist in the network using Ethernet 802.3 or Ethernet II, one or more routers should be configured with all frame types in use. This will allow those legacy devices to reach the 802.2 IPX network without requiring the servers to support multiple frame types.
Servers	Limit all servers to one frame type only. The preferred frame type is 802.2. By limiting the frame type to one, the servers are acting only as file servers, not routers. This will increase their performance and decrease the RIP and SAP broadcast traffic on the switched network.

Optimization Techniques

Using the rules outlined above, a large IPX flat network can be implemented. There are some additional processes that can be used to optimize that network. These suggestions are presented in order to minimize the overall broadcast rate of the network and maximize its growth potential.

Single Frame Type

The first optimization technique has already been discussed: Standardize only on 802.2 framing on your IPX network. The reasons for doing so include the simplicity of configuration; increased server performance; complete interoperability over Ethernet, Token Ring, and FDDI from the LLC perspective; lower broadcast rates; and even increased router performance. The only disadvantage to implementing 802.2 is that the clients may require a one-time reconfiguration or upgrade to support this mode. It is the recommendation of almost every vendor involved in IPX networking that the 802.2 frame type be used exclusively.

If your network is currently a mix of 802.2, Ethernet 802.3, and even Ethernet II and SNAP, the migration to a pure 802.2 network is relatively simple. The steps are as follows. If followed, the end result will be a much simpler, higher-performance network.

Step 1: Configure at least one server or router (preferred) interface in each LAN for 802.2 in addition to the existing LLC types.

Step 2: Configure your remaining file servers for 802.2. In networks that already have a majority of clients using 802.2, remove all other frame types from the server. If non-802.2 clients wish to reach the server, they must use the router configured in step 1.

Step 3: Configure your clients that are currently using non-802.2 frame types for 802.2. This may be done by a simple change in a network control panel (NT and 95) or a change in the net.cfg for DOS ODI drivers. Be sure to also disable "auto frame detect" features on operating systems that have them, since they may allow 802.2-capable devices to use other frame types.

Step 4: Once a layer two LAN is configured entirely for 802.2 at the clients, remove the other frame types from the routers and servers used in step 1. This will reduce broadcast SAP and RIP traffic significantly.

This process can be done on any LAN over as much time as you require. Once completed, the network will be much better optimized for IPX traffic.

Disable Routing at Servers

A Novell server has the ability to not only act as a file and print server but also as an IPX and even IP router. While this capability is very useful in small networks that require limited routing, it is not the best use of the server's resources in larger networks. In large networks with high traffic levels and user demands, the file server should be focused on only being a file server. To require it to also be a router in the network will usually result in mediocre performance in both roles. Because of this fact, it is highly recommended that the routing functionality of any servers be disabled. The actual methods of disabling routing include using only one interface card and one frame type, disabling the router function through the IPX router NetWare loadable module, or even using third-party load balancing software such as balance.nlm.

Disable Give Nearest Server Function

In a large flat-switched network, there is one potentially disruptive effect when large numbers of servers are present on the same switched fabric. When a client enters the network and loads its IPX NetWare drivers, the client will broadcast a get nearest server SAP request in order to find an available server. This message will be flooded across the entire switched domain and ultimately reach all servers. By default, any server that receives a get nearest server request will respond with a unicast give nearest server offering its services to the client. In a large switched network containing a very large number of servers (e.g., over 50 servers), this could result in a large traffic peak at the client. Additionally, responding to these requests is wasteful at the server. In order to optimize the IPX network for this situation, it is recommended that in a switched domain with large numbers of servers, the ability to respond to get nearest server requests should be disabled on some of the servers. The choice of servers to be disabled is somewhat arbitrary but should always include several servers with large server licenses and free connections. The actual method of disabling this property is through the commands in the Autoexec.NCF file.

Utilize NLSP

The majority of broadcast-related traffic on a NetWare LAN is due to the periodic SAP and RIP advertisements generated by routers and servers. In very large networks the number of SAP and RIP advertisements can number in the hundreds. This does not result in an extremely high average broadcast rate but can result in reasonably high peak broadcast rates. One method of reducing the broadcast rate used by routers in the network is by utilizing the newest NetWare routing protocol: Novell Link Service Protocol, or NLSP. This protocol is a link state routing protocol similar to Open Shortest Path First (OSPF) routing in Internet Protocol. As a link state protocol, each router tracks the complete topology and calculates its own routes. By doing this, there is no need to advertise routing tables, and the total broadcast rate is reduced significantly. The decision to use NLSP instead of RIP and SAP is significant, since a new routing protocol and all of its configuration and troubleshooting issues must be learned. If the option to utilize NLSP is available, it should be seriously considered. For more information on the operation of NLSP, consult the architectural specifications from Novell or any of the newest texts about NetWare 4.x.

Future IP Support

One final step that can be taken to ultimately support a large flat-switched network is to migrate towards the newest transport option for NetWare: Internet Protocol. The latest version of NetWare 4.1x contains support for native Internet Protocol transport for NetWare Core Protocol (NCP). While this option is not available for older versions of NetWare, new installations should consider it. There is a tremendous saving in complexity and support by operating all networking services over one core protocol. Since IP is by far the most flexible and open of the major protocols, it is the obvious choice. If the reader is considering a new installation of NetWare in his or her switched LAN, a thorough evaluation of NetWare over IP should be done. The rules for implementing NetWare over IP in a flat network are the same as for native IP, which is covered in Chapter 4.

Troubleshooting Novell Networks

Once a switched NetWare network has been implemented, it is necessary to support and maintain it. Chapters 3 and 8 examine most maintenance and troubleshooting processes for switched networks. This section will examine the issues associated with some specific NetWare-related troubleshooting scenarios.

Connectivity Failure

The most significant problem in any network is the failure of connectivity to a needed resource. NetWare networks can also experience situations where clients simply cannot reach their servers. In some cases, the

Figure 5.16

Connectivity failure.

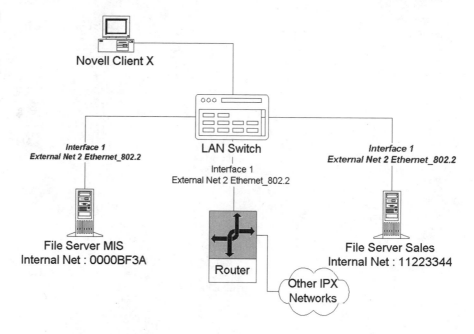

connectivity is related to the switched network failing to deliver the packets, but in most cases the issue lies with the end-system's configuration. By understanding the details of communication between the client and server, any failing connectivity should be identifiable. The following text will examine the process of identifying a failure between a client and a server.

In Figure 5.16, client X is unable to communicate to either file server. The symptom that the end user sees is simply that there are no available servers. In Windows 95 and NT 4.0, this shows itself as an empty network neighborhood. The process for troubleshooting this issue is as follows.

Step 1: Follow the flow charts in Chapter 8 to troubleshoot connectivity issues in switched networks. This process will identify conditions such as physical disconnection, failing switches, congested networks, and faulty cables.

Step 2: If step 1 indicates that the switched network is operating properly, a network analyzer should be utilized. Two placement options for the analyzer are shown in Figure 5.17. The first option involves using a small repeater at the client, while the second makes use of port mirroring or redirection on the switch. Port mirroring is a proprietary option most high-end switch ven-

Figure 5.17

Analyzer
placement options.

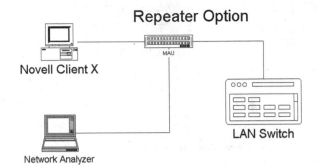

Repeater Option

Novell Client X

MAU

LAN Switch

Network Analyzer

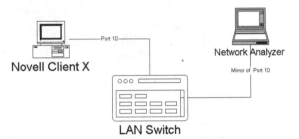

Port Mirror Option

Novell Client X

Port 10

Network Analyzer

Mirror of Port 10

LAN Switch

dors provide. Other, more advanced options such as conversation tapping could also be used in this step to replicate the client/server conversation to the analyzer's port.

Step 3: Once the analyzer is placed either on a repeater with the client or the client's port, or conversation has been mirrored, the analyzer should start a bidirectional capture of all packets to or from the client.

Step 4: As the capture is running, the client should attempt to attach to any NetWare server. This can be done by reloading the NEXT.EXE or VLMs in DOS or by restarting Windows 95 or NT. Once the failure occurs, stop the capture and examine the trace.

Step 5: From the previous discussion, the Novell login process always follows the same basic process. The first packet is a get nearest server followed by give nearest server responses from one or more servers. Next, the client sends a RIP request (get local target) followed by a RIP response from the server or router with a route to the nearest server. If these are successful, the next packets are the actual NCP attachment and login unicast messages. Examine the trace and determine if the login process happened as expected. Use Table 5.2 to identify failures in the trace and possible causes.

If the login process completes successfully, but there is still no server seen, the issue is most likely related to the client's operating system failing. Some common troubleshooting steps at this point include verifica-

TABLE 5.2

Possible Connectivity Failure Causes

Issue in Trace	Possible Cause	Resolution
No get nearest server sent	NetWare drivers are not loaded on the client or the network interface card is not operational.	Troubleshoot the adapter card and verify that the network drivers are installed by checking network properties.
Get nearest server but no response	The client is utilizing the wrong LLC type (e.g., Ethernet 802.3 in a pure 802.2 network).	Check the LLC type of the client by examining the analyzer trace or the client configuration for "frame type." Correct the frame type to match the server's and reboot.
No NCP	The servers may have no free connections.	Increase the server license or log out unneeded users.
Get nearest server with responses but no RIP requests	If Token-Ring segments are present, the switches may not be translating the MAC addresses properly.	Examine the trace for MAC addresses that are inconsistent at layers two and three (the IPX node ID) in the give nearest server. If the addresses are not the same for the destination MAC address and the destination IPX node address, the switch connecting the Token Ring to the Ethernet segments is not translating IPX packets.

tion that another device can communicate to the servers (already done in step 1) and reinstalling the client's operating system's networking drivers.

Slow Response Times

The second NetWare-related troubleshooting situation deals with slow response times. There are many causes of perceived slowness on a network, including network overload, end-system overload, errored packets, and retransmissions. Most of these issues are identifiable using the techniques described in Chapter 8. It is possible that the actual cause of the slowness on a NetWare network may be related to the actual path taken from client to server. One would assume that the path in a switched network would be direct and without significant latency. That assumption is usually valid in switched networks, since it is the primary reason for deploying a switched infrastructure in the first place. It is possible though in a NetWare network to have the client and server communicate via less than optimal layer three paths simply based on how they are configured. In the situation shown in Figure 5.18, client X

Figure 5.18

Troubleshooting poor response time.

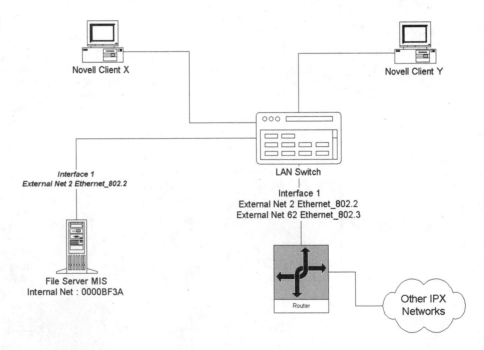

is experiencing very poor performance to server MIS compared with the client/server performance of client Y to the server MIS.

Since this is a switched network, it would be logical to assume that the communication between client X and server MIS should be direct at layer two using the switch. This assumption should not be made without more information, because IPX protocol is a layer three protocol that is ultimately responsible for determining the route between the client and server. In most cases, IPX would use the layer two switched network to communicate directly between the client and server. In this case, a simple misconfiguration at the client has resulted in a significantly different path. Client X has been configured for Ethernet 802.3 LLC framing, and, because of this, the path used to ultimately reach server MIS has been reconfigured to that shown in Figure 5.19.

Because client X is configured with the Etherent_802.3 LLC, the router has provided the response to the get nearest server and RIP request messages. The client is able to see all servers and reach them through the router. Unfortunately, the path taken involved sending packets to the router, who must convert the LLC to 802.2 and then forward the packets to the server using the same interface. This path results in unnecessary traffic and router intervention in the flow of IPX packets. Because of

Figure 5.19

Actual path used in misconfigured NetWare client scenario.

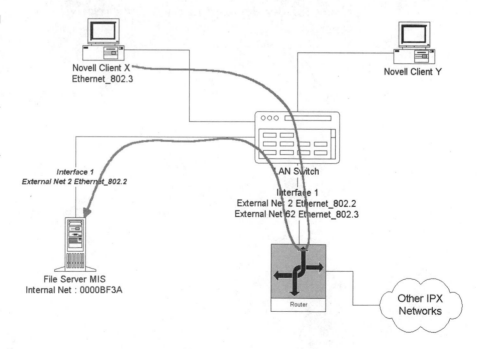

these extra steps, the performance from X to server MIS is significantly slower compared with the performance of Y to server MIS.

One simple way to detect this condition is to use a network analyzer and capture the conversation between X and server MIS. It would be obvious that the layer two destination MAC address was the router's and that should immediately cause concern. As previously discussed, it is very important to standardize on 802.2 LLC and remove support for other frame types if your NetWare network is to operate at its peak efficiency.

Summary

Novell NetWare is the dominant client/server network operating system in use today, based on its flexibility and simplicity. It is a mature system and provides excellent services to a large-scale network. From the discussions in this chapter, it should be clear that the implementation of NetWare on a switched LAN is a relatively simple process as long as external network numbers and frame types are kept consistent. With the information gained from this chapter, the reader should be able to successfully deploy and maintain a relatively large-scale switched IPX network.

CHAPTER 6

Other Protocols in Flat Networks

The previous two chapters examined how the two most common network layer protocols can exist and operate in large-scale, flat-switched networks. Internet Protocol and NetWare must be able to operate in your network as switched areas are added and the router hierarchy is reduced. In addition to these two protocols, all other protocols should be able to operate successfully in switched LANs. Given the vast number of protocols in use on LANs today, this book cannot address each of them fully. Instead, this chapter will provide some guidance in evaluating protocol operation in general on a switched LAN and then focus on some specific protocols in more detail. By understanding what elements of any protocol are affected by implementing the protocol over a switched LAN, readers should be able to make correct decisions regarding the suitability of any specific protocol running on their switched network.

Factors in Evaluating Protocol Operation on Switched LANs

In order to decide if a particular protocol can operate successfully in a switched network, it is necessary to understand the protocol's operation. If your network is utilizing several protocols, such as IP, IPX, and AppleTalk, it will be worth your time to learn how these protocols operate. There are many excellent references on just about every major protocol. Once you understand how that protocol operates generally, evaluating its behavior over a switched LAN will be a simple process of verifying that each of the factors described in the following sections will not cause that protocol to fail.

There are several areas that should be evaluated for every protocol when one is considering implementing a large switched network. It is important to remember that almost all protocols were initially designed to operate over bridged networks and then evolved to support routed networks. As such, it is very likely that any protocol you are using will operate perfectly well on a large switched network. The only issues you will face will relate to just how many devices using that protocol can operate on the switched LAN. In order to evaluate a protocol, the following areas should be examined.

Broadcast and Multicast Rates

Chapter 3 dealt with the scalability of switched networks. It was seen in that chapter that there are very few real limits in terms of how large a switched network can grow. The one real limit that still exists today is based on the broadcast and multicast rates on the network. If you have not read Chapter 3 on switched network scalability, now would be an excellent time to do so. As discussed in Chapter 3, broadcasts and multicasts are necessary components of all major protocols. The broadcasts in NetWare, for instance, allow clients to find servers, servers to communicate with each other, and routers to understand the network. If the normal NetWare-related broadcasting were stopped, the protocol would also stop. In evaluating protocols for use in large switched networks, it is necessary to understand what broadcasting and multicasting services exist within the protocol and if they will cause the overall switched network to have an excessive broadcast/multicast rate.

There are two broadcast- and multicast-related services used in most protocols. The first is the use of broadcasts to find services or advertise them. NetWare SAP and IP ARP are examples of these types of broadcasts. This type of service is usually the cause of the average broadcast rate on any network. Since these broadcasts and multicasts are necessary, the only issue one faces in determining if a particular protocol will be suitable for a switched network is determining if these advertisement and request broadcasts will increase the overall broadcast and multicast rates to an unacceptable level, as discussed in Chapter 3. In order to make this determination, use of a network analyzer with a filter set to the protocol in question on an active segment will provide an approximate measurement of the broadcast and multicast rates generated by that protocol for a given number of users. If the rate for the number of users you expect to use this protocol on the switched network will not create an excessively high rate, the protocol can be implemented without further examination. If the rate is excessive, implementation should be monitored using proper baselining techniques.

The second broadcast and multicast services that must be examined regard the use of true broadcast and multicast packets for applications. An example of this type of service is the IP multicast services. IP multicast uses an IP class D address but also uses a MAC layer multicast destination derived from the class D address. Since IP multicast is often used for high-bandwidth applications such as video conferencing, it can contribute significantly to the multicast rate of the overall network. When evaluating a protocol for its use on a switched network, it is important to identify if any applications use multicast or broadcast packets for communication not related to advertisements and requests. If such applications exist, the rate of multicasts or broadcasts must be determined and a decision made as to whether this additional rate will cause an overall excessively high rate on the switched LAN. If it will, the application is not suitable for a switched network. If it will not, the application should be allowed onto the network but monitored closely to identify any increase in the broadcast or multicast rates attributed to that service.

Logical Address Space

If the protocol under examination uses a logical address with the network:node format, as IP and IPX do, the addressing format needs to be examined to ensure that there are enough logical node addresses for the single switched network area. Each layer three protocol uses its own method of addressing. From the previous chapters on IP and IPX, it is obvious that while IP and IPX addresses have the same general functions, they are very different in actual structure.

Most protocols allow for a relatively large number of nodes in any one network or allow for multiple networks in one layer two area. IPX is an example of a protocol with a very large node count. IPX addresses allocate 48 bits of addressing for the node identifier, allowing for almost unlimited numbers of nodes in one IPX external network. Class A and B IP networks also allow for large numbers of nodes in one network, with class A supporting 16 million nodes and class B supporting over 64,000. Class C IP networks and AppleTalk phase 2 networks support relatively few nodes, with both supporting about 255 nodes per network. These protocols overcome this limit by allowing multiple IP class C networks or AppleTalk networks to exist in one layer two area. Multiple class C IP networks are supported by secondary IP addressing at the attaching routers, and multiple AppleTalk networks are supported through the use of extended networks with multiple cable ranges. Figure 6.1 illustrates this concept of multiple logical networks sharing one layer two switched area.

At this time, all major protocols support very large numbers of nodes in a single layer two switched LAN either directly, as is the case for IPX and class A and B IP networks, or indirectly, as is true for class C IP net-

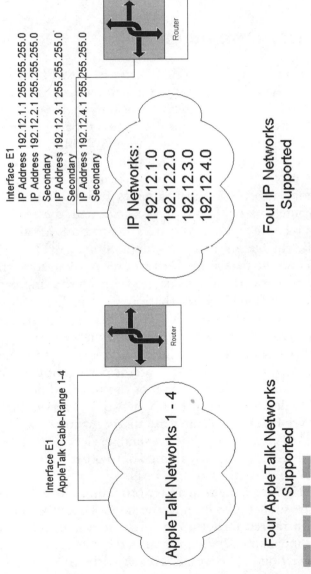

Interface E1
IP Address 192.12.1.1 255.255.255.0
IP Address 192.12.2.1 255.255.255.0
Secondary
IP Address 192.12.3.1 255.255.255.0
Secondary
IP Address 192.12.4.1 255.255.255.0
Secondary

IP Networks:
192.12.1.0
192.12.2.0
192.12.3.0
192.12.4.0

Four IP Networks
Supported

Interface E1
AppleTalk Cable-Range 1-4

AppleTalk Networks 1 - 4

Four AppleTalk Networks
Supported

Figure 6.1 Configurations for multiple logical networks in one layer two LAN.

works and AppleTalk networks. It is necessary that you evaluate your protocols and determine what must be done, if anything, to support the number of nodes you have in your switched network. Failure to examine this aspect of switched network deployment could result in protocol-related failures. In the case of AppleTalk, failure to increase your cable range when deploying a switched network could cause significant problems if more than 255 Macintosh computers using AppleTalk phase 2 tried to exist in a single AppleTalk network.

Router Dependencies

Routers in today's networks are not just used for routing. Many protocols and services that do not operate natively through routers have defined roles that the routers perform to enable their protocol to operate in a router network. Examples of this type of service include BOOTP/DHCP relay agent functions and NIS YPBIND redirectors for Internet Protocol. Routers also can play significant roles in the basic operation of some protocols, such as AppleTalk phase 2, by providing a focal point for zone information and name resolution. If a network is flattened and the routers are either removed or relocated, these services may be affected. It is necessary to verify that the protocols in use will not be affected by the changes in the router hierarchy.

In order to determine if the router is involved in the protocols in use on your network in ways beyond simply relaying packets, examine the router's configuration for that protocol. If there are any entries for service beyond basic routing (addresses, masks, etc.), each entry should be examined to determine if it is necessary on the network and, if so, whether another device will serve the same role after the router is removed. In most cases, the services the router is performing can be relocated to another router on the periphery of the switched network or onto another class of device such as a UNIX host or NT server. Figure 6.2 illustrates a network before implementing a larger switched area. The routers in the switched area are providing several services to the LAN. Figure 6.3 shows how those services are realigned onto other routers and servers to enable successful flattening of this LAN.

In Figure 6.2, the routers are providing the DHCP relay agent services for the subnets not local to the single DHCP server. This service allows for centralized DHCP server placement in a routed network (discussed fully in Chapter 7). Additionally, the routers are the source of all zone information in the AppleTalk network. An AppleTalk zone is a logical

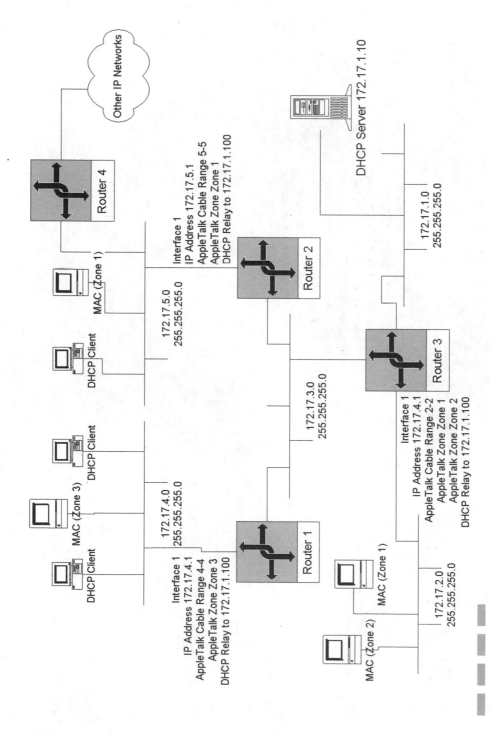

Figure 6.2 Example of router dependencies for client services.

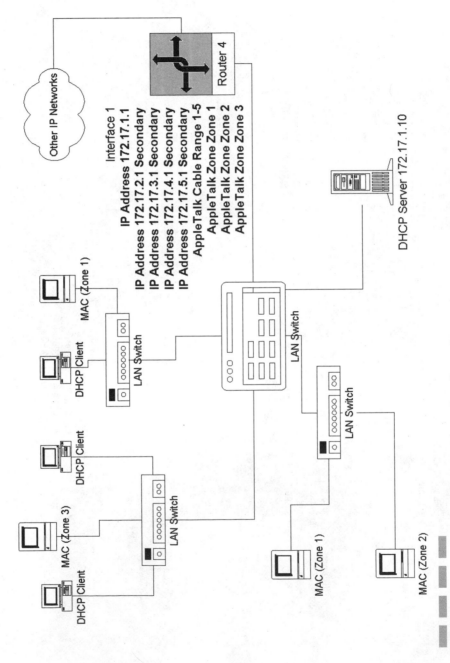

Figure 6.3 Relocation of client services after flattening.

grouping of users for the purpose of organizing resources in the Apple-Talk chooser application. In flattening this network, these services must be accounted for.

Figure 6.3 illustrates one possible configuration for flattening these segments while maintaining the service provided by the routers in the segmented network shown in Figure 6.2. All the routers are removed, except one, providing access to other IP networks or possibly the Internet. The remaining router is assigned secondary IP addresses to accommodate the five subnets present before flattening. The router is also configured with extended AppleTalk networks with a cable range of one through nine. This allows for five AppleTalk networks in the switched LAN. The DHCP relay agent services are not placed on the remaining router, because the server is no longer separated from the clients by routers. It can respond directly to the DHCP discover messages. Its local scope will need to be changed to reflect the new flat area. Once that is done, all service defined in the routed segmented network shown in Figure 6.2 will be present in the final switched LAN shown in Figure 6.3.

End-System Dependencies

When considering the impact of changing a network structure from a highly segmented routed network to a switched LAN with less router hierarchy, it is important to understand the impact such a change will have on the end systems of the network. Previously we saw that the routers provide some services to the end systems, such as zones in Apple-Talk and DHCP relay agent functions for IP. Additionally, the end systems have developed a relationship to the router at layer three in terms of their logical network identifiers and any cached routing information. If the routers are removed or altered, the end nodes may not realize this and they may continue to believe that the router structure has not changed. There are two categories of end systems in terms of how they relate to the routers on the network. They are those that have learned the router identity dynamically and those that are statically configured with routing understanding. Both are affected when changes in the router hierarchy occur.

Static routing understanding is primarily found on Internet Protocol end systems. As discussed in Chapter 4, the end nodes can be configured with a static IP address and static routing information such as default gateways and static routes. This kind of end system always requires consideration when router changes occur. In most cases, these end systems are modified to know less about the router placement so they are less affected by it when changes occur. The typical IP configurations to do this include natural network masks and a default gateway set to the host's own IP address.

End systems that learn router information dynamically are also affected when router structure changes. While this kind of end system does not require any configuration defining who the routers are, it will ultimately learn this information through its protocols. That information is cached and used. If the router is removed or changed, the information the end system has is no longer valid and needs to be discarded. On host nodes of this type, the only real way to relearn new router information is through a system reboot. Examples of this type of end node include IPX clients. They learn their external network number from their first service attachment. If that network number is no longer needed or is changed, the clients will continue to use the one they had learned until they are rebooted. AppleTalk nodes have a similar issue in that they listen to the Routing Table Maintenance Protocol (RTMP) messages sent from the local routers to determine what AppleTalk network they are on. Once that information is known, the node must be reset if changes occur. IP clients using proxy ARP will dynamically populate their ARP cache with MAC addresses of local routers providing reachability to other nonlocal nodes. If the network is flattened, the IP end system (unaware of the flattening) will continue to attempt to reach its IP destinations using the MAC address of the router used previously. This situation is shown in Figures 6.4 and 6.5.

In Figure 6.4, the IP host communication is using the MAC address of the router as the destination of the initial packet from X to Y. This information was obtained using the ARP process at user X and the proxy ARP services of the router. When the router is removed and replaced with a switch, the communication between users X and Y will fail, because the MAC address user X knows as user Y's is really the router's. Since the router is no longer present, user X will continue to send MAC layer packets to the MAC address of the router until its ARP cache times out or user X is rebooted.

In general, because of the fact that end systems cache dynamic information about routers in most routable protocols, it is always recommended that changes in the routed infrastructure be done during network downtime. Additionally, it is also recommended that the end users in the newly created switched area be reset to ensure that all dynamic information about the removed routers is purged.

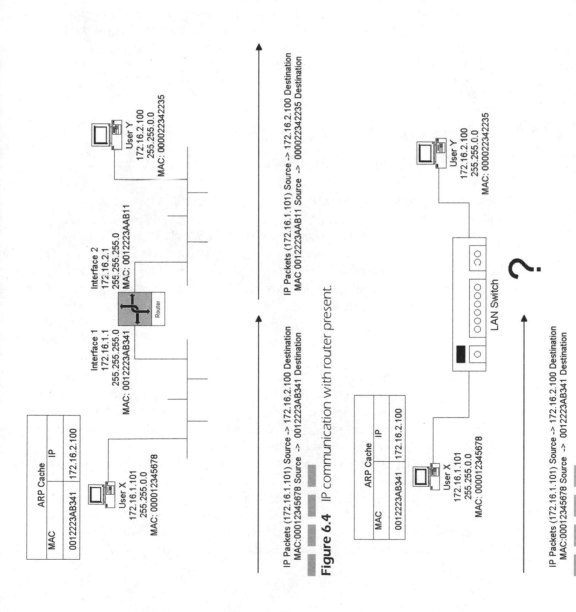

IP Packets (172.16.1.101) Source -> 172.16.2.100 Destination
MAC:000012345678 Source -> 0012223AB341 Destination

IP Packets (172.16.1.101) Source -> 172.16.2.100 Destination
MAC 0012223AAB11 Source -> 000022342235 Destination

Figure 6.4 IP communication with router present.

IP Packets (172.16.1.101) Source -> 172.16.2.100 Destination
MAC:000012345678 Source -> 0012223AB341 Destination

Figure 6.5 IP communication if router is removed and end systems are unaware of change.

Examination of Specific Protocols

From the previous discussion, specific areas of any protocol should be examined to identify their suitability on a switched LAN. The remainder of this chapter will examine specific protocols in order to provide some additional information helpful in understanding their operation on switched networks. For more detailed information on any of the discussed protocols or those that are not covered in this book, please refer to the reference texts in the bibliography.

Microsoft Networking in Flat-Switched Networks

Overview of Microsoft Networking

With the advent of Microsoft Windows for Workgroups, Windows NT, and Windows 95, client operating systems moved to an entirely different level of integration with their networks. This change was based primarily on the integration of what is known as Microsoft networking as a networking option for these operating systems. This Microsoft networking consisted of a set of client/server and peer-to peer services that allowed network access to other Microsoft networking devices. Since these services were integrated directly into the operating systems of the client devices, the types of network services became much more usable and transparent to the end user. Instead of simply seeing additional services as additional drives and printers, the resources were integrated into more advanced local interfaces, which blurred the distinction between what was local and what was remote. While the Windows 95 and NT clients can still map drives and printers explicitly, if they are attached to a network, those services will also be accessible without an explicit mapping. They are simply part of the network neighborhood.

In order to make this type of service possible, Microsoft had to utilize additional protocols and services. The major service utilized by the Microsoft network is the Network Basic Input Output System, or NetBIOS.

There are two services provided by NetBIOS: data transfer and access and a resource naming system. NetBIOS has been used for many years by a variety of networking services, ranging from older LAN Manager operating systems to current IP name services. Microsoft utilizes its services to provide a generic interface into the underlying network transports for its file sharing and resource identification. By utilizing a NetBIOS interface for its networking system, the Microsoft networking services can effectively operate over any lower-level media and transport protocol. By default, Windows NT and 95 can support Microsoft networking over Internet Protocol, IPX, and NetBIOS Extended User Interface (NetBEUI). This wide variety of protocols allows for almost universal support for the Microsoft networking services.

NetBIOS provides a data transport service based on Server Message Blocks (SMBs). When data are to be moved between nodes using NetBIOS, the actual data are formatted as SMBs and then transported over the network using the rules of the lower-level protocols such as IP or IPX. The SMB interface is important, since it abstracts the upper-layer applications from the lower-layer protocols. An application must only understand NetBIOS and its SMBs to use the Microsoft networking service, regardless of transport protocol.

The second service provided by the NetBIOS interface is a common naming service. NetBIOS defined services based on names. One of the significant advantages of Novell NetWare over other network operating systems such as IP was its ability to define services by name rather than logical address. The Service Advertisement Protocol (SAP) provided this service. For Microsoft networking, the NetBIOS interface provides a similar service. NetBIOS defines each device as a name and allows for the advertisement and location of that name. The actual mechanisms for doing the advertisement and location will vary, based on the lower-level protocol, but they all provide the ability to browse the network for services defined by name without direct understanding of the lower-layer protocol. This feature allows for a much more user-friendly interface and thus creates a more useful network operating system.

Since this is a book about implementing large-scale switched networks and not about NetBIOS, the rest of this chapter will focus on the layer three implementation of Microsoft network's protocols. If the reader is interested in more detailed aspects of the Microsoft networking services, several excellent texts are listed in the bibliography.

IP/IPX/NetBEUI Options in Switched LANs

Microsoft networking allows for a variety of layer three transport protocols. The three primary options are Internet Protocol, IPX, and NetBEUI. Each of these protocols will support the upper-layer Microsoft networking NetBIOS interface and services, but at layer three each operates based on its layer three protocol. Given this choice of several protocol options for layer three transport, a conscious evaluation should be made to determine which protocol is best suited for any individual network. This section will attempt to explore the details of each of these three implementations for Microsoft networking.

IPX Implementation

Microsoft networking can be implemented using IPX protocol as its layer three transport. At layer three, the frame structure and protocol addressing are as they are in any IPX implementation, such as NetWare. The significant differences are in terms of how services are defined and how the layer three protocol is used to provide upper-layer connectivity. In a network in which Novell NetWare and Microsoft networking coexist on the various network clients, the system administrator may wish to select IPX as the transport for the Microsoft networking service. In doing so, the number of protocols in use on the client is reduced and the configuration simplified. If other protocols such as IP are also needed, either protocol could be used for Microsoft networking.

The operation of IPX as the transport protocol for Microsoft networking is basically the same as it is for NetWare at layer three. Each area of the network is defined as a network, based on frame type (see Chapter 5 for more details). The logical addressing is based on an external network number and a node identifier based on the client's MAC address. The IPX protocol can be routed if IPX routing is present and the other aspects of layer three IPX such as frame format are the same as they are in NetWare. Microsoft networking uses the IPX transport for a very different role than NetWare in terms of the service provided. IPX in NetWare was used primarily for transporting NCP, RIP, and SAP between client and server devices. IPX in Microsoft networking is used to transport NetBIOS SMBs over the LAN and to transport name advertisements and queries.

The IPX implementation of Microsoft networking provides NetBIOS services, data transfer, and naming services. The services are provided through IPX by utilizing type 20 NetBIOS over IPX messages as its transport. For name services, the Microsoft networking device will broadcast its name to the network periodically using IPX broadcasts (which is also a MAC layer broadcast destination of ff.ff.ff.ff.ff.ff). To find services on the network, the device will also broadcast IPX NetBIOS name query messages. In most situations, the fact that the device is sending IPX broadcasts would prevent this protocol from passing through a routed network. Routers will typically not forward broadcasts. It is possible to configure the routers to forward these type 20 IPX NetBIOS broadcasts to other segments to allow name advertisements and name queries to reach all segments. This configuration, while possible, generally is not desirable, since it results in the routers no longer providing a broadcast boundary for all broadcasts. In a switched LAN, the use of IPX NetBIOS broadcasts is acceptable, since the switched area is a single broadcast domain. This does not mean that other protocols should not be used instead of this option.

NetBEUI Implementation

A second transport protocol option for Microsoft networking is the NetBIOS Extended User Interface, or NetBEUI. This protocol is based on NetBIOS services riding over the IEEE 802.2 LLC type 2 protocol for transport over a LAN. Since the NetBIOS service uses the layer two LLC services directly, there is no layer three protocol involved. This means that this service has no logical address and as such is not routable. NetBEUI is most suitable for small LANs consisting of only a few hundred users at most. It is very simple and very high performance, since it is not encumbered by all the complexities of layer three protocols. Given this role, it is recommended that NetBEUI transports be used only in LANs that do not require routing between users and that have relatively few users.

In order to provide the data transport and naming services of NetBIOS, NetBEUI utilizes a MAC layer multicast to resolve names and unicast MAC layer packets for data transport. Every end device using

NetBEUI will periodically multicast to the LAN to advertise its name. When connectivity is required, the node will again multicast a NetBIOS name query message to the LAN looking for the MAC address of the service it requires connectivity to. This broadcasting will only work on the local layer two network if routers are present, because the routers will not forward any NetBIOS multicasts unless they are configured to act as bridges for this protocol.

Internet Protocol Implementation

Internet Protocol is the third option for transporting NetBIOS services of Microsoft networking. This option makes use of the Internet Protocol Suite for NetBIOS services based on RFCs 1001 and 1002. These RFCs define how to utilize NetBIOS services over an IP network. Microsoft implements its networking services over IP in compliance with these RFCs' recommendations. In most networks, this choice of transport is preferred, since it provides better support for large networks with routing present. Additionally, this choice allows for significantly more complex naming services compared with the basic broadcasting mechanisms of IPX and NetBEUI. Even if routing is not present, this option is the recommended protocol choice for implementing a Microsoft networking environment.

The operation of NetBIOS over IP is significantly more complex than its operation over IPX or NetBEUI, based on the large number of options the protocol provides for name services. IP clients implementing NetBIOS operate in one of four modes. They are known as B-Nodes, P-Nodes, H-Nodes, and M-Nodes. These names refer to how the device will attempt to resolve NetBIOS names when attempting to find the IP address of a particular service. Each of these modes of operation is discussed below in order to fully understand the impact nodes in each mode have on the overall broadcast rate of the switched network.

B-Nodes: Broadcast Nodes   A B-Node operates much like the behavior of a NetBIOS node using IPX or NetBEUI. When a name is being queried, this type of node will use IP over MAC layer broadcasting to find the node on the local layer two network. In general this behavior is not desirable on switched LANs, since it results in broadcasts that must be propagated to all nodes in the switched area.

P-Nodes   A P-Node takes advantage of a service defined in RFC 1001 called a NetBIOS Name Server (NBNS) in order to resolve NetBIOS names to IP addresses. This server consists of a dynamic database of registered names and IP addresses. If P-Nodes are to operate properly, they must perform two tasks. They must register their NetBIOS names and IP addresses with the NBNS on initialization and then consult it using unicast IP messages to determine the IP address of any other registered P-Node on the LAN. This process essentially eliminates the broadcasting seen in the B-Node operation and allows the name resolution requests to traverse a routed infrastructure, since they are simply unicast IP messages, not broadcasts.

In Microsoft networks the role of the NBNS is found in the Windows Internet Name Service (WINS). WINS servers are NBNSs. Their role is to dynamically track any registered NetBIOS names and provide the corresponding IP address to any station requesting that information. By centralizing the IP to name bindings, the server can provide any node on the LAN complete information about any IP to name binding registered from any location. This mechanism has one potential failing: It requires that all nodes participate and register for it to function effectively using P-Nodes. If a node does not register because it cannot support NBNS service or simply does not know the IP address of a WINS server, that device will not be in the WINS database and as such will simply not exist to the P-Nodes on the network.

M-Nodes: Mixed Nodes   An M-Node provides a combination of the B-Node and P-Node functions to provide name resolution services over NetBIOS. This type of node will always utilize the B-Node method of name resolution first. If that method fails, the destination name is queried using the P-Node method of consulting the WINS server. This method allows a client to use the quicker B-Node method to find local resources and the more complex P-Node option in finding devices located across routers. This option is acceptable but does not minimize broadcasting on a switched network. The node will always broadcast as a B-Node regardless of the destination's actual location. As such this M-Node will generate as many broadcast messages as a B-Node would.

H-Node: Hybrid Node   The final node option for NetBIOS over IP is called an H-Node, or Hybrid Node. This configuration is similar to an M-Node in that both broadcast- and server-based resolution methods are used. It differs in that the H-Node reverses the methods of the M-Node. An H-Node will always use the NBNS or WINS server to resolve names first. If that fails, the node assumes that the node is not registered or is unable to use WINS and can be reached using B-Node functions. This combination is very effective in eliminating name query broadcasts from a switched LAN. If most devices register with the WINS server as P-, M-, or H-Nodes, there will be almost no broadcast name queries sent, since the server will be able to resolve almost all requests to register devices. If WINS is utilized on typical Microsoft networking clients such as NT and 95, the H-Node is the default mode of operation.

Given these modes of operation of the clients, implementation of an IP-based Microsoft network can result in variable amounts of broadcast traffic attributed to NetBIOS name resolution, depending on the node types in use. In general, the H-Node using WINS is the preferred option for client configuration in an IP-based Microsoft network.

Flat Network Evaluation of Microsoft Networking

Given the different protocol options available in implementing Microsoft networking, some comparison of the methods is justified. Using the criteria outlined in the first section of this chapter, the various Microsoft networking implementation options will be evaluated.

Option 1: NetBEUI Protocol for Microsoft Networking

Criteria	Effect	Notes
Broadcast and multicast rates	Medium	NetBEUI uses MAC layer multicasting for all NetBIOS name advertisements and queries.
Logical address space	N/A	There is no network layer address used in NetBEUI.
Router dependencies	High	Routers *must* bridge this protocol. Failure to do so will create isolated Microsoft networks on each side of the router.
End-system dependencies	Low	End systems believe that they are already in a flat network. Adding switches will not change their operation.

Criteria	Effect	Notes
Other issues	Low	NetBEUI uses the IEEE 802.2 LLC type 2 framing. As such it is interoperable over all major layer two network types (Ethernet, Token Ring, FDDI).

Conclusion: NetBEUI provides simple NetBIOS service to individual layer two networks. It cannot be routed and it is somewhat multicast intensive. This option should only be used on small isolated networks.

Option 2: IPX Protocol for Microsoft Networking

Criteria	Effect	Notes
Broadcast and multicast rates	Medium	IPX NetBIOS services use type 20 IPX messages. Name resolution is performed using IPX broadcasts that are transported by MAC layer ff.ff.ff.ff.ff.ff broadcast packets.
Logical address space	Good	IPX provides 48 bits for node identifiers within one logical 32-bit IPX network. The actual node address is typically the MAC address of the client. There is no danger of having insufficient node addresses for any size switched network using IPX NetBIOS.
Router dependencies	High	Routers must be configured to flood type 20 IPX broadcasts to allow name advertisements and requests to traverse the routed network. This eliminates the broadcast boundary created by routers for IPX NetBIOS.
End-system dependencies	High	If changes are made in the external IPX network number for a given frame type or if frame types are changed, all end systems on that network must be reconfigured and reset. Failure to do so will result in clients configured with incorrect IPX network addresses or incompatible frame types.
Other issues	Medium	If NetWare is in use on the switched network, any changes in the clients for NetWare will affect the NetBIOS services over IPX.

Conclusion: IPX NetBIOS transport is only desirable in networks that use IPX NetWare and wish to limit protocols on the network. In general, this method generates more MAC layer broadcasts than any other option and requires significant end-system configuration coordination to effectively provide large-scale NetBIOS support. Router reconfiguration is also necessary if multinetwork environments are desired.

Option 3: Internet Protocol B-Node Configuration for Microsoft Networking

Criteria	Effect	Notes
Broadcast and multicast rates	Medium	B-Nodes broadcast for all name advertisements and name queries.
Logical address space	Medium	Based on IP network type and subnet mask (see Chapter 4 for details), logical address space can be exhausted. Class C networks will be limited to 255 nodes unless secondary IP networks are supported.
Router dependencies	High	Even though IP can be routed without router knowledge of NetBIOS, an IP router will not forward the name advertisement and request broadcasts. B-Node functions are limited to isolated layer two networks unless manual name resolution is configured at the NetBIOS clients.
End-system dependencies	Medium	Changes in the IP network structure may affect clients if their logical network is removed. In most cases, the logical networks will be combined using secondary IPs at the remaining routers. The end systems need only purge their ARP cache to adapt to the new network.
Other issues	Low	Possible issues with IP subnet broadcasts can occur in flat areas with multiple subnets and B-Node operation.

Conclusion: B-Node IP operation is the least desirable option for Microsoft networking in switched areas. It cannot operate through routers without manual address resolution and generates significant broadcast traffic on the LAN. This mode should not be used in medium- to large-scale networks.

Option 4: Internet protocol P-Node configuration for Microsoft Networking

Criteria	Effect	Notes
Broadcast and multicast rates	Low	P-Nodes do not broadcast name queries on the LAN. This mode has almost no effect on the overall broadcast rate of the LAN.
Logical address space	Medium	Based on IP network type and subnet mask (see Chapter 4 for details), logical address space can be exhausted. Class C networks will be limited to 255 nodes unless secondary IP networks are supported.
Router dependencies	Low	Since name-to-IP resolution is centralized on a known server(s), this mode of operation interacts with routers seamlessly.
End-system dependencies	Medium	Changes in the IP network structure may affect clients if their logical network is removed. In most cases, the logical networks will be combined using secondary IPs at the remaining routers. The end systems need only purge their ARP cache to adapt to the new network.
Other issues	Low	This mode does not interact with B-Node devices.

Conclusion: P-Node operation provides very low broadcast effect on the switched network. This mode can be fully routed and provides centralized management of name-to-IP bindings. It does not interact with B-Nodes, so it may be unsuitable for some environments.

Option 5: Internet Protocol M-Node Configuration for Microsoft Networking

Criteria	Effect	Notes
Broadcast and multicast rates	Medium	M-Nodes broadcast for all name advertisements and name queries before using the WINS server. This mode has the same broadcast effect as a B-Node.

Criteria	Effect	Notes
Logical address space	Medium	Based on IP network type and subnet mask (see Chapter 4 for details), logical address space can be exhausted. Class C networks will be limited to 255 nodes unless secondary IP networks are supported.
Router dependencies	Low	When broadcast resolution fails, an M-Node will use the centralized WINS services to resolve remote devices. This allows the nodes to fully communicate through routed networks.
End-system dependencies	Medium	Changes in the IP network structure may affect clients if their logical network is removed. In most cases, the logical networks will be combined using secondary IPs at the remaining routers. The end systems need only purge their ARP cache to adapt to the new network.
Other issues	Low	Possible issues with IP subnet broadcasts can occur in flat areas with multiple subnets and M-Node operation.

Conclusion: M-Node operation provides both B- and P-Node functions. Because the B-Node resolution method is utilized first, the broadcast rate generated by an M-Node is the same as for a true B-Node. This fact makes this option less desirable in large switched networks. It is recommended that this mode not be utilized if P- or H-Node functionality is available.

Option 6: Internet Protocol H-Node Configuration for Microsoft Networking

Criteria	Effect	Notes
Broadcast and multicast rates	Low	H-Nodes broadcast for name advertisements and name queries only if the WINS service cannot resolve the NetBIOS name. If P-, H-, or M-Node functions are deployed on all end nodes, there is very little need for the H-Node to broadcast.

Criteria	Effect	Notes
Logical address space	Medium	Based on IP network type and subnet mask (see Chapter 4 for details), logical address space can be exhausted. Class C networks will be limited to 255 nodes unless secondary IP networks are supported.
Router dependencies	Low	Since name-to-IP resolution is centralized on a known server(s), this mode of operation interacts with routers seamlessly. Only when centralized name resolution is unsuccessful, are H-Nodes affected by the router's inability to forward IP NetBIOS broadcasts.
End-system dependencies	Medium	Changes in the IP network structure may affect clients if their logical network is removed. In most cases, the logical networks will be combined using secondary IPs at the remaining routers. The end systems need only purge their ARP cache to adapt to the new network.
Other issues	Low	This mode allows complete interaction with all IP NetBIOS options.

Conclusion: H-Nodes provide the best set of services for Microsoft networking using IP in a switched LAN. The nodes do not broadcast often, because centralized name services are available through WINS. This mode can operate over both switched and routed networks and is the recommended mode of operation.

Overall, the suitability of Microsoft networking in large-scale switched LANs is dependent on the choice of transport protocol used. All of the transports will operate in a switched environment, but in such an environment broadcast and multicast rates used by specific protocols should always be minimized. If you choose to implement Net-BEUI in your switched LAN, that system's broadcast and multicast rates may be significantly higher than had you implemented H-Node IP NetBIOS functionality with WINS servers. Using the information outlined in this chapter and any of the reference material on Microsoft networking, you should be able to implement any of the above transports successfully on your switched LAN.

AppleTalk Protocol Evaluation

AppleTalk protocols exist in many LANs. Even though the protocol is not as common as IP or IPX, it exists in sufficient quantity to be of concern when implementing a large switched LAN. This section will briefly introduce the protocol and its operation. The protocol will then be evaluated for its suitability in switched LANs.

AppleTalk Overview

AppleTalk, as with IP and NetWare, is a protocol suite consisting of many independent protocols working together to provide user communication. Most of the protocols used in AppleTalk have no real impact on the protocol's operation over a switched versus a routed network. This section will address the overall protocol suite and then cover the protocols that do affect AppleTalk's operation in a switched LAN. For more detailed information on the AppleTalk Protocol Suite or any of its sub-protocols, please consult the reference material cited in the bibliography. Figure 6.6 illustrates the protocol structure of AppleTalk.

AppleTalk operates over a variety of physical media using specific AppleTalk frames and services including LocalTalk, EtherTalk, Token-Talk, and FDDITalk. Above the physical and link layers AppleTalk uses its own Address Resolution Protocol (AppleTalk ARP) and provides its own routable protocol known as Data Delivery Protocol (DDP). For routing advertisements, the Routing Table Maintenance Protocol (RTMP) is used and for name resolution, the Name Binding Protocol (NBP) is provided. A basic test protocol known as AppleTalk Echo Protocol (AEP) and the Zone Information Protocol (ZIP) also are present. These protocols provide the basic infrastructure for AppleTalk communication.

Above the protocols listed are the protocols used for actual data communications. They include AppleTalk Data Stream Protocol (ADSP) for low-speed, connection-based communications, AppleTalk Transaction Protocol (ATP) as the primary transport layer protocol, AppleTalk Session Protocol (ASP) as the primary session layer protocol, and AppleTalk Filing Protocol (AFP) to interface into the local operating system. For print service, Printer Access Protocol (PAP) and PostScript are provided. Only four protocols—AppleTalk ARP, ZIP, NBP, and RTMP—are sig-

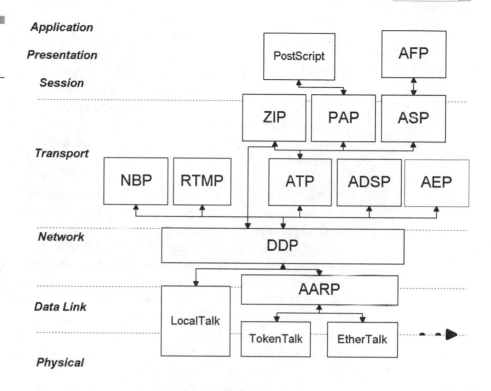

Figure 6.6

AppleTalk Protocol Suite.

nificant to the protocol's operation over a switched LAN. Each will be discussed in the following paragraphs.

AppleTalk ARP When operating over physical networks such as Ethernet or Token Ring, AppleTalk requires a mechanism to determine the MAC layer addresses of devices its upper-layer logical protocols wish to communicate with. This requirement is not uncommon in layer three protocols and was examined in some depth in Chapter 4. AppleTalk uses a protocol similar to IP ARP. It is known as AppleTalk ARP and provides several key services to the AppleTalk network. The primary service provided by AppleTalk ARP is the resolution of layer three AppleTalk addresses to MAC layer addresses. Whenever new communication is required to an AppleTalk destination, the AppleTalk source will send an AppleTalk ARP multicast to resolve the layer three known address to a MAC address. A second service provided by AppleTalk ARP occurs when an AppleTalk client first enters the network. The client must assure that its layer three address is unique. Since AppleTalk nodes randomly choose their address, the AppleTalk ARP protocol is used to verify that the one chosen is not in use. This process is known as probing the network. The new AppleTalk client will always send ten AppleTalk ARP messages to look for its own AppleTalk address. If none of the other devices on the segment responds, the AppleTalk client can assume that it has a unique layer three node address. This protocol can be of concern on a switched LAN, since it makes use of MAC layer multicasting, which must be propagated to all nodes in the LAN. This protocol is necessary and cannot be altered to operate in any way other than that described.

Name Binding Protocol   NBP provided a mechanism to map logical service names to devices on the LAN, just as SAP and WINS in NetWare and Microsoft networking provided this service. NBP operates in two entirely different ways, depending on whether the LAN has AppleTalk routers present. If the LAN has no routers present, the NBP makes use of MAC layer multicasts to request the names and AppleTalk addresses of devices providing file or print services to the LAN. Any node seeing an NBP lookup message requesting the type of service it provides is obligated to respond directly to the requesting device. This mode of operation is relatively uncommon, since most LANs contain at least one AppleTalk router.

The second mode of operation for NBP occurs when the AppleTalk client has seen a router. In this case, the router becomes a focal point for all NBP lookup messages. Now, when a client wishes to find names and AppleTalk addresses of other nodes, it will unicast an NBP message to the local router. The routers of the network will then multicast the message onto all segments where the service could exist. This logical area is usually known as a zone. Now the devices seeing the request respond through the routed network to the source. This method is much more efficient in most networks, since the services being queried usually do not exist on all networks. In most cases, the services in a single zone exist only on a few selected networks. By allowing the routers to control the multicast requests so that they only reach the network segments containing the given zone, the protocol saves many unneeded multicast messages.

Routing Table Maintenance Protocol   RTMP provides routing table updates to the AppleTalk routers on the LAN. There are two levels of RTMP possible in AppleTalk networks. Initially, AppleTalk provided only eight bits of logical address space for the node ID within a given network. It also did not allow for multiple networks to occupy the same segment. This limitation forced AppleTalk networks to limit the number of nodes per network to 253. Additionally, the initial AppleTalk protocol, known as phase I, allowed only one logical group (zone) to exist in a given AppleTalk network. This phase I AppleTalk was upgraded to phase II. Phase II supports extended networks in which multiple logical AppleTalk networks can exist on a single layer two LAN. This allows a single LAN to support about 16 million nodes. Additionally, phase II added support for Token Ring and FDDI and allowed a single network to contain AppleTalk nodes belonging to up to 255 different zones. RTMP was enhanced to support phase II AppleTalk. Its primary role is to propagate routing table information to other AppleTalk routers in the network, much in the same way as the IP or IPX Routing Information Protocol (RIP). RTMP advertisements also allow AppleTalk clients to locate the local routers on their segment. This feature is useful, since it eliminates the need for static routing configuration, as is found in IP, at the AppleTalk clients.

Zone Information Protocol   ZIP provides AppleTalk with a mechanism for logically grouping services together without regard for their actual physical location. A zone is simply a logical group of AppleTalk devices. Devices grouped into zones are accessible through a local service known as the "chooser." The chooser uses ZIP to ask a local router for a list of all zones. It then displays them to the user, who selects one to browse. Once one is selected, the chooser utilizes NBP to find all devices in that zone meeting the requested service type. This process is shown in Figure 6.7.

In Figure 6.7, MAC X asks the router for a list of all zones. This request occurs when the user opens the chooser. When X clicks on the zone sales and the apple file server icons, an NBP lookup is sent to the router requesting the names and AppleTalk addresses of all servers in the sales zone. The router then sends this request to all segments containing the sales zone. At this point MAC Y sees the request and responds. MAC Z never sees this request, since it is not on a network containing the sales zone.

AppleTalk Protocol Evaluation

Given the basic introduction to the various protocols that make up the AppleTalk Protocol Suite, it is now possible to evaluate AppleTalk for use in a flat-switched network. AppleTalk is one of the most multicast-

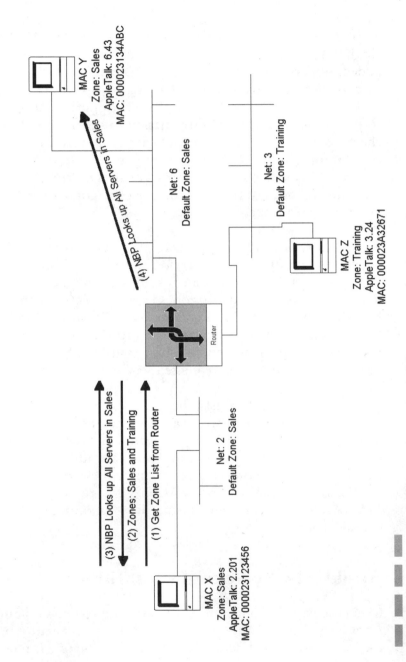

Figure 6.7 ZIP and NBP interaction with AppleTalk router.

intensive protocols available. This "chattiness" is primarily the result of its desire to be plug and play. Because the end systems require almost no configuration and there are no centralized name servers, AppleTalk must utilize broadcast and multicast protocols for resource location. This is similar to the way NetBIOS over IPX functions in the Microsoft networking architecture. Routers exist in the network, but instead of stopping broadcasts and multicasts, they are configured to forward and manipulate them. This results in higher overall broadcast and multicast rates on any network using AppleTalk, as compared with other protocols. Because of the potential for higher than normal broadcast and multicast rates on a LAN with AppleTalk present, long-term broadcast rate baselining (as discussed in Chapter 3) is critical in determining the size of an AppleTalk switched network.

Using the criteria outlined at the beginning of this chapter, AppleTalk is evaluated as follows.

Criteria	Effect	Notes
Broadcast and multicast rates	High	AppleTalk nodes and routers generate significant multicast traffic for AARP and NBP messages.
Logical address space	High	Each AppleTalk network can contain only 253 nodes. In phase I, that limit translates into only 253 nodes per switched network. With phase II AppleTalk, extended networks using multiple network numbers can be used. This allows for up to 16 million nodes per switched network.
Router dependencies	High	Without AppleTalk routers, zones do not exist and NBP must be handled directly by the end nodes. In most AppleTalk networks, at least one AppleTalk router is needed. Fortunately, many servers, such as NT and Novell, can fill this role.
End-system dependencies	Low	End nodes on their next reboot dynamically discover changes in the AppleTalk network. This allows for relatively little configuration in changing the shape or logical structure of an AppleTalk network.
Other issues		None

Conclusion: AppleTalk can exist in switched networks with some constraints. Generally, if more than 253 AppleTalk nodes are to exist in the network, phase II routers must be used. Additionally, at least one Apple-Talk router (or server with AppleTalk routing capabilities) must be present to handle NBP and zones. It is also critical to monitor the broadcast rate of the LAN to watch for excessive broadcasting and multicasting, since AppleTalk nodes can generate significant numbers of AppleTalk ARP and NBP multicasts. When the overall broadcast rate of the network becomes excessive, you have reached the switched LAN's maximum size. In most cases, this size will be in excess of 1,000 Apple-Talk nodes.

Summary

In this chapter, the process of evaluating protocols for use in flat-switched networks was outlined. The criteria given provide some guidance in determining how your protocols should exist in the switched LAN. It is critical that you establish a basic understanding of the protocols you wish to utilize before you attempt to implement these protocols on any network, switched or not. The key point to always remember is that most protocols were designed to operate over bridged networks and, as such, can operate over today's switched LAN systems. It is just a matter of determining what elements of that protocol must be monitored and considered in order to implement the protocol successfully over large-scale switching systems.

Dynamic Host Configuration Protocol (DHCP) in Switched Networks

Overview of DHCP

Simplicity and speed: These are the two goals of every network being implemented today. Enhanced performance is necessary, as users move towards faster computing platforms and bandwidth-intensive multimedia applications. Simplicity is necessary in order to maintain the simple model of the local area network and to keep management and maintenance tasks to a minimum, thereby controlling the costs of the increased capacity. In an effort to increase performance through newer technology and more efficient network layer protocols, such as TCP/IP, while maintaining the current level of support and management, new methods of network administration have come into existence. One such new feature is Dynamic Host Configuration Protocol, or DHCP.

This chapter will explain the operation of DHCP in general and describe the specific implementation issues involved in using DHCP in both routed and switched networks. Examination of the protocol will involve packet flow through the network, configuration of the systems involved, and some vendor-specific implementation issues. Additional design rules for implementing DHCP in switched networks will be discussed.

The primary objective of the Dynamic Host Configuration Protocol is defined in RFC 1541 as follows: "The Dynamic Host Configuration Protocol (DHCP) provides a framework for passing configuration information to hosts on a TCP/IP network. DHCP is based on the Bootstrap Protocol (BOOTP), adding the capability of automatic allocation of reusable network addresses and additional configuration options."

This objective provides a vital service to networks that wish to implement Internet Protocol for data transport but are concerned about the cumbersome manual administration of client addresses. When evaluating the implementation of various layer three protocols, two issues are obvious. Some network operating systems and their associated protocols focus on ease of administration through server-based addressing models, while others focus on client-based addressing mechanisms. What is evident, however, is that the peer-to-peer systems such as Internet Protocol provide superior protocols in terms of performance and flexibility but lack the simplicity of configuration of the less efficient protocols such as Internetwork Packet Exchange (IPX). Figure 7.1 compares network operating systems in terms of efficiency and simplicity.

Figure 7.1

Simplicity and
performance
perception of
various network
operating systems.

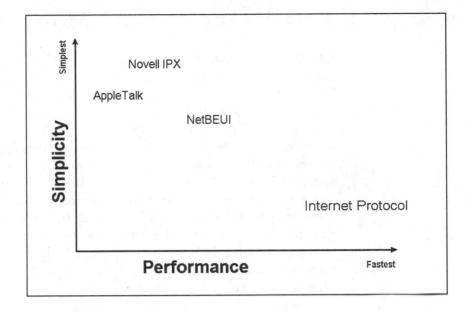

Figure 7.1 is by no means an absolute definition of the performance
or simplicity of the various operating systems but is reflective of the
perception and in some cases the reality of how these systems function.
It is generally true that Novell NetWare has become a dominant network operation system but not because of its layer three performance.
Instead, NetWare is popular due to its simplicity of implementation:
Clients need almost no configuration to operate it using IPX. In con-
trast, Internet Protocol is perceived as being extremely high performance yet complex to implement due to the static client-based addressing
scheme.

It would seem that given a choice between Internet Protocol and IPX,
one is faced with a trade-off: ease of administration but lower performance with IPX or high performance and configuration complexity with
Internet Protocol. Ideally, one would prefer a layer three system that is
both high performance and simple to administer. DHCP attempts to
provide the simplicity of operation for Internet Protocol by removing
the static addressing requirement of the end systems through a centralized address distribution mechanism.

DHCP Operational Model

DHCP operates in a client/server model. The client is the end system in the Internet Protocol network that requires an IP address. The server is the depository of the available IP addresses for use by clients. DHCP defines the method of communication between the client and server to allow clients to obtain a valid IP address. DHCP also defines how the server will provide this requested address with no prior knowledge of the specific client (unlike other IP assignment protocols such as BOOTP and RARP). A third element is defined in DHCP systems: the relaying agent. This represents a device that is neither a client nor server in DHCP. Its role is to forward DHCP messages between remote IP networks to allow DHCP servers and clients to operate in routed networks without requiring local DHCP servers on all networks. The DHCP relay agent is usually a router device but can be implemented in any device capable of relaying layer three data units and understanding DHCP messages.

Figures 7.2 and 7.3 illustrate the relationships between the three components of DHCP. Figure 7.2 defines the relationship in a nonrouted or local subnet configuration, while Figure 7.3 defines the relationship in a routed multisubnet configuration.

Figure 7.2

DHCP operational model in flat network space.

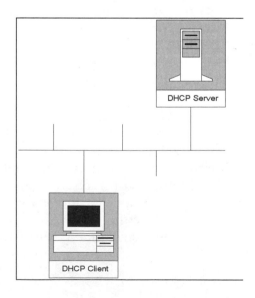

Figure 7.3
DHCP operational model in routed networks.

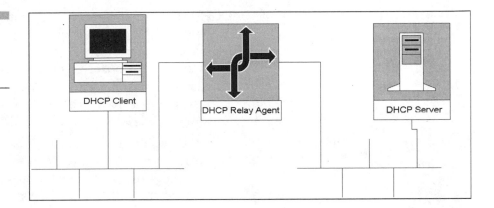

Defining Standards

DHCP is defined as a series of RFCs under the Internet Engineering Task Force. These documents define the scope of DHCP and its operations. The included RFCs are 1533, 1534, and 1541.

Since DHCP is defined as a series of RFCs, there are various interpretations and options, which may or may not be included in all vendors' interpretations of the standard.

Server Configuration

DHCP servers act as the distribution point for all configuration parameters. They are the focal point for all DHCP communication, even though all DHCP communication is initiated by the clients. Configuration of the DHCP server involves three general steps.

1. Scope creation
2. Assignment of configuration value to scopes
3. Activation of scopes

Each of these steps will be examined more closely in the following sections, but first, some general terminology must be discussed.

DHCP Lease: DHCP provides IP addresses to clients for a finite duration. This duration is known as the lease duration.

DCHP servers specify for each scope how long a client will be able to utilize an IP address. When the lease is close to expiration, the client must try to renew the lease in order to keep its IP address. If the lease expires, the client must attempt to rebind to the address if it is still available. If it is not, a new IP address must be leased.

DHCP Scope: DHCP provides automatic assignment of configuration parameters (including IP address), based on logical groupings of users called "scopes." Each subnet (as defined by the subnetwork mask) in an IP network has its unique configuration parameters defined in a unique scope. Each subnet can have only one scope defined, consisting of a continuous range of IP addresses to participate in DHCP. Addresses in the subnet that are not to be used in DHCP must be excluded from the continuous range after the range is defined.

Exclusion Range: Since each subnet can only have one DHCP scope, it is necessary to allow administrators to exclude some addresses from the leasing process. These addresses would be those of non-DHCP clients, the DHCP servers, any routers, and in some cases remote access devices such as terminal servers having their own mechanisms of dynamically assigning addresses.

Scope Creation

Scope creation is the process of defining the address ranges to be used by DHCP for a particular subnet. The process is simple in that the administrator defines a starting IP address, an ending address, a subnet mask, and any excluded addresses. Figure 7.4 shows the interface in Windows NT 3.51 server used to create a scope.

In this scope, called "MIS Group Subnet 12," the entire 132.111.12.0 subnetwork is to be used for DHCP, except the 12.20–12.50 range and the IP addresses 132.111.21.1 and 132.111.12.250. A client residing in the 132.111.12.0 subnet and requesting an IP address from this server could get any address in the range except those excluded.

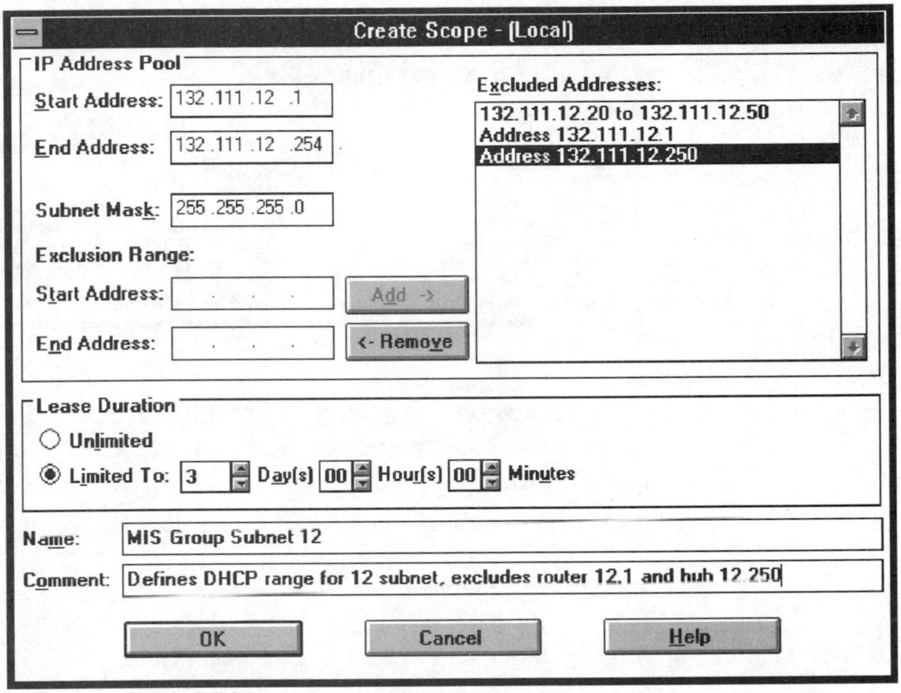

Figure 7.4

Windows NT DHCP
scope creation.

Assignment of Configuration Value to Scopes

Once the scope has been created, it could be used, but it would only provide the IP address and subnet mask to the clients if they made a request. Since one reason to use DHCP is its ability to provide a great deal of configuration parameters, it is necessary to define the customized parameters for the DHCP scope prior to allowing clients to use the scope.

The definitions of the configuration values are usually created from a given list of well-known parameters. These will usually be supported by all DHCP clients. Additional parameters can be created at this point if the clients are able to request them. The Windows NT 3.51 server interface used to accomplish this is shown in Figure 7.5.

Activation of Scopes

Once the scope has been created and the various options defined, the scope can be activated to allow this server to process DHCP requests

Figure 7.5

DHCP scope
options
configuration.

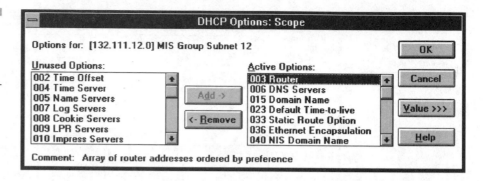

from clients on the subnet defined in the scope. It is important to note that a particular scope will only provide service to clients on its subnet as determined by the relay agent forwarding the request or the DHCP server recognizing the request as local.

Client Configuration

DHCP clients require no initial configuration to operate in this process. They, by default, will request service from any DHCP server on the network upon initialization. The RFCs defining DHCP specify only generic rules for DHCP clients. It is important to note that the DHCP client need not support all configuration options defined at the server.

Some common software implementations that support DHCP client functionality are listed on the Internet as the DHCP Frequently Asked Questions (FAQs) list at http://www.syr.edu/~jmwobus/comfaqs/dhcp.faq.html.

Relay Agent Configuration

A DHCP relay agent provides the service of forwarding DHCP requests across subnets to enable remote DHCP clients to contact DHCP servers that do not reside on the client's subnetwork. The implementation of a DHCP relay agent is defined in RFCs 1532, 1533, and 1541. In reality, the DHCP relay agent is exactly the same as a BOOTP relay agent in terms of operational characteristics. Unfortunately, the BOOTP relay agents that have existed prior to DHCP will typically not operate correctly when forwarding DHCP requests and responses, since DHCP makes use of a broadcast flag in the datagram that was typically not utilized in BOOTP. In order to guarantee compatibility with DHCP, most router vendors have been forced to update their BOOTP relay agents to properly handle the broadcast flag indicator. The current status of DHCP support for some router vendors is as follows.[1]

ALANTEC Router Software for DHCP Support: The switches' router function has been handling BOOTP forwarding since 1993. Support for the broadcast flag was introduced in maintenance release 2.5 of their software and is in version 2.6 and later.

Cisco Router Software Update for DHCP Support: If you use Cisco routers with software versions prior to versions 9.21 (3.2) and 10.0 (2.1), and use DHCP servers in your network, you must obtain a software update from Cisco Systems. BOOTP extensions to support DHCP (per RFC 1542) were integrated into 9.21 (3.2) and 10.0 (2.1) Cisco software. It is recommended that you use these versions of the router software for better compatibility with DHCP servers.

IBM 2210 Router Software for DHCP Support: Version 1 release 2 has a BOOTP relay agent. There is no official confirmation of support for the broadcast flag.

Microsoft Windows NT Server DHCP Relay Support: The DHCP relay agent is supplied with Windows NT Resource Kit (version 3.51).

Novell NetWare DHCP Support: For Novell servers, there are NLMs that forward BOOTP requests and, therefore, DHCP requests. The "forward BOOTP NLM" is included in NetWare 4.1. You can get this support in NetWare 3.11 and 3.12 also, but you must apply the TCP31A.EXE patch, which is located on NetWire. An example of one such NLM is available online: ftp://netlab2.usu.edu/misc/bootpfd.zip (unsupported Novell software, 1993).

3Com Router Software Update for DHCP Support: If you use 3Com routers with software versions prior to version 7.1, and use DHCP servers in your network, you must obtain a software update from 3Com. BOOTP extensions to support DHCP (per RFC 1542) were integrated into versions 7.0.04, 7.1, and later systems. It is recommended that you use these versions of the router software for better compatibility with DHCP servers.

---

1. Information obtained from Microsoft Windows NT resource pack and DHCP FAQs.

Ungermann-Bass Networks Router Software for DHCP Support: If you use Ungermann-Bass ASM83xx routers with software versions prior to version 7.2 and use DHCP servers in your network, you must obtain a software update from Ungermann-Bass Networks. BOOTP extensions to support DHCP (per RFC 1542) were integrated into version 7.2 router software. It is recommended that you use these versions of the router software for better compatibility with DHCP servers.

Wellfleet Communications Router Software for DHCP Support: If you use Wellfleet router software versions other than 5.75, you should contact Wellfleet Communications and update to the version that fully supports DHCP. Version 5.75 supports BOOTP extensions that support DHCP (per RFC 1542). However, if you move a client from the same network segment of a DHCP server to a remote network segment (across a wide area network), the client starts with the original IP address. You must issue the commands ipconfig\release and then ipconfig\renew from the command prompt on the client. Contact Wellfleet for a version that fixes this problem. BOOTP extensions to support DHCP (per RFC 1542) were integrated into Wellfleet version 7.71 (fix4) software. It is recommended that you use these versions of the router software for better compatibility with DHCP servers.

Xyplex Router Software for DHCP Support: Version 5.5 of their routing software supports DHCP.

Configuration of a DHCP relay agent involves the creation of either UDP broadcast redirectors or helper addresses. These two terms describe the same function. When a router has been configured with a UDP redirector or helper address, it is given the IP address of a server (in this case a DHCP server) that can service DHCP requests. Refer to the relay agent's user manuals for specific commands used to configure IP helper addresses. The exact operation of the relay agent in a routed DHCP network will be discussed in more detail later in this chapter.

DHCP in a Simple Network

The operation of DHCP in a simple network (one not requiring the services of a relay agent) is discussed in this section. The two physical components necessary for simple DHCP operation are the DHCP clients and the DHCP server(s). DHCP communication always begins with the client initiating a DHCP DISCOVER to find available DHCP servers. If a DHCP server is able to provide the requested service, it will respond with a DHCP OFFER of service. The client will then decide to accept the OFFER and send a DHCP REQUEST indicating the specific server whose offer it accepted. The server will then send a DHCP ACK message acknowledging the acceptance of the offer and providing the requested scope parameters. The process may or may not contain all four steps depending on whether the client had an IP address previously.

Detailed DHCP Communication

For the purpose of describing simple DHCP communication, the network configuration shown in Figure 7.6 illustrates the parties involved and their connections.

On the DHCP server, a single scope has been defined with the following parameters.

Scope ID:	176.16 Network
Start Address:	176.16.10.1
End Address:	172.16.10.254
Excluded IPs:	176.16.10.10
Lease Time:	259,200 Seconds (3 Days)
Subnet Mask:	255.255.0.0

Figure 7.6

Simple DHCP
network diagram.

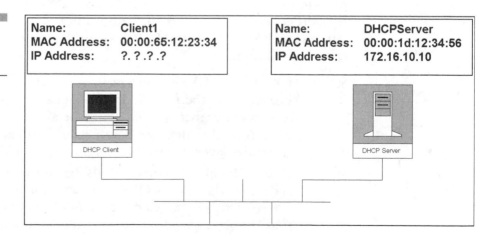

Name:	Client1
MAC Address:	00:00:65:12:23:34
IP Address:	?. ? .? .?

Name:	DHCPServer
MAC Address:	00:00:1d:12:34:56
IP Address:	172.16.10.10

DHCP Client

DHCP Server

Figure 7.7

DHCP message
exchange flow.

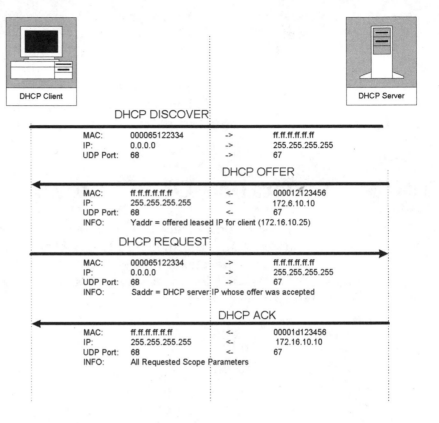

The communication begins when the DHCP client initializes. For the purpose of this discussion, we will assume the client has never leased an IP address. Figure 7.7 outlines the communication steps involved in obtaining an IP address for the DHCP client. The following list discusses these steps in more detail.

Step 1: DHCP DISCOVER: This message is sent as a MAC and IP broadcast by the DHCP client. Its goal is to find any DHCP servers on the network that may be able to provide an IP address and other network parameters. This packet should cross the entire layer two network and reach all local servers.

Step 2: DHCP OFFER: This message will be sent by all servers that receive the DHCP DISCOVER message and are able to provide the requested parameters. The OFFER message tells the client that the server is willing to provide parameters but does not mean the parameters are accepted by the client. Note that the destination address can be either a MAC and IP broadcast or a unicast MAC and leased client IP. The broadcast or nonbroadcast return option is set by the client as a flag in the original DHCP DISCOVER message.

Step 3:   DHCP REQUEST: This message is sent as a MAC and IP broadcast by the DHCP client. It is the client's attempt to accept an OFFER from a specific server. The server whose offer is to be accepted is designated by the DHCP server IP address field within the DHCP packet.

Step 4:   DHCP ACK: This message is send by the DHCP server as either a unicast or broadcast, depending on the client's request. It is the final message in the process. It includes the requested parameters. The client's lease on that address begins with this message.

Once the DHCP ACK message is received by the client, the client should have a valid IP address and any other necessary parameters for IP host communication. There are two additional messages that can occur in this process. They are the DHCP NACK, which allows a client to refuse a DHCP OFFER or a server to deny a client request, and the DHCP RELEASE, which allows the client to give up its address during a graceful shutdown.

DHCP in Routed Networks

DHCP is not restricted to single network support. What this means is that a single DHCP server can provide configuration information to clients that reside on several different subnets with the assistance of DHCP/BOOTP relay agents. This allows centralized configuration administration for a great number of subnetworks using a limited number of DHCP servers.

The protocol used for configuration of clients does not change significantly to support remote subnets. However, the DHCP network now requires three components (the server, client, and relay agent) to participate in the configuration process.

Relay Agent's Role

The relay agent is responsible for forwarding DHCP communication from remote segments to the server and back. In order to do this properly, the relay agent must understand the DHCP process to some degree. In reality, the DHCP configuration messages are extensions of the BOOTP REQUEST and BOOTP REPLY frames. This similarity allows most existing routers and BOOTP relay agents to support DHCP with little or no modification. Previous sections in this chapter examined the various vendor implementations of DHCP relay agents.

Detailed DHCP Communication with Relay Agents

For the purpose of describing the multisubnet operation of DHCP, the network illustrated in Figure 7.8 will be used.

On the DHCP server, two scopes are defined (see Table 7.1).

The communication begins when the DHCP client initializes. For the purpose of this discussion, we will assume the client has never leased an IP address. Figure 7.9 outlines the communication steps involved in obtaining an IP address for the DHCP client. The following list discusses these steps in more detail.

Step 1: DHCP DISCOVER: This message is sent as a MAC and IP broadcast by the DHCP client. Its goal is to find any DHCP

TABLE 7.1

Comparison of Two Scopes

Parameter	Scope 1	Scope 2
Name:	172.16 Network	172.17 Network
Start address:	172.16.10.1	172.17.10.1
End address:	172.16.10.254	172.17.10.254
Excluded IPs:	172.16.10.1 172.16.10.10	172.17.10.1
Lease time:	3 Days	3 Days
Subnet mask:	255.255.0.0	255.255.0.0

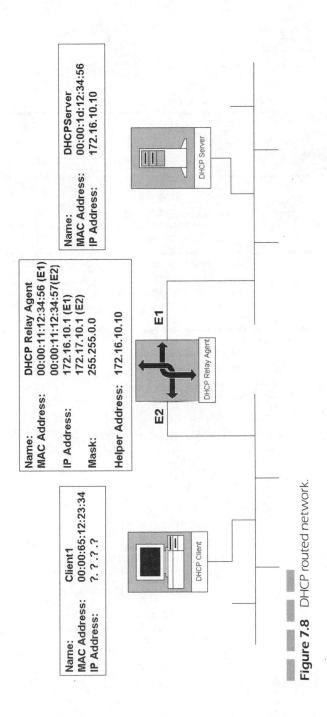

Figure 7.8 DHCP routed network.

Figure 7.9

DHCP communication flow with relay agents.

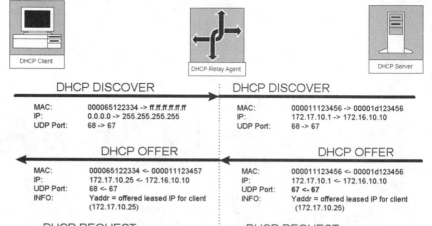

servers on the network that may be able to provide an IP address and other network parameters. This packet crosses the client's layer two network only. The router configured as a DHCP relay agent recognizes this UDP broadcast to port 67 and accepts the frame. Once the router receives this frame, it then changes the source and destination IP address to reflect source IP = the router and destination IP = the helper address (preconfigured to point to a DHCP server). The router also modifies the gateway IP address to match the router's client-side interface IP. The DHCP DISCOVER is then forwarded through the network directly to the DHCP SERVER.

Step 2: DHCP OFFER: This message will be sent by all servers that receive the DHCP DISCOVER message and are able to provide the requested parameters. The OFFER message tells the client that the server is willing to provide parameters but does not mean the parameters are accepted by the client. In this network, the server, having just received a DHCP DISCOVER message with the GATEWAY IP field set (giaddr ≠ 0.0.0.0 indicates a remote client), sends the DHCP OFFER directly to the relay agent's IP and MAC address. This message is also unusual in that the source and destination UDP ports are both 67 (server to server). Once the relay agent receives this DHCP OFFER message, it forwards it to the interface the client is located on (known by the IP destination and GATEWAY IP [giaddr] fields). The final delivery from the relay agent to the client involves either a unicast or broadcast MAC and IP frame, depending on the setting of the broadcast flag in the BOOTP header.

Step 3:   DHCP REQUEST: This message is sent as a MAC and IP broadcast by the DHCP client. It is the client's attempt to accept an OFFER from a specific server. The server whose offer is to be accepted is designated by the DHCP server IP address field. This frame also is intercepted by the relay agent and redirected to the server (helper address).

Step 4:   DHCP ACK: In this network, the server, having just received a DHCP REQUEST message with the GATEWAY IP field set (giaddr ≠ 0.0.0.0 indicates a remote client), sends the DHCP ACK directly to the relay agent's IP and MAC address. This message is also unusual in that the source and destination UDP ports are both 67 (server to server). Once the relay agent receives this DHCP ACK message, it forwards it to the interface the client is located on (known by the IP destination and GATEWAY IP [giaddr] fields). The final delivery from the relay agent to the client involves either a unicast or broadcast MAC and IP frame, depending on the setting of the broadcast flag in the BOOTP header. It is the final message in the process. It includes the requested parameters. The client's lease on that address begins with this message.

Once the DHCP ACK message is received by the client, the client should have a valid IP address and any other necessary parameters for IP host communication. There are two additional messages that can occur in this process. They are the DHCP NACK, which allows a client to refuse a DHCP OFFER, and the DHCP RELEASE, which allows the client to give up its address during a graceful shutdown.

DHCP in Switched LANs

DHCP, as a protocol, is designed to operate in routed and nonrouted networks. The only significant difference in DHCP's operation in a routed network is the addition of relay agent functions. There are some issues that must be covered concerning the practical deployment of DHCP in a switched network to ensure that the proper configuration is used to prevent unwanted complications. These issues are related to the fact that DHCP is a relatively new protocol, and, as such, all vendors' implementations have not evolved and matured enough to fully support all possible network configurations.

Using DHCP in a large switched network is a very useful tool in managing the distribution of IP addresses and parameters. Depending on the configuration of your IP addressing scheme in and out of the switched network, specific configurations and features may be required. In general, there are two types of IP addressing schemes found in switched networks considering the use of DHCP.

1. Class A or class B networks: The switched network is using a class A or class B network address, the deployment of DHCP is a reasonably simple operation. In general, the switched area of the overall network will consist of several subnets of the class A or B network. Through the use of either a dedicated server for the switched area, new superscoping features, or multiple DHCP servers, a solution can be found to fully support DHCP in this type of network. Implementation plans discussed in the following text will describe each option in depth.

2. Multiple class C networks: If the switched network consists of several separate class C network addresses, the process of implementing DHCP is slightly more complex than with a class A or B network. It is very possible to support DHCP in this type of network, mainly due to second-generation DHCP server features, such as superscoping and the server's ability to set the leased IP address as the default gateway of a DHCP client. Older, first-generation servers did not support this type of IP addressing scheme well, but the latest servers from companies such as Microsoft have added support for this type of switched network. An implementation plan for this type of switched network will also be described in the following text.

DHCP Implementation Plan 1: Class A or B Network Only

Network Configuration   The network shown in Figure 7.10 consists of a single class B network. There are no routed subnets and all hosts exist inside of the switched network. This type of network configuration is not extremely common today given the past decade of router-based segmentation. As that segmentation is reversed, networks will begin to look much more like a single address space with no router-based segmentation.

DHCP Configuration   A single scope should be created on the server spanning the entire class A or B network. If the network consists of more than 250 users, consideration should be made to place multiple DHCP servers on the network and allow the address pool to be split between the servers. This would allow a server failure to occur without shutting down DHCP operations, since other servers would remain. As an example, two servers could be used to provide DHCP service to the

Figure 7.10

Single class A or B network address space example.

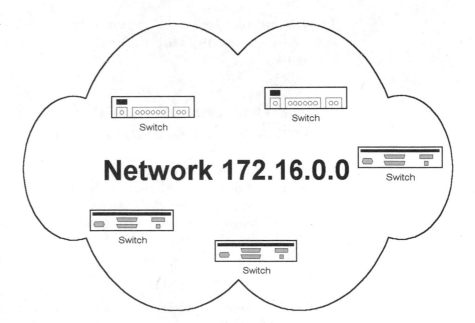

Network 172.16.0.0

172.16.0.0 network. Each server would have one scope defined, as shown in the following chart.

Parameter	Server 1	Server 2
Start IP address	172.16.0.1	172.16.127.0
End IP address	172.16.127.254	172.16.255.254
Network mask	255.255.0.0	255.255.0.0
Excluded range	Any static devices, such as the DHCP servers, UNIX hosts, Novell servers, and Internet firewalls	Any static devices, such as the DHCP servers, UNIX hosts, Novell servers, and Internet firewalls

Given this configuration of the two servers, any DHCP client sending a DISCOVER message would get two responses (one from each server). The servers would both lease out addresses to clients on a first-come, first-serve basis. If one server failed, the other would still be online to provide half of the total addresses.

Implementation Issues   There are no real implementation issues in this configuration. Any existing DHCP server should support this basic configuration.

DHCP Implementation Plan 2: Class A or B Network with Local and Remote Subnets

Network Configuration   This type of IP address network consists of a single class A or B network that has been subnetted. Some of the subnets exist across routers and WAN links. The remaining subnets exist inside a large flat-switched LAN. This combination is extremely common in switched LAN implementations. In this situation, two options exist for DHCP server configuration. Figure 7.11 illustrates this type of network.

Option 1: Separate Local Servers for Switched LAN and Remote Subnets   This option uses a separate server for the switched LAN. That server would define a single scope as follows.

Figure 7.11

Subnetted class A
or B network.

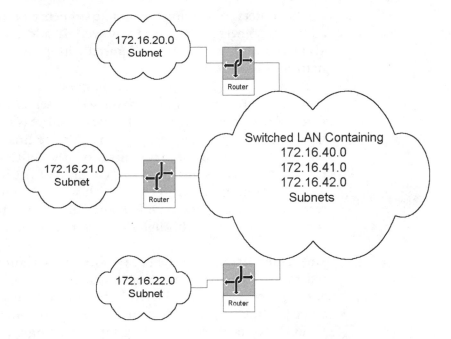

[Scope 1, Start IP: 172.16.40.1, End IP: 172.16.42.254, Mask 255.255.0.0, Excluded IPs: all servers, routers, static devices, and network management devices]

A second server would then be configured to support the DHCP requests from the remote subnets. Given the current generation of servers, this server would have to have its local network interface configured with a subnetted mask of 255.255.255.0 to operate properly in this role. It would also be possible to place servers in those subnets, but that option would decentralize the DHCP management. The second server would define one scope for each remote subnet as follows.

[Scope 20, Start IP: 172.16.20.1, End IP: 172.16.20.254, Mask 255.255.255.0, Excluded IPs: all servers, routers, static devices, and network management devices, Default Gateway = remote router interface]

[Scope 21, Start IP: 172.16.21.1, End IP: 172.16.21.254, Mask 255.255.255.0, Excluded IPs: all servers, routers, static devices, and network management devices, Default Gateway = remote router interface]

[Scope 22, Start IP: 172.16.22.1, End IP: 172.16.22.254, Mask 255.255.255.0, Excluded IPs: all servers, routers, static devices, and network management devices, Default Gateway = remote router interface]

The routers connecting the remote subnets would also require helper addresses pointing to the second server's IP address. The routers would also require all ports to be configured with proxy ARP enabled, since a natural mask is being utilized.

In this configuration, DHCP requests on the switched LAN would be handled by the first server, since the second server has no local scope defined. When DHCP clients on the remote subnets send DISCOVER messages, the routers should intercept them and redirect the messages to the second server. As part of that redirection, the routers insert their remote interface IP address into the GIADDR field of the message. This address allows the second server to pick which scope the message is tied to. The second server then should OFFER an address to the remote host by sending the message back through the router acting as the relay agent.

Implementation Issues   The two-server configuration is required for older DHCP servers, because of limitations internal to most first-generation servers. The older DHCP servers could only support one local scope (a scope whose address pool is in the same network as the server's IP address). The servers also only support a single scope per network or subnet address. These limitations make it impossible to use a single server for the multiple local subnets (255.255.0.0 mask) and each of the remote subnets (255.255.255.0). By splitting the responsibilities between two servers, one can use the natural 255.255.0.0 mask for the switched network, while the other uses the 255.255.255.0 mask to define the remote subnets. Most servers should allow this combination.

Option 2: Utilize Second-Generation Services for Switched Networks
This option takes advantage of two features found on newer servers to explicitly support switched networks. In this configuration, a single server could be used. That server would have a 255.255.255.0 mask on its local interface and a default gateway set to its own IP address. The DHCP configuration would define a separate scope for each of the six subnets involved as follows.

[Scope 20, Start IP: 172.16.20.1, End IP: 172.16.20.254, Mask 255.255.255.0, Excluded IPs: all servers, routers, static devices, and network management devices, Default Gateway = remote router interface]

[Scope 21, Start IP: 172.16.21.1, End IP: 172.16.21.254, Mask 255.255.255.0, Excluded IPs: all servers, routers, static devices, and network management devices, Default Gateway = remote router interface]

[Scope 22, Start IP: 172.16.22.1, End IP: 172.16.22.254, Mask 255.255.255.0, Excluded IPs: all servers, routers, static devices, and network management devices, Default Gateway = remote router interface]

[Scope 40, Start IP: 172.16.40.1, End IP: 172.16.40.254, Mask 255.255.255.0, Excluded IPs: all servers, routers, static devices, and network management devices, Default Gateway = leased IP address]

[Scope 41, Start IP: 172.16.41.1, End IP: 172.16.41.254, Mask 255.255.255.0, Excluded IPs: all servers, routers, static devices, and network management devices, Default Gateway = leased IP address]

[Scope 42, Start IP: 172.16.42.1, End IP: 172.16.42.254, Mask 255.255.255.0, Excluded IPs: all servers, routers, static devices, and network management devices, Default Gateway = leased IP address]

Scopes 40, 41, and 42 would be grouped together in a superscope called Super_Scope_40. The routers would be configured with helper addresses pointing to the single DHCP server.

The two features that make this configuration possible are as follows.

1. Superscopes: This option allows several separate scopes to be grouped together to form one large pool of addresses. Super_Scope_40 would define a pool of addresses ranging from 172.16.40.1 through 172.16.42.254 that would be given out in order to users on the local network. By having this option a consistent mask of 255.255.255.0 can be used for network 172.16.0.0, allowing all subnets to exist on one server.

2. Switched network flag: Microsoft 4.0 DHCP servers with service pack 2 and beyond added support for an option to allow the DHCP server to set the default gateway of the DHCP client to the leased IP address. This configuration allows the client to be completely flat, as discussed in Chapter 4. That client will ARP directly for any IP address on any network. In this network, the devices in the switched LAN will have this configuration enabled, allowing all devices in the switched LAN to communicate directly even though their mask defines them as being in different subnets. The routers on the switched network boundary must have proxy ARP enabled to allow these devices to exit the switched network and reach remote subnets. The devices in the remote subnets can be configured in the same way, or, since only one subnet is local to each, they can be configured with the traditional router set to default gateway.

Implementation Issues Most older servers do not support super-scopes or the switched network flag for setting the default gateway to the leased IP address. If this option is to be used, the servers should be evaluated based on their support for these second-generation features.

DHCP Implementation Plan 3: Multiple Class C Networks

Network Configuration This configuration consists of a switched network comprised of several distinct true class C networks. Because these networks separate logical networks, the devices making up each of the separate addresses will not talk to other networks without an IP gateway defined. This type of network is the most difficult to implement DHCP on and, with first-generation servers, is usually impossible to make work well. Figure 7.12 illustrates this type of configuration.

DHCP Configuration This network consists of three class C networks in the switched LAN and three other class C networks in remote networks. DHPC configuration for the three remote networks is rela-

Figure 7.12

Multiple class C networks configuration.

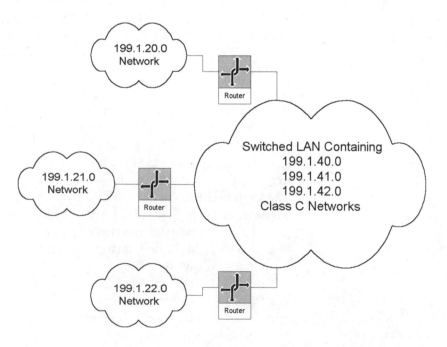

tively simple. A single server is used with a scope defined for each remote network as follows.

[Scope 20, Start IP: 199.1.20.1, End IP: 199.1.20.254, Mask 255.255.255.0, Excluded IPs: all servers, routers, static devices, and network management devices, Default Gateway = remote router interface]

[Scope 21, Start IP: 199.1.21.1, End IP: 199.1.21.254, Mask 255.255.255.0, Excluded IPs: all servers, routers, static devices, and network management devices, Default Gateway = remote router interface]

[Scope 22, Start IP: 199.1.22.1, End IP: 199.1.22.254, Mask 255.255.255.0, Excluded IPs: all servers, routers, static devices, and network management devices, Default Gateway = remote router interface]

The routers configure helper addresses for each remote network pointing at the DHCP server.

The DHCP support inside the switched LAN is much more difficult when using first-generation servers. Since each server only supports a single local scope, a total of three servers could be used. Each server could define a local scope for its network address. This would allow the three network addresses to be distributed to the clients on this network but would result in a very poorly configured network. The reason for the poor configuration is based on the fact that the first-generation servers cannot set the default gateway to the leased IP address. Instead, they must configure the clients with the default gateway as a router in the switched network. This configuration would result in router-based communication between two devices having different class C network numbers but residing on the same switched LAN. For this reason, it is suggested that DHCP not be used if only first-generation servers are available and your configuration is similar to this example.

If a second-generation server such as Microsoft NT 4.0 service pack 2 is available, the switched LAN DHCP configuration is significantly easier. The server would define a scope for each local class C network. A superscope would then be defined grouping the three into one address pool. The switched network flag would be set on these three scopes. The result would be a DHCP configuration in which users in the switched LAN would receive addresses from the superscope and be configured with the default gateway set to the leased IP address. Users configured in this manner would be able to communicate directly to the other local class C networks and, through the router's proxy ARP, be able to reach any known external network.

Implementation Issues This configuration should only be implemented if second-generation DHCP server functions of superscope and switched network flag are supported. Without these features, the DHCP can be made to lease addresses, but routers will still be used for communication, even between local users having different network numbers.

Summary

Simplicity and speed: These two goals of networks today are closer to reality through the addition of Dynamic Host Configuration Protocol (DHCP) in IP networks. Internet Protocol and its many options (UDP, TCP) provide a flexible, high-performance layer three protocol suitable for both local area and wide area networks. DHCP enhances Internet Protocol's usability by simplifying the single biggest configuration task: client IP configuration. In most switched networks, DHCP can be easily implemented to allow this configuration simplicity. With the latest generation of server functions, even the most complex switched networks and IP address configurations can take advantage of DHCP.

Advantages of DHCP include the following.

- Provides network administrators with simple server-based configuration mechanisms to assign client configurations
- Direct knowledge of the clients is not necessary
- Provides adaptable IP address assignment to accommodate mobile users
- Allows centralized control of DHCP even in highly segmented networks
- Supports routed environments
- Supports a large number of configuration options
- Supports customized configuration options
- Provides IP address assignment with limited duration

Limitations of DHCP include the following.

- The end nodes must be capable of DHCP communication.
- The end nodes must be able to request all necessary information required for IP host communication.

- The DHCP servers must support all requested necessary parameters.

- Routers must support DHCP (specifically the BOOTP broadcast flag).

- Administrative tasks for IP address assignment are not eliminated; they are just centralized at the server.

- DHCP is generally not compatible with decentralized name resolution services such as NIS and DNS. This is due to the client IP address potentially differing with each new lease.

CHAPTER 8

Troubleshooting and Maintaining Switched LANs

Once you have built a well-designed switched network, your overall network performance should be greater, and the new simplicity of end-system configuration should allow the network administrator additional time for other tasks. It is important to realize that simply building the network is not the end of the process of implementing a switched LAN. Once the system is running, the focus now must shift to maintaining and operating that network. There are two main areas of switched LAN operation.

1. Maintaining the network: This is the process of observing network behavior in order to track overall network health and detect potential problems before serious network failures occur. This proactive monitoring of the network is vital to maintain continuous system availability. The task of maintaining a switched network will be significantly simpler than the process of maintaining and administering a highly segmented router-based network.

2. Troubleshooting network-related issues: This is the process of identifying and solving network-related problems as they occur. This reactive task must be well defined in advance in order to quickly resolve any network-related failures. Key in this process is the understanding of the tools used for network troubleshooting and the processes in which these tools will be used to solve problems.

This chapter will focus on these two areas of switched LAN operation. The tools available to system administrators of switched networks will be examined, and the processes of maintaining and troubleshooting the network will be defined.

Maintaining a Switched Local Area Network

Most networks in use today are far too large for the system administrators to effectively manage all of their elements, given the current methods and tools used. The system administrators must focus on the operation of the network above all else. They must make sure it is working now. If the network is stable, their time is now in demand for configuration of end systems and servers. And, finally, if they have some time left over, they may perform some network optimization and baselining and growth planning. The unfortunate part of this set of priorities is that the proactive monitoring and baselining are viewed as the least important tasks. By having effective baselining and proactive monitoring capabilities of the networking hardware enabled, the network will usually be much more stable. Additionally, troubleshooting problems will generally be faster, since more information and tools will be available to solve problems. With a switched LAN, the system administrator can make use of several networking tools to automate network analysis and monitoring functions. By simply investing a small amount of time in the configuration of the switched LAN's native monitoring capabilities, the system administrator is potentially saving hundreds of hours of downtime later related to simply not having enough information to solve problems quickly.

Two major tasks are involved in the maintaining of a switched LAN: network baselining and configuring automated management tools. Network baselining is the process of determining the network health in terms of utilization, error rates, number of users, and possibly protocol distribution. In order to effectively manage any network, it is vital to understand just how that network operates in a normal situation. If the administrator understands how the network characteristics appear when the network is fully functional, changes in those characteristics can be cause for concern. A significant change in the basic characteristics of any part of the network may be a sign of an error condition or may be an indicator that the network is becoming saturated and requires increased capacity. The second element, configuration of automated management tools, involves the system administrator allowing the devices in the switched network to watch for changes in the network health and even take actions based on those changes. In order to configure these tools, an accurate understanding of exactly what denotes a functional network is required. That understanding is gained by the network baselining process.

Network Baselining Overview

Understanding the network health is the goal of network baselining. Network health is a general term used to define the major network statistics that characterize the operation of the network at any particular time. A variety of tools are available to gain insight into the health of a switched network. These tools include RMON probes, vendor-specific statistical MIBs, network analyzers, and a variety of specific software-based applications. Before specific techniques of network baselining can be described, the tools that will be used must be examined. Rather than focusing on a specific set of tools, it is best to discuss the two basic categories of network baselining tools: historical statistics gathering tools and absolute statistics gathering tools.

Historical statistics gathering tools are defined as those tools that provide statistical information over a period of time that includes a time reference. An example of this kind of tool might be the RMON history groups, which calculate and store network statistics as time-specific samples. An RMON history could tell a system administrator what the utilization of a segment was each minute for the past five hours, as an example. Other tools of this type are statistics logging applications, such as the statistics gathering tools found in all major network management platforms, in which a management computer polls a network device and logs specific statistics on some cycle. The time-specific statistics are then provided to the network management software's graphical interface for analysis. These tools are vital in gathering a long-term perspective of network health. Using either mechanism, the system administrator could gather statistics from several parts of the network and be able to correlate them based on the time they occurred.

Absolute statistics gathering tools are those tools that show an absolute statistical value of some network characteristic. A tool that showed the immediate utilization or collision rate on a segment would be useful in determining whether the network was operating as expected at that time. Examples of this type of tool are the RMON statistics group; the RMON host and matrix groups; and any vendor-specific statistical counters, such as those displayed in element management–based device views. In addition to providing an immediate view into various network statistics, these tools provide information related to the absolute effect stations and conversations have had on the network—for example, the RMON host group cannot tell the system administrator when a particular station generated broadcasts, but it can show how many broadcasts the end system generated during its time on the network. By understanding how many absolute broadcasts each station generates, this tool can provide a listing of which stations are the primary generators of broadcast packets. That information can then be used to focus on reducing the broadcast rates of the network by further examination of the identified highest broadcast generators.

Since each network is different in both design and operation, the remainder of this section will focus on the process of determining a network's health by focusing on the characteristics of each general area of a switched LAN. Both historical statistics and absolute data will be defined that allow a proper view into the network's health. Figure 8.1 illustrates the total switched local area network in terms of its three major areas: the network core, the centralized resources area, and the periphery user areas of the network.

Figure 8.1 represents a possible construction of a switched LAN. It consists of three general areas based on function. Chapter 2 provided insight as to the rationale behind each of these areas. Since each of these areas has a different role in the overall network operation, each area must be treated separately in terms of how network baselining should be done.

Figure 8.1

Switched network areas.

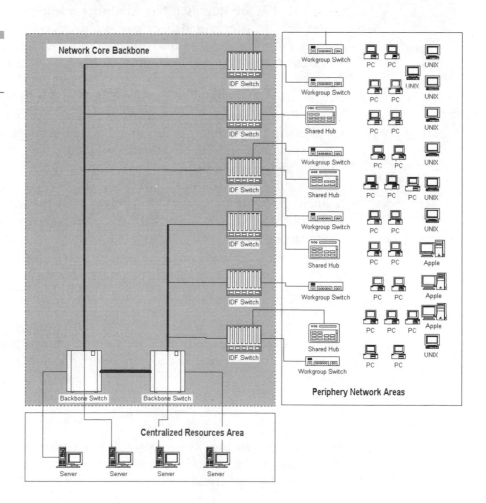

Baselining the Network Core

In a switched LAN, the network backbone, or core, is easily the most important component. This area, as defined in Chapter 2, is the aggregation point for most network traffic. It is usually the area of the network with the highest bandwidth capacity. If it were to fail, end users would most likely lose contact with their centralized resources and the company business operations could stop. Because of the critical nature of this section of the network, companies are usually willing to purchase costly but very fault-tolerant backbone switches. These switches have redundant systems throughout them and are usually designed to prevent any one component failure from disabling all the switches. Even though these switches are designed for reliability and high capacity, they can fail or become overloaded. Because a failure is possible, it is critical that the system administrator not make the mistake of installing the network backbone and then not monitoring it for network changes and failures.

Monitoring backbone switches involves much more than just a periodic polling of the devices, indicating they are still running. It involves monitoring the traffic on the switches' segments to determine if the network capacity is being overloaded. It involves monitoring the switches' resources to make sure they have ample capacity internally to maintain their forwarding capabilities. It involves monitoring the network segment error rates to detect rising error rates before they become critical problems. There is no such thing as having too much information about the network health of your backbone.

The exact information that can be gathered from the network to determine its operational health will vary based on the tools used. The minimum necessary information required to baseline a backbone is listed in Table 8.1.

Table 8.1 provides a basic list of critical information needed to monitor a backbone. The method of gathering this information is not as significant as the fact that without this information, the network health of your backbone is unknown. Given the network core of the sample network shown in Figure 8.1, the following plan could be used to gather the necessary network core statistics.

Baselining Plan for Network Core Backbone This network backbone consists of six distributed switches located on individual floors of a building. Each of the six switches is connected to one of two core back-

TABLE 8.1

Minimum
Statistics for
Backbone
Monitoring

Network Information	Description
Long-term utilization	This historical information should include at least seven days' statistics on network load. Each backbone link requires this information in order to determine which links are utilized most heavily and which are utilized most lightly. Given this information, growth in network utilization will be obvious before the network is saturated.
Short-term utilization	The utilization of the network over a typical workday should be tracked. This information is useful in determining the highest demand times on the network. If this demand overloads the network segments involved, upgrades should be considered.
Top 20 users	A tracking of the top 20 addresses generating traffic should be generated for each workday. These data permit an understanding of which stations are requiring the most network bandwidth. If new stations appear in this list, additional examination of those stations' roles should be examined. The RMON HostTopN could be used for this purpose.
Long-term error rates	The total error counts of the individual backbone links should be tracked. It is not unusual to experience a small number of errors on network segments. If that error counter increases beyond a very small number, the segment involved is in danger of failure.
Switch status	The operation of each backbone switch should be monitored. A minimum monitoring would consist of periodic ICMP PINGs indicating system status. More comprehensive monitoring would include polling internal status indicators for CPU utilization, memory usage, address table saturation, etc. Each vendor's switch will provide different statistics regarding its health.
Long-term broadcast and multicast rates	This historical statistic should be logged to indicate the weekly rates of nonunicast packets over time. If the network nonunicast packet rate begins to climb beyond the acceptable level discussed in Chapter 3, further investigation should be made to determine the source of this change.
Top 20 broadcast and multicast users	The top 20 addresses generating broadcasts or multicasts on the network should be tracked. Significant changes in this listing should be grounds for further examination. These data should be collected approximately every workday.

bone switches via full-duplex 100Base-FX links (see the following plan). The backbone switches are connected together via redundant gigabit Ethernet links. Each backbone link must be monitored for long- and short-term utilization and error rates. The entire backbone must be monitored for broadcast and multicast rates. Each switch must be monitored for status and resources.

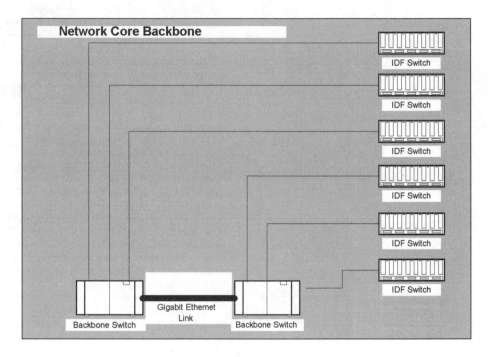

Utilization and Error Rate Monitoring Plan:

- RMON History (7-day duration, 1-hour sample) on each backbone link
- RMON History (10-hour duration, 5-minute sample) on each backbone link

Broadcast and Multicast Rate Monitoring:

- RMON History as above
- RMON HostTop20 at one switch (8-hour duration) on broadcasts out
- RMON HostTop20 at one switch (8-hour duration) on multicasts out

Switch Status Monitoring Plan:

- SNMP get against SytemUpTime of MIB-II system group
- SNMP get against Dropped Events of the RMON etherstats group

This plan will provide logging of utilization and error rates of all backbone segments, allowing proper understanding of the network capacity and availability. Broadcast and multicast data will be collected long term and the top 20 list of broadcast- and multicast-intensive stations will be tracked to understand broadcast use on network and determine if the rate is growing. Switch status will be logged by watching the system uptime of MIB-II and the dropped events value of each interface's RMON statistics. Loss of contact or overload and the loss of the ability to count all incoming packets will be identified.

Baselining the Centralized Resources Areas

Centralization of server resources is commonplace in networks today. Servers are becoming larger and more powerful but are also more difficult to maintain. In order to minimize the administrative issues of high-end servers, network administrators are moving those servers to central locations, where they are easily accessible and protected from environmental issues such as overheating and power failures. This choice of physical location for servers places more of a burden on the network, because now end users must almost always traverse the network backbone to reach these centralized resources. The area where these resources are connected to the network is known as the centralized resources area. This area is almost as critical as the backbone, because failure here will remove key servers from the network. This failure will affect not only the server but also all the users logically attached to that server. Management of this part of the network involves baselining of key statistics to determine the operational status of the network links used by the servers and additional monitoring of the servers themselves if possible. The basic statistical information required to monitor this part of the network is listed in Table 8.2. The focus of this information is mainly concerned with the status of the links connecting the servers to the network core. This focus is necessary, because these links represent possible congestion points in the network if the total client/server communica-

TABLE 8.2

Centralized
Resources Area
Monitoring
Statistics

Network Information	Description
Link utilization	This historical information would provide an indication of the capacity of this link. Since the server is attached directly to the switch in most cases, this number represents the traffic level into and out of the switch. If this number is relatively low (under 70 percent of the link's capacity), the current physical link is adequate for the server. If the link utilization is consistently high (over 70 percent of the link's capacity), the link is possibly inadequate and may need an upgrade to a higher-capacity connection.
Link error rate	The error rate of the link is a useful proactive management statistic. If this error rate begins to increase, the link is in danger of failing or the adapter in the server is faulty. Early detection of error rates is vital in detecting faults early and preventing significant network breakdown.
Server status	The actual operation of the server should be monitored. Since a variety of server types exist, each will have inherent monitoring tools. At a minimum, contact status via ICMP PINGs should be used. If the server can support a CPU capacity-reporting capability, that statistic is very useful in detecting server overload. A server attached to a 100 megabit link may simply run out of CPU resources long before the link is saturated. As such, simply monitoring high-speed link capacity is not always adequate to determine when a server is overloaded. In switching systems today, it is not unusual for the server to become overloaded as the network bandwidth capacity grows. This is simply because the slower router-based networks introduced a bottleneck limiting the traffic a server would see. Now, as switching is used, that bottleneck is removed and the server's CPU capacity could become the bottleneck in the network.

tion on the network is greater than the servers' capacity. Monitoring these links also assists in planning server network capacity. As an example, a Novell server with an ISA bus 10Base-T network interface card attached to a switch link operating at 95 percent utilization would be an ideal candidate for an upgrade to a PCI 100Base-TX interface attached to a fast Ethernet switch port.

In addition to the basic statistics listed in Table 8.2, other statistics listing the conversation matrix on the link could be useful in determining the breakdown of the servers' conversations. Overall, by monitoring the basic statistics in Table 8.2, the system administrator can gain an understanding of the load each server link usually operates under. As that link utilization or CPU utilization increases, the administrator can examine the cause and, if justified, increase the servers' network capacity before a serious network bottleneck occurs. A sample plan follows below to monitor the centralized resources area of the network shown in Figure 8.1.

Centralized Resources Area Monitoring Plan The centralized resources area of this network consists of four large servers providing a variety of network resources to the end users of this network. The servers are located in the central operations room of the network. Each server is connected via a 100Base-TX connection to one of two backbone switches. Each of the servers must be monitored for link utilization, contact status, link error rates, and server CPU capacity.

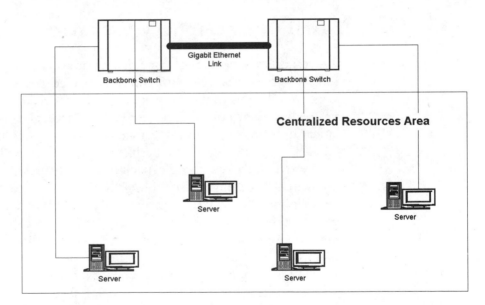

Link Utilization and Error Rate Monitoring Plan:

- Long-term RMON History (duration 5 days, interval 1 hour) against each server link
- Short-term RMON History (duration 9 hours, interval 5 minutes) against each server link

Contact Status Monitoring:

- SNMP polling of the server's SystemUpTime

CPU Utilization Monitoring:

- Dependent on the server type
- Statistics to be monitored include CPU utilization, memory utilization, and user count

This plan will provide information related to the capacity and operation of the servers in this centralized resources area. If the network capacity begins to be exhausted by increased utilization, the output of the RMON history will show this change. If the link begins to fail, the RMON history error rates will show this; and if the server fails or becomes overloaded internally, the polling of status and resource utilization will show this state.

Baselining Periphery User Areas

The periphery areas of the network are the areas where end users are attached. These areas make up the majority of the switched network's ports. Monitoring these areas is necessary to make sure users are not overloading their current connectivity. In general, this area is the least critical in terms of baselining, since individual users are not as vital as the backbone or servers. The periphery of the network is the area that requires the least switching capacity and is usually built using lower-cost switches. An interesting point here is that the switches making up the periphery of the network are usually capable of more complex management tasks, since they are not required to focus on forwarding capacity above other roles as a backbone switch is. Because of this, many tasks involving traffic matrixing and protocol operation are best done on the periphery switches of the network. The basic information necessary to monitor this area of the network is listed in Table 8.3. This information is primarily focused on the current status of each switch and traffic and error rates on each port. It is not vital to monitor each port on the network in order to understand the overall network health, since the statistics gathered from the backbone and centralized resources areas give a very good picture of the overall network operation.

In addition to basic status and utilization information gathered from periphery switches, these switches can be used to gather more complex information about the network traffic matrix and protocol distribution. The port or ports used to uplink the periphery switch to a back-

TABLE 8.3

Minimum
Periphery Switch
Monitoring
Statistics

Network Information	Description
Contact status	Each switch in the network should be polled for contact status. This polling can indicate the failure of a switch or possibly indicate that the switch is overloaded and unable to respond to management polls.
Port utilization	If desired, selected ports containing key resources can be baselined for utilization and error statistics. This historical information would allow tracking of the particular attached device's network requirements. This process in not required on all periphery switch ports but should be used for ports containing faster devices. Switch ports connecting shared hubs should also be monitored for historical utilization and error statistics if the hub itself cannot manage the segment.

bone switch could be configured to monitor the RMON matrix, host, and HostTopN groups and possibly the RMON2 protocol distribution group. By having the periphery switch do this monitoring, the backbone switch is spared this complex management burden and should be able to forward packets at a higher rate. This distribution of more complex tasks to the periphery switches allows for complex network information to be gathered with a minimum impact on any one switch area. A plan follows to configure the monitoring operations of the periphery area of the network shown in Figure 8.1.

Periphery Network Monitoring Plan   The periphery area of this network is distributed on several floors of a building. Each floor's switches and shared hubs are attached to a backbone area switch. The attached users are a mix of end users, including PCs, UNIX machines, Apple Macintoshes, and other devices. Some areas provide dedicated switch ports for users, while other areas utilize existing shared hubs connecting multiuser Ethernet segments to a switch port. The monitoring plan for this part of the network involves monitoring the contact status of all switches and hubs in the periphery areas. It also involves gathering historical statistics of all uplink ports and some critical user ports. RMON host, HostTopN, and matrix groups are configured for uplinks on each switch in the periphery area to allow an understanding of the traffic patterns into and out of each periphery area. If available, the switches can also be configured to use RMON2 or vendor-proprietary tools for some protocol distribution data collecting. These protocol-specific data can assist in understanding what types of network communication are utilizing the network resources.

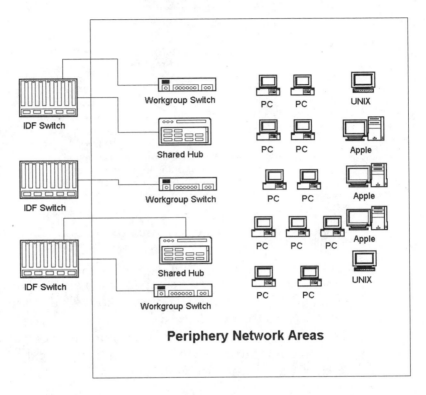

Periphery Network Areas

Contact Status Monitoring:

- Each switch and hub will be polled for SNMP SystemUpTime to determine operational status

Uplink and Critical User Port Utilization Monitoring:

- RMON History (7-day duration, 1-hour interval) configured on all uplinks and ports containing critical or very active users
- RMON History (9-hour duration, 5-minute interval) configured on all uplinks and ports containing critical or very active users

Traffic Pattern Monitoring:

- RMON host and matrix groups configured on all uplink ports
- HostTop20 (Octets Out, Packets Out: 8-hour duration) configured and run periodically on all uplink ports

Protocol Distribution Monitoring:

- RMON2 Protocol Distribution or vendor-proprietary tools used to log protocol use on all uplink ports

This plan should allow for a basic view of the operational status of the periphery switches. Additional baselining information related to the uplink ports and critical users can also be obtained to monitor for overloading of these links. If links are seen to be overloaded, further analysis of the specific users on the periphery switch utilizing that uplink will be required. After those data are collected, those users can be relocated on an additional switch with its own uplink or the current switches' uplink capacity can be increased using full-duplex of alternative technologies. Traffic pattern data collected using the host, HostTopN, and matrix groups should provide the required information to determine which users are saturating the uplinks.

Presenting the Information

Once the information regarding the various areas of the network have been baselined, those data must be extracted and processed. Most RMON network management tools allow some graphing and tabular viewing of the data they have gathered. Those graphs can be utilized if the tool chosen provides sufficient graphs of each segment's utilization, errors, broadcasts, overall contact, and top N users. If it does not, it is recommended that data be exported into a spreadsheet such as Microsoft Excel or a database application such as Microsoft Access for further processing. These tools usually have easy-to-use graphing engines and allow more complex analysis of the data collected. Figure 8.2 shows a sample chart of the core statistics of a switched network produced by exporting baselined data into Microsoft Excel version 7.0 and using its chart wizard to produce the 3-D graph.

Regardless of the tools used to produce the baselining data output, it is critical that this process be done and some form of data be produced that will allow the system administrator to understand the operation of the switched network in a normal situation. These reports should be generated on a periodic basis to verify that the network is continuing to operate as expected. Most of this process can be automated using any one of a variety of tools, ranging from those built into the network management platforms to simple macros in Microsoft Excel.

Figure 8.2

Baseline chart sample.

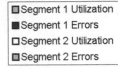

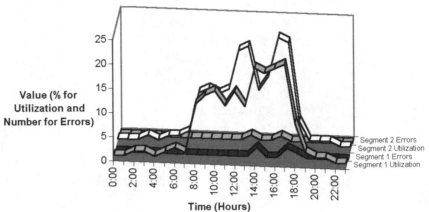

Baselining Summary

The baselining of a network is a critical part of monitoring any complex network. Without the information described above, the system administrator has no information describing the operational status of the network. If those basic data are gathered, the status of each part of the network can be understood and monitored. Once the baseline operation of the network is known, ongoing monitoring will make significant changes in the operation of the network extremely obvious. If the load on a particular uplink begins to increase, this may indicate that the users on that segment are either more active or more numerous. If no action is taken, and the link cannot provide enough capacity to forward all data sent to or from those users, the network response time and overall performance for that part of the network will degrade. With simple baselined statistics and ongoing monitoring, this bottleneck should have been seen and corrected before the users were impacted. Even if the problem was not prevented, when it occurred the baselined statistics should have quickly identified the cause of the performance degradation as the saturated link. This baselining process is not required to use a switched network, but, if it is done, the job of keeping that network operational with high performance will be significantly easier.

Configuration of Automated Management Tools Overview

In addition to the process of baselining the network's health to monitor the overall network capacity and operation, monitoring a switched network involves the configuration of automated tools integrated into the switch to detect immediate changes in the network. These tools monitor many of the same statistics as the baselining process discussed previously. Instead of gathering long-term statistical data, these tools are concerned only with the immediate state of the network in order to quickly detect when critical thresholds have been exceeded. By implementing these tools, the network can be configured to continuously watch for potential error conditions and notify the system administrator of these conditions.

In order to properly configure the automated management tools of a switched network, the baselining process described previously must be completed. By having a comprehensive set of statistics describing how the network normally operates, it is possible to decide what value a particular network statistic must reach to be cause for concern. In this section, some of the tools commonly available to automate network monitoring will be examined. If the system administrator devotes a small amount of time to configure these tools, the network will essentially monitor itself. Instead of having to periodically examine each device for potential error conditions, the system administrator can simply watch the network management software for messages from the switches indicating defined network fault conditions.

Alarm Limits and Thresholds

Alarm limits and thresholds are the primary tools for automated management of a switched network. This category of network monitoring tool defines any embedded threshold monitoring capability of a network device. If the network device can be told to watch a network statistic and notify a network management station if a threshold is crossed, that operation is considered an alarm limit or threshold function. There are two types of alarm limit and threshold implementations available in most LAN switches.

1. RMON Alarm and Events: Any RMON version 1–compliant network device implementing groups 3 and 9 has the capability to watch for network events.

2. Vendor-Specific Thresholds: Most vendors have proprietary monitoring functions that watch a fixed set of statistics on the device's ports. The statistics monitored are usually focused on the traffic and error rates of individual ports. This capability is usually less flexible than RMON in terms of choices of statistics but simpler to configure, because the vendors provide prebuilt configuration tools.

Either of these mechanisms can be used to monitor a switched network if available on the devices being configured.

TABLE 8.4

Configuration Parameters for Alarm Limits

Parameter	Description
Statistics	This parameter defines what statistic should be watched. When configuring with RMON alarms, the choice of statistics usually includes all MIB values in the device. When configuring with a vendor-specific tool, the choice of statistics is limited to a predetermined set of statistics.
Threshold	This is the value the statistics must reach for this alarm to be activated. This value is time dependent, based on the next parameter. If the network has been properly baselined, the values to be used here will be known. If the network has not been baselined, this value will be an unknown. If the system administrator simply guesses at this value, it is unlikely that the alarm will be useful. If the guess is too low, many false alarms will be generated. If the guess is too high, a network failure could occur without an alarm. If alarms are to be used, it is best to have done the baselining described previously, so that proper values can be known and used in the configuration of alarm limits.
Time frame	This value defines how often a statistic should be sampled to determine if an alarm threshold has been reached. If this value was set to one minute, the threshold for that statistic would be checked every 60 seconds. If the cumulative value of the statistics for the past 60 seconds exceeded the defined threshold, an alarm would be generated.
Type of threshold	Usually, alarms are configured to be triggered if a value exceeds a certain level. In RMON alarms it is possible to also configure falling alarms to watch for statistical values below a defined level.

To use these alarm limits and threshold tools, the usual configuration requires several parameters, listed in Table 8.4. Each of these parameters must be known before any automated monitoring can be used effectively.

The statistics that are useful in automated monitoring of switched networks will vary, depending on the role each switch plays in the overall network structure. Switches in the core of the network will focus on watching for excessive backbone link traffic levels, while a switch in the periphery area of the network may be more concerned with monitoring broadcast rates to protect against excessive broadcast rates generated from an attached device or segment. A sample alarm configuration plan for the sample switched network seen in Figure 8.1 follows. This plan specifies a set of alarm configurations for each of the three major areas of this switched network.

Switched Network Alarm Limit Configuration Plan   In order to maximize the system monitoring capabilities of a switched network, configuration of integrated alarm limits should be used on all switches. Specific configurations should be used in the network core, the centralized resources areas, and the periphery network areas. For these switches, RMON alarms and events should be used to enable this monitoring capability.

Network Core Switch Alarm Limit Configuration:			
Alarms configured on each backbone link			
Alarm	Type	Value	Time Frame
EtherStats Octets	Rising	62,500,000	10 Seconds
EtherStats Octets	Falling	40,000,000	10 Seconds
EtherStats CRCAlignment Errors	Rising	25	10 Seconds
EtherStats CRCAlignment Errors	Falling	1	10 Seconds

Centralized Resources Area Alarm Limit Configuration:

Alarms configured on all server ports operating at 100 megabits per second

Alarm	Type	Value	Time Frame
EtherStats Octets	Rising	62,500,000	10 Seconds
EtherStats Octets	Falling	40,000,000	10 Seconds
EtherStats CRCAlignment Errors	Rising	25	10 Seconds
EtherStats CRCAlignment Errors	Falling	1	10 Seconds
EtherStats Broadcasts	Rising	7,500	10 Seconds
EtherStats Broadcasts	Falling	5,000	10 Seconds
EtherStats Multicasts	Rising	7,500	10 Seconds
EtherStats Multicasts	Falling	5,000	10 Seconds

Periphery Network Area Alarm Limit Configuration:

Alarms configured on all user ports operating at 10 megabits per second

Alarm	Type	Value	Time Frame
EtherStats Octets	Rising	6,500,000	10 Seconds
EtherStats Octets	Falling	4,000,000	10 Seconds
EtherStats CRCAlignment Errors	Rising	25	10 Seconds
EtherStats CRCAlignment Errors	Falling	1	10 Seconds
EtherStats Broadcasts	Rising	7,500	10 Seconds
EtherStats Broadcasts	Falling	5,000	10 Seconds
EtherStats Multicasts	Rising	7,500	10 Seconds
EtherStats Multicasts	Falling	5,000	10 Seconds

These alarm limits should provide automatic monitoring for several network conditions that could indicate network failure or overload. By monitoring octets at the above rates, an average load of about 50 percent would trigger the alarm. This 50-percent level is arbitrary and can be adjusted if the network's overall performance does not seem impacted by traffic levels of this size. The CRCAlignment Error alarm will provide notification of an error rate of 25 corrupted frames within ten seconds. This level may seem low but in reality may be too high. Any CRCAlignment errors seen on a network segment are an indication of potential physical failure of that network segment. If this alarm is triggered on certain segments often, those segments most likely have bad cable, connectors, or devices attached. The broadcast and multicast alarms are put in place to identify an excessive broadcast or multicast rate on a port. This 7,500 packet per ten seconds alarm rate would be appropriate for this network given broadcast analysis baselining, indicating an absolute peak normal broadcast rate of 400 packets per second. If 7,500 broadcasts were seen over a period of ten seconds, this alarm would trigger. That 750 packet per second rate is far beyond the expected peak value and thus is an indicator of a potential network failure.

RMON History

The RMON history tool was used extensively in the network baselining process described previously. In that role it provided a historical view of the network capacity and allowed the network administrator to understand growth patterns and potentially disruptive error and broadcast rates. All of these tasks were focused on understanding network health. This tool can also be used in conjunction with the alarm limits discussed in the previous section to provide more information about the network if an alarm is triggered. In this capacity, shorter-duration RMON histories are generally more useful. By setting up additional RMON history groups with shorter duration and closer intervals, specific information about network operation at the time of an alarm can be obtained.

When configuring RMON histories for use as a tool to examine the network following an alarm, choosing an appropriate duration is critical. The general rule is to use a duration a few hours longer than the average response time the support staff spends identifying the problems. In most network support roles, network problems are detected either via an alarm in a network management system or a call from an end user

▬▬ ▬▬ ▬▬ ▬

Figure 8.3

RMON history for
packets and errors
on user port.

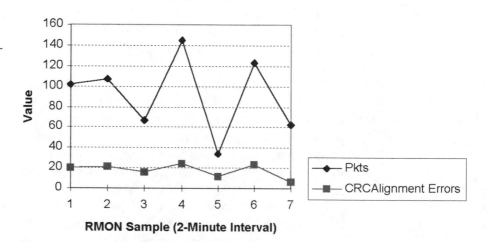

Packets and Errors on User Segment

RMON Sample (2-Minute Interval)

complaining about network connectivity. Once the alarm is seen or a
call is received, the support staff begins the process of diagnosing the
real issue. This process varies based on the severity and type of network
issue. In most cases, though, the support staff will need to determine if
network statistics indicate an obvious issue, such as a high error rate or
excess broadcast level. The RMON history is an excellent tool for this examination. In order to successfully use the history, it should collect data
for at least a few hours longer than the time it takes the support staff to
detect a problem and begin the information gathering process.

An example of using this RMON history in support situations is as
follows.

RMON history configuration:	Each interface on the switches is configured for RMON history with a duration of four hours and an interval of two minutes. The choice of these times is based on the average response time of two hours and the need for detailed statistics every two minutes to gauge exactly how statistical values change within reasonably short periods.
Problem trigger:	A problem trigger is a call to the support center complaining about network performance being slow to reach a specific centralized resource.

Initial response process:	The network management system is examined for alarms and indications of failed devices. None are found in network core or centralized resources areas. Since these areas have alarm limits set to detect high average traffic rates, high error rates, and excessive broadcast rates, it is assumed that those events are not the cause of this response-time issue. A single network rising alarm for error count is received on a periphery switch in the user's area.
Secondary response process:	Using RMON history on the segments containing the client complaining about response time and the server being contacted, the data shown in Figure 8.3 are seen on the port containing the user reporting the problem.
Response conclusions:	The port containing the user complaining about network connectivity appears to have a consistent low error rate. Because the packet rate is very low and the error rate is remaining above the alarm falling threshold for this port, only the rising alarm is generated. The low rate does impact the user's communication to the server to cause failures in the login process. The cause of this error rate is probably based on a failing cable from the user to its switch. Support personnel are dispatched to examine and possibly replace the cable segment. It is also suggested that the alarm threshold on these ports for errors be lowered to ten per two minutes to allow quicker automated management detection for this condition in the future.

Statistics Logging Applications

In addition to the RMON history groups, any one of various vendors' statistics logging tools can be configured to assist in the automated management of a switched network. These tools are usually included by default in all major network management applications, such as SunNET Manager, Hewlett-Packard OpenView, Cabletron Spectrum for Open Systems, and IBM NetView 6000.

Each of these network management platforms allows any MIB variable to be polled periodically and logged to a database. That information can then be used to produce reports and graphs regarding that statistic. In the process of automating the management of a switched network, the gathering and observation of critical information is vital. If critical statistics are constantly observed, major changes in those network values can be observed before the change is detrimental to the network operation. RMON history provides a mechanism to observe and record the network segment's operation for a variety of statistics but does not provide the flexibility to log other statistics. The RMON version 2 user history will allow this operation, but it is usually not available on switches and other devices critical to the network.

Using a statistics logging application is usually a simple matter of specifying the MIB variables to be logged and an appropriate duration and interval to log at. The only difficult part of this process is identifying what statistics should be logged. The two major areas of statistics that may require logging beyond the basic RMON segment histories are device operation statistics and additional network segment statistics.

Device operation statistics are the MIB values on a particular network devices such as a server, switch, or gateway that defines its current condition or capabilities. Additional network segment statistics are MIB variables on switches and probes that define additional network-specific statistics, such as protocol breakdown, frame size distribution, and address count. Since each device will have a proprietary MIB, there is no common value that can be used to observe all critical statistics. Table 8.5 lists some typical device and network statistics that should be logged on the network.

Any other statistics that define critical functions of either network devices or the network itself can be added to the list in Table 8.5 as long as an SNMP MIB attribute is available defining them. When choosing the statistics to watch on your network, the process is usually a simple question of what statistics on this device would indicate its proper or improper operation. Once that question is answered, the device's MIB should be obtained from either the vendor or an Internet FTP site such as venera.isi.edu. If the MIB defines a value for that statistic, configure the network management system to poll and log that value. A periodic report should be created to monitor that value. If this is done, most changes in the overall operation of those network components will become obvious and the network operation much more predictable.

TABLE 8.5

Sample
Statistics to Be
Logged

Statistic	Devices	Description
Average CPU load	Servers, routers	Polling a server or router for average CPU load is an excellent gauge of the operation of that device. Since servers and routers are primarily software-driven devices, extremely high average CPU load could be an indication that they are unable to perform their specified tasks. Most servers and routers support private MIBs to allow SNMP management stations to poll these statistics.
User count	Servers	On servers with a specified number of licenses, monitoring the current user count is critical to prevent a situation in which authorized users are unable to attach to that server. In a Novell network, for instance, if a 250 user license server is contacted by the 251st user, that user will be unable to attach and reach the resources. By watching the user count on the servers over time, proper decisions can be made regarding increasing the user license on a particular server before the maximum user limit is reached.
SAT size	Switches	On traditional LAN switches, the source address table should be monitored to determine the number of active users on the switched network. Generally, only a few switches should be logged, since the size of the SAT will be almost the same on all switches in complex networks, based on the normal function of switched LANs. By watching this number, the system administrator gains some understanding of the actual user population on the network. If this number changes drastically, further investigation should be made as to why. A sudden increase in the user count could indicate that another separate network has been added to the current network. A sudden drop could indicate that the network has failed in some area, isolating some users. Note that proper alarms should indicate any physical failures.

Automated Management Tools Implementation Process

Given the tools of RMON history, alarm limits, and statistics logging, a switched network can be configured to essentially monitor itself. Once a proper baselining is done, and these tools configured, the system administrator should be confident that the network is operational and stable as long as no alarms are seen and the logged and monitored statistics do not show significant changes from the baseline. In order to get to this stage of automated switched network management, the steps shown in Figure 8.4 should be followed. Given a minor investment of time to baseline and configure the network, the return will be a much more manageable network that allows far quicker response time to problems.

Troubleshooting Switched Networks

Even the most soundly designed and built networks will eventually experience some type of failure. This statement is based on the fact that it is impossible to control all elements of any large network. Without total control, a variety of disruptive or faulty devices can be added to the network by the user community. It is important to recognize that sooner or later the system administrator will have to troubleshoot a problem affecting network operations. Once that fact is understood and accepted, the process of preparing the tools, methods, and data to quickly and effectively solve these problems becomes necessary. In the previous section on maintaining a switched network, the system was configured to watch for potential failures. The network was also configured to activate alarms and provide indication of changes when issues occurred. These baselining and monitoring tools provided an excellent window into the network's health and provided a great deal of information concerning problems, but they did not solve those problems. This section is focused on the processes and tools that will allow identified network-related problems to be resolved. By understanding and anticipating many categories of network problems, the network support personnel will be far better prepared to handle network failures.

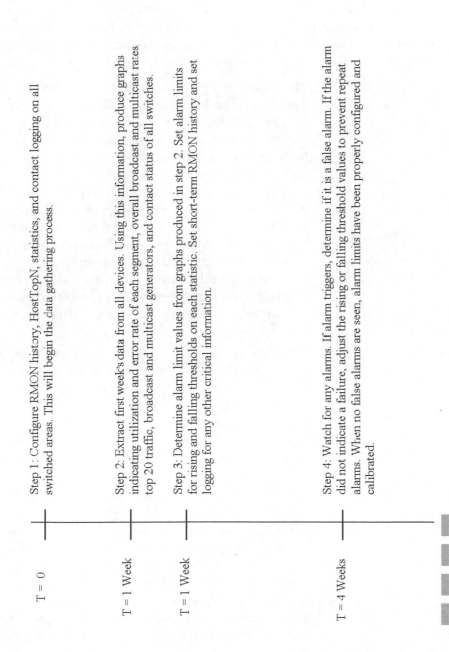

Step 1: Configure RMON history, HostTopN, statistics, and contact logging on all switched areas. This will begin the data gathering process.

Step 2: Extract first week's data from all devices. Using this information, produce graphs indicating utilization and error rate of each segment, overall broadcast and multicast rates, top 20 traffic, broadcast and multicast generators, and contact status of all switches.

Step 3: Determine alarm limit values from graphs produced in step 2. Set alarm limits for rising and falling thresholds on each statistic. Set short-term RMON history and set logging for any other critical information.

Step 4: Watch for any alarms. If alarm triggers, determine if it is a false alarm. If the alarm did not indicate a failure, adjust the rising or falling threshold values to prevent repeat alarms. When no false alarms are seen, alarm limits have been properly configured and calibrated.

T = 0

T = 1 Week

T = 1 Week

T = 4 Weeks

Figure 8.4   Timeline for baseline and monitoring implementation.

Troubleshooting Tools and Processes

There are many specific tools that can be utilized to troubleshoot switched networks. Each tool provides some level of information that can identify causes of network-related failures. In this section, some of the more common tools will be examined for use in solving specific types of network-related problems.

LAN analyzers: The most common tool utilized in network trouble-shooting is the LAN analyzer. There are many high-quality LAN analyzer products available, including the Network General Sniffer, the Azure Technologies LAN Pharaoh, Domino Analyzers, and so on. Each of these analyzers, while physically different, performs the same basic task. All LAN analyzers are designed primarily to monitor network segments, capture the traffic, and decode the packets into a usable form. Most are able to recognize well-known types of failures and provide a summarized symptom report describing a possible cause of this failure. For this discussion, the analyzers will be used for their primary purpose: to capture packets for further examination.

RMON: RMON tools are also very powerful troubleshooting tools, since they allow the network support personnel to quickly gather very detailed information regarding the operation of network segments. The RMON statistics and history groups are most useful in troubleshooting faulty network segments, while the host, HostTopN, and matrix groups are best used to identify end-system-related issues. In most situations, RMON can be used as the primary troubleshooting tool when network connectivity is failing.

Other MIBs: While RMON is a very good standard MIB for segment and network analysis, most vendors of networking hardware will support a very comprehensive set of proprietary and standards-based MIBs. These MIBs will provide a variety of information related to other areas of network operation. The IETF Bridge MIB is an example of a very useful MIB that shows the operational state of a switch and the details of its SAT and spanning tree. It is usually a good idea to obtain the MIBs of any device on your network that can be managed, in order to understand what kinds of information can be obtained. In most large networks almost every statistic and operational event is being counted or logged somewhere. The key is to know where that information exists and how to retrieve it. Having and reading the vendors' MIBs provides the answer to what can be counted, and obtaining good network management software for those devices provides the mechanism to obtain the data.

Network maps: A comprehensive physical and logical map of the network is an invaluable troubleshooting tool. This type of map can be in the form of the view of a network management software interface or can be CAD drawings of the network connectivity. In general, network problems are usually related to specific areas of a network. If a good map of the network is available, it is usually possible to determine if the failures on a network have some common element. An example of the value of a comprehensive network map can be seen in the situation where ten switches simultaneously lose contact with the network management system and the users lose access to their resources. This catastrophic failure could be ten separate failures or there could be some common cause. If a map of the network were available, such as the one shown in Figure 8.5, the real cause of the failure would be obvious. The backbone switch has failed. Without having this connectivity map, this problem could have been incorrectly viewed as ten separate switch failures.

Using these tools, the network support personnel should be able to execute a variety of troubleshooting processes. This set of tools could be considered the basic toolkit of the network support person. In the following text, the application of these tools will be discussed. Various network-related troubleshooting situations will be examined and these tools will be applied to determine a solution.

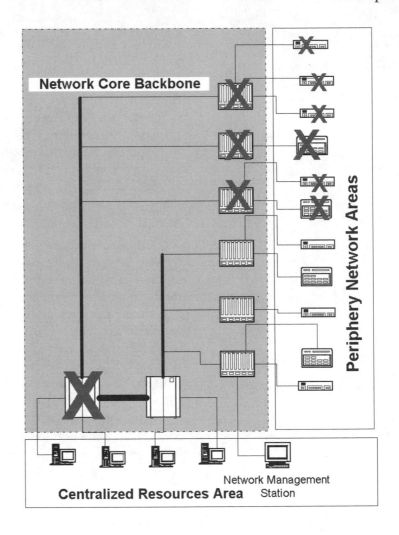

Network failures are usually related to two broad causes: topology failure and user connectivity issues. There two areas encompass a variety of situations, but most problems do fall into one of these categories.

Topology Failure   A topology failure is defined as any condition in which the physical network connectivity becomes unreliable or fails completely. This type of failure is limited to the infrastructure of the network, consisting of all the switches, hubs, cables, and connections. If any of these components fails to operate properly, the network integrity is lost and some portion of the network will lose reliable connectivity. In general, symptoms of this kind of failure are seen through alarms

TABLE 8.6

Symptoms of Topology- Related Failures

Symptom	Description
Intermittent network access to resources	This symptom describes situations where groups of users are unable to access their resources. In general, the users will lose contact with file servers, printers, and other network resources. The loss of contact will be intermittent and should affect more than one specific user.
End-system isolation	The users affected are unable to see any resources. This could manifest itself in the form of Novell shell failure (unable to find any file server), an empty browser (network neighborhood) in the Microsoft networking environments, or just simply the inability of an IP end system to PING any network resources beyond its local switch.
Slow transfer times and network time-outs	Users attempting to reach other network resources experience slow transfer times and periodic session time-outs. The definition of slow transfer time must be based on known transfer times experienced on a regular basis. Time-outs are usually indicated by messages to the user indicating a loss of contact or possible system lockup at the end user while connectivity is restored.

and loss of contact to network devices. Table 8.6 describes the most common symptoms of a topology failure. Any of these symptoms could indicate the failure of the topology to reliably deliver user data.

When end users lose contact with network resources or experience unreliable or unstable connectivity, the usual reaction is to blame the network infrastructure. It is important to recognize that until some analysis is done, it is as likely that the user's PC card has failed as it is that the backbone is down. In dealing with topology-related failures, following a logical troubleshooting flow to isolate the cause and resolve the issue is critical in coming to a quick resolution. Most networks are far too large to try to guess what component is failing. The specific process flow for dealing with a topology-related issue is dependent on what the symptoms are. In the following text, several process flows will be defined to provide a basic framework for dealing with topology-related failures.

Topology Troubleshooting Flow 1: Intermittent Network Access Experienced by Multiple Users

Description of problem: Absolute loss of network connectivity is experienced for periods of time. Connectivity is available at some times while unavailable at other times.

Possible causes and probability:

- Frequent topology convergence caused by changes in the spanning tree topology (high probability)
- Network overload on the backbone links or user links (high probability)
- Resource overload internal to service (medium probability)
- Excessive error rates on interswitch or user links (low probability)
- Intermittent failing switch in the path (low probability)

From the above list of potential causes of this intermittent loss of network connectivity, some causes are more probable than others. Each of these situations will be tested to ultimately reach a conclusion regarding the cause of this problem.

Figure 8.6 provides a process for initially identifying the major symptoms of a topology-related failure. In this flowchart, several possible alarms could exist in the network management system. If spanning tree alarms such as root bridge changes are seen, the issue is related to the spanning tree topology. If error rate, broadcast rate, or traffic rate alarms are seen on devices or links, the issue is a topology-related failure or overload. If critical resources such as servers are indicating alarms, those devices should be specifically examined. The final indicator is if contact is lost to a switch or multiple switches in the fabric. Loss of contact requires its own analysis process to determine exactly what failure has occurred.

Figure 8.7 provides a suggested path for dealing with spanning tree–related failures or changes. Since the entire switch topology is built using a single spanning tree, any change or failure in that topology will cause network disruptions. Most switches can provide indications of changes in the topology by implementing the IETF Bridge MIB. This flowchart provides a path for determining if the topology has changed and if that change is acceptable.

Figure 8.8 defines the process for dealing with traffic-related alarms. If an alarm is seen indicating excessive traffic levels on a link, examination must be made to determine if this is just a burst of traffic or if this is an indication that the network capacity is being overloaded. If this is a burst, the process then identifies the sources of most traffic and suggests methods of relocating them nearer their resources or providing additional switch capacity to those users. If the traffic level is constantly above this alarm limit, the flowchart suggests a variety of reconfiguration options to increase network capacity.

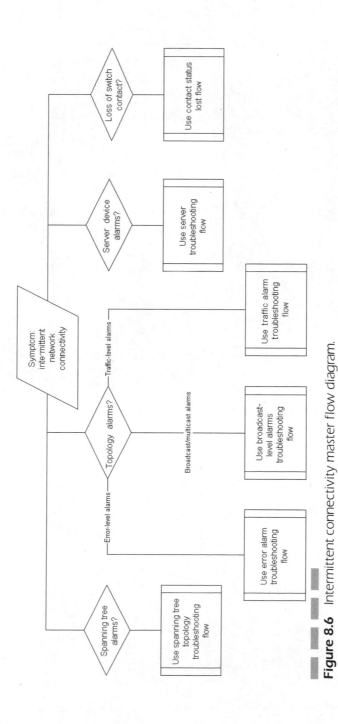

Figure 8.6 Intermittent connectivity master flow diagram.

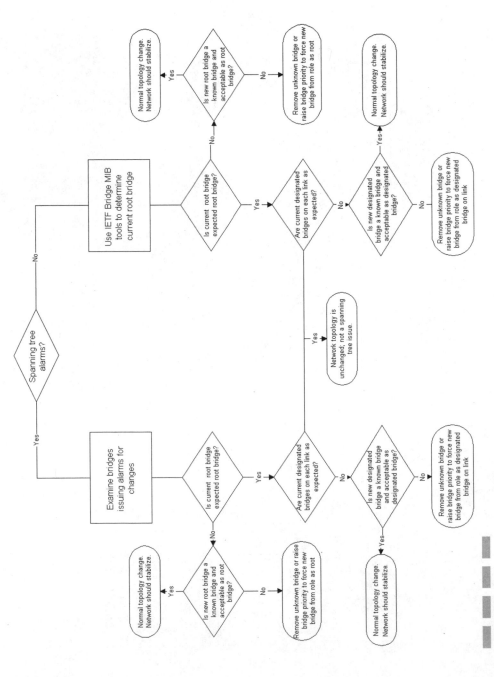

Figure 8.7 Spanning tree failure flow diagram.

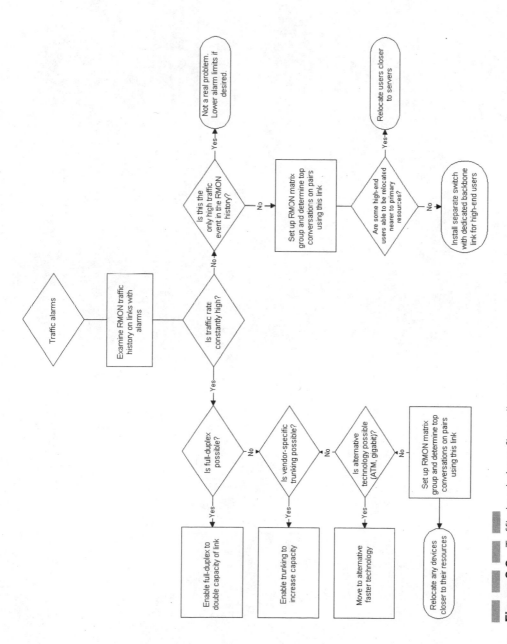

Figure 8.8 Traffic-level alarm flow diagram.

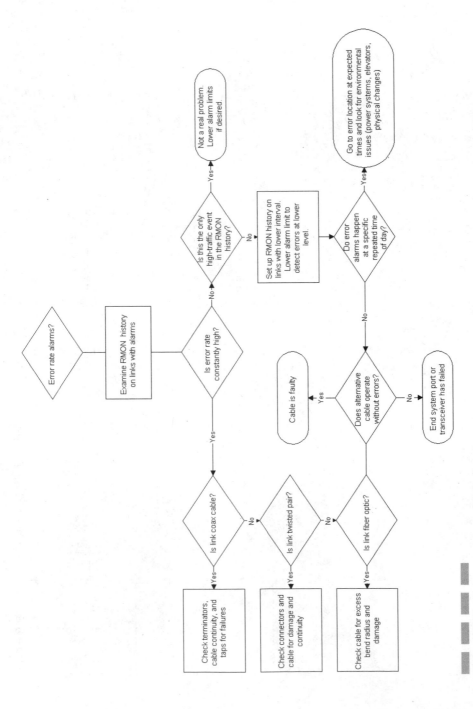

Figure 8.9 Error rate alarm flow diagram.

Figure 8.9 describes the action to be taken when error rate alarms are seen. If physical layer errors are seen on a link or port, immediate action should be taken. This flowchart uses RMON history to determine if this error condition is constant or intermittent. If RMON shows a constant error rate, the problem is most likely due to damaged cable, connectors, or faulty interfaces. If the problem is intermittent, the issues may be more likely related to some interference event, such as an elevator being active or a person stepping on coaxial cable.

Figure 8.10 examines how to handle alarms indicating excessive broadcast or multicast rates. In this flowchart the alarm could indicate a constant broadcast rate or an intermittent burst. If the rate is constantly high, tools such as RMON hosts should be used to determine the source and identify whether the broadcasts are necessary. With a constantly high broadcast rate, the dramatic step of disabling the user's interface may be used as a last resort if the network is beginning to completely fail.

Figure 8.11 deals with troubleshooting server overload. Two possible alarms can be generated related to the server: alarms dealing with network link saturation and alarms dealing with internal resource depletion. If the alarms indicate a network link overload, several options are available, including upgrading to full-duplex, faster technologies, and realigning end users to other servers. If the alarms are indicating a lack of CPU capacity, drive space, or memory, the server can be upgraded or its responsibilities distributed to other servers on the network.

In Figure 8.12, troubleshooting situations where your management station loses contact with a switch or multiple switches are examined. If only a single switch is not reachable, the flowchart suggests trying other methods of communication, such as ICMP Echo Requests (PINGs). If that fails but devices on the other side of the switch are still reachable, then the switch's IP stack or management interface has failed or is improperly configured. If no devices are reachable beyond the switch, then the switch has completely failed and must be replaced. If multiple switches are unreachable, then the process of using your network maps to identify the closest failing switch to the management station must be completed. Troubleshoot that switch once it is identified.

Topology Troubleshooting Flow 2: Total End-System Isolation

Description of problem: Absolute loss of network connectivity is experienced for a specific set of users. No network resources are visible to affected users.

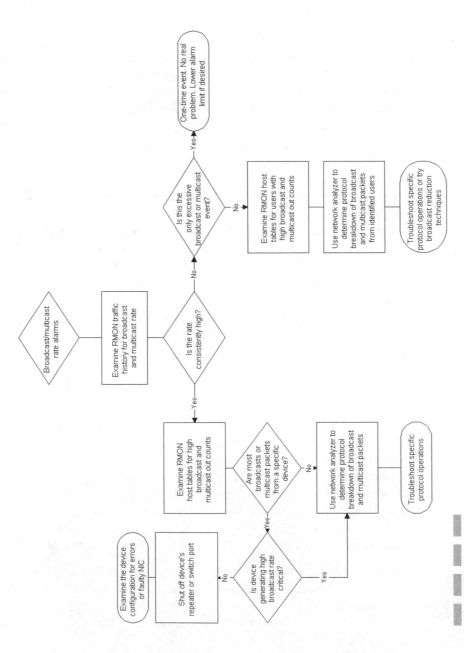

Figure 8.10 Broadcast and multicast alarm flow diagram.

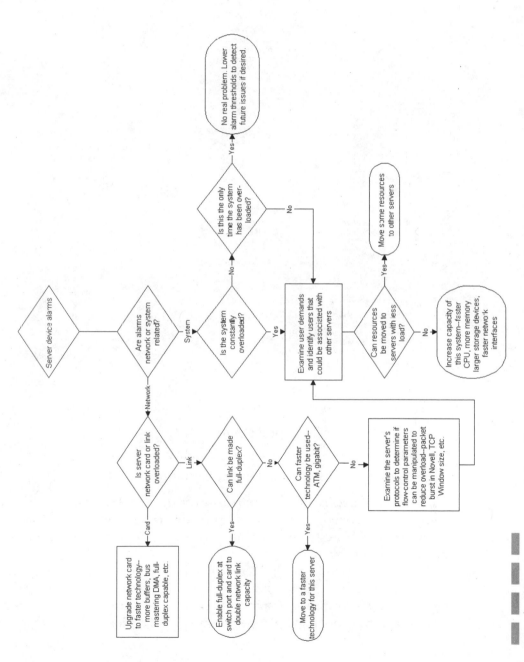

Figure 8.11 Server overload alarm flow diagram.

Figure 8.12

Loss of switch
contact flow
diagram.

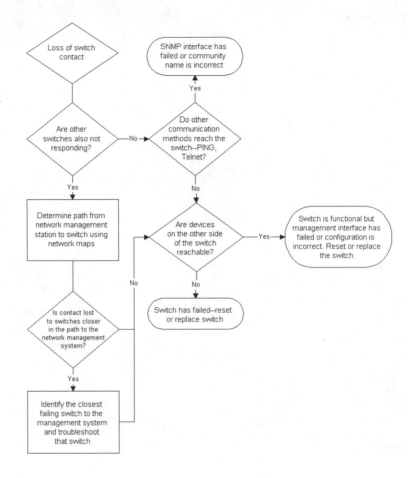

Possible causes and probability:

- Switch failure (high probability)
- Physical cable failure (high probability)
- Network segmentation (low probability)

From the above list of potential causes of this absolute loss of network connectivity, some causes are more probable than others. Each of these situations will be tested to ultimately reach a conclusion regarding the cause of this problem.

Figure 8.13 provides a high-level decision tree for dealing with end systems that have no network connectivity. There are three major paths to examine. The presence of spanning tree changes requires an examination of the network topology (see Figure 8.7). The loss of contact with

Figure 8.13

Master flow for
troubleshooting
end-system
isolation.

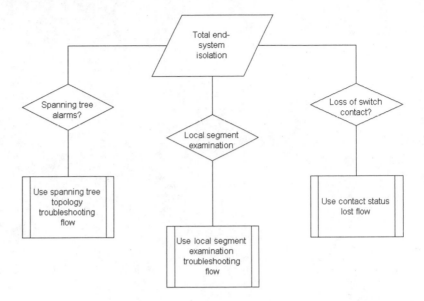

any switches requires the steps shown in Figure 8.12. And, finally, the possibility that the end user may be disconnected or failing requires a third path, shown in Figure 8.14.

In Figure 8.14, the end-system connectivity is examined. It is possible that the user's port is disabled. In the flowchart, it is necessary to determine why a port is disabled before it is reenabled. Many switches and repeaters have the ability to disable ports automatically on certain alarm levels. This end-system isolation could also be related to the fact that the device is not connected to the network. Examination of the station's link condition is also required. If link is OK and the port is not disabled, then the port statistics should be examined for error rates. If no error rates are found, then a decision should be made using the statistics or host groups to determine whether the user is sending data. If the user is not, then this is an end-system failure. If the user is, this is protocol related and requires further analysis with a network analyzer.

Topology Troubleshooting Flow 3: Slow Network Operation and Frequent Network Time-Outs

Description of problem: Network connectivity is always available, but performance levels vary tremendously. This change in performance is intermittent.

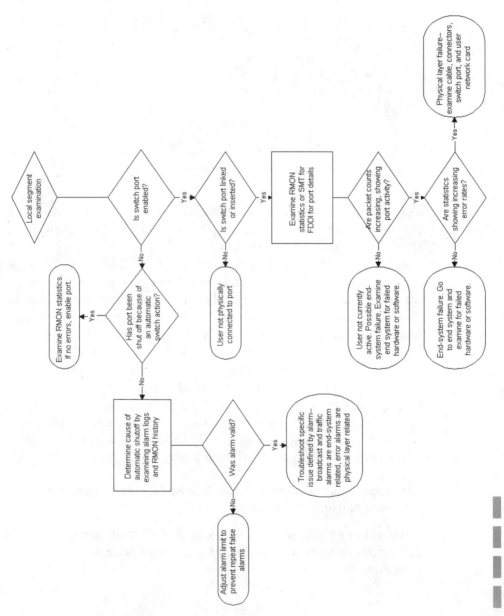

Figure 8.14 Network segment examination troubleshooting flow diagram.

Figure 8.15

Slow Performance or frequent time-outs troubleshooting flow diagram.

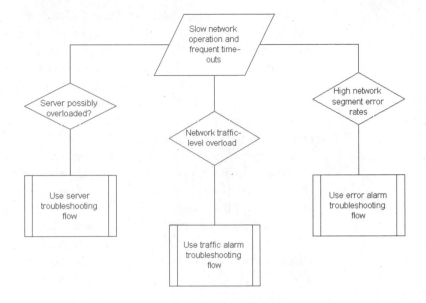

Possible causes and probability:

- Resource overload internal to service (high probability)
- Network overload on the backbone links or user links (high probability)
- Excessive error rates on interswitch or user links (medium probability)

From the above list of potential causes of this poor performance network connectivity, some causes are more probable than others. Each of these situations will be tested to ultimately reach a conclusion regarding the cause of this problem.

Figure 8.15 provides three possible paths for troubleshooting slow network performance. The first path uses Figure 8.11 to determine if the server is internally overloaded or its network link is saturated. The second uses Figure 8.8 to identify traffic alarms on the network and find and upgrade saturated network links. The final option uses Figure 8.9 to identify error rates on the network that could be impacting overall performance.

User Connectivity Issues   The second major area of network-related failures is that dealing with individual users unable to access network resources. This category of failure is different from the topology issues discussed previously, because these failures assume that the switch topology is on line and stable. This type of error is more frequently encountered than the topology-related failures, mainly because the end systems' specific configurations could be the cause of the failure. If an end user has an improperly configured or failing PC or even has accidentally disconnected the PC from the network, his or her first reaction is typically to blame the network for lack of connectivity. It is important to develop efficient processes to quickly identify whether the network is functional for the user who claims that the "network is down." If the network support staff can verify that the network is operational, the focus of the troubleshooting can be directed to the end-user's configuration. This section will focus on the process of proving that the network is functional for the user who claims it has failed. The process of then troubleshooting the end-system's configuration is beyond the scope of this discussion. For more details regarding potential failure scenarios for specific protocols, see Chapters 4, 5, and 6.

Connectivity issues have one primary symptom: a specific user claims that he or she cannot contact a known network resource. That user may be unable to log into a Novell server, may be unable to reach an Internet gateway, or any similar situation. When dealing with this, it is important to recognize that the network may in fact be failing to provide connectivity for this user. Until some analysis is performed to examine the actual state of the network, it is not safe to assume that the user's configuration is to blame.

The analysis procedure to determine whether the network is functional for a specific user involves systematically confirming that each network component in the user's path is operational. While this process may seem complex, it is usually a very simple task, given properly configured network management systems. In the following text, a typical process flow for this kind of troubleshooting is outlined. It is important to develop a similar flow for your network support staff to consult when users complain about lack of connectivity. If this kind of procedure is in place, the support staff will be able to quickly identify network-related issues versus end-system issues.

Using Figure 8.16, the complaint of end user X failing to reach network resource Y can be addressed. Following the flowchart, the topology is examined for alarms first. This is always the first step, because, if the topology is failing, there will always be some users affected. If topology alarms are present, this is not an end-user issue; it is a topology issue and should be troubleshot using the above processes. If the topology appears stable, the process continues with a simple test: Can other devices

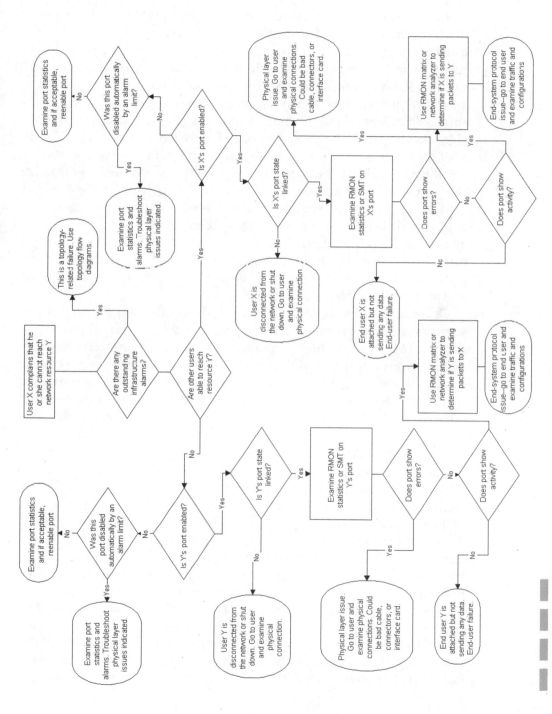

Figure 8.16 End-user connectivity troubleshooting process flow.

reach Y? If other devices cannot reach Y, the failure is most likely related to Y.

The flowchart then tests the port status and port state. If the port is disabled, the user will obviously not be able to communicate. The next question is why the port is disabled. Some switches and repeaters implement alarm limits that can disable ports if traffic, errors, or broadcast rates exceed a certain limit. On Token-Ring devices, most vendors disable ports where beacon conditions can be isolated. If this port were shut off because of one of these conditions, it is not advisable to reenable the port until the cause has been identified and resolved. Use the RMON statistics and history to identify the conditions seen on the disabled port. If all statistics seem normal and the end system seems stable, the port can be turned on. It is advisable to further test the network card, cables, and end station if any unusual statistics or alarms are logged against that port prior to reenabling. If the port were not disabled, the flowchart determines its link status. If the link status indicates no link, the end user is not even connected to the network. If that is the case, have the end user or a support person go to the end station and examine the cable connections.

Once the port has been determined to be on and linked, the RMON statistics and history groups are to be examined for traffic and error statistics. If the port has a high error rate, the cause of the problem has been found. Excess errors on a link are an indication of a cable, connector, or interface card failure. All three components will need to be examined to identify the actual failing component. It is also advisable to lower the error alarm limits of this port so that this condition can be detected sooner.

The RMON statistics should then be examined for activity. Activity is unicast packets in the RMON statistics. If this port is directly connected to the user and no activity is seen, the user is not even attempting to communicate. This inactivity is usually caused by the end system failing or being misconfigured. Maybe the user forgot to load the network drivers or maybe the drivers are conflicting with other newly installed hardware. If the user is not sending packets, the switch fabric cannot be blamed for failing to deliver them. If the port is on and linked, there are no error issues, packet activity is present, and the topology is stable (no alarms), the problem is most likely related to a protocol or configuration issue at the end system. Using the RMON matrix group or a network analyzer, the last step is to determine if traffic is seen between user X and user Y. If traffic is present, the issue is most likely related to a protocol failure. If there is no Y to X or X to Y traffic seen, the issue is most likely related to end-system failure. At this time, further analysis is needed either at the end system or on the network itself to determine just where the user's configuration or protocol is failing. What is nearly certain at this point it that the switched network is functional and is not to blame for this connectivity issue.

Summary

By following the steps outlined in this chapter to maintain and troubleshoot your switched network, your ability to keep this complex network operational will be significantly enhanced. Through the baselining process, you will gain an understanding of your network's normal operation. If those statistics begin to change, you will recognize the change and be prepared to adapt the network to its new demands before a network failure occurs. If the network fails and the proper automated management processes are in place, flashing icons in your management system's map will notify you, and alarm messages will identify the conditions. In most cases you would be the first to know a network failure has occurred, so your response time will be far quicker than if user complaints identified the failed network. Using the information provided by the alarms and the troubleshooting processes outlined here, you should then be able to identify the cause of the condition and isolate the failure's location. You may even be able to correct some of the problems remotely. In all cases, however, the small amount of time you spent configuring alarm limits and monitoring the network's health will provide you with vast amounts of information, which will be invaluable when you must troubleshoot your switched network.

Virtual LANs

Overview

The term *Virtual LAN,* or VLAN, has become another industry marketing term. It is used freely by almost all vendors of switches but lacks a detailed definition. With no definition, any vendor with any VLAN technology is free to use the term. This results in different vendors using a common term to describe completely different and usually incompatible technologies. This chapter will attempt to provide a generic definition of the term *VLAN* and then outline the basic functions any vendor's implementation should provide to be of use in a switched network. Once the definition and goals of generic VLANs have been outlined, an examination of the features of VLAN systems will be examined. To conclude this chapter, an examination of the IEEE 802.1Q specification for Virtual Bridged LANs will be investigated for both functions and limitations when compared with the current range of vendor-specific VLAN solutions.

Industry Definition

Individual vendors, when describing certain enhancements to their LAN switches, use the term *VLAN* very freely. Since vendors' technologies are very different, why do they all utilize the same term to describe their services? The primary reason this is done is simply based on marketing. VLAN has a very strong appeal to the networking community, since it promises better performance and simplicity over the basic LAN switch. Since the term is appealing, most vendors have adopted it as the name of their assorted LAN switch technologies in order to capitalize on the marketing value of the word.

Even though the term *VLAN* is used by many different vendors to describe very different technologies, it is possible to develop a common industry definition. That definition is: *Virtual LAN—A logical layer two broadcast domain.*

This definition is very simple. A VLAN has exactly the same function and behavior as a layer two broadcast domain. A bridged network is an example of a layer two broadcast domain. In bridged networks, if a broadcast packet is sent into any port, it is flooded out to all ports in the broadcast domain. A VLAN has exactly the same operation. If a broadcast is sent into a VLAN, it is flooded to all members of the VLAN. The difference, however, between the bridged network and the VLAN is that the VLAN is a logical broadcast domain, while the bridged network is a physical broadcast domain. This means that the boundaries of the VLAN are created logically by rules in the switches. A bridged network has boundaries that are physical. The bridged network's boundaries are defined as the end of the cable plant. Bridged networks end when the LAN cables end. VLANs end when a logical rule defines that they end. This concept of a logical broadcast domain (or logical bridged network) allows for tremendous flexibility. Since the VLAN is simply a logical broadcast boundary implemented over a switched LAN, its shape can be changed as users move, and, more importantly, the switched LAN can support many overlaid VLANs on the same switches.

The logical model of a switched LAN without VLANs is shown in Figure 9.1. It describes the entire switched LAN area as one single broadcast domain. With VLANs, Figure 9.2 shows that the switched LAN can support several logical VLAN broadcast domains. Note that in Figure 9.2, the VLANs overlap, so that they can exist anywhere in the switched LAN. Their logical boundaries are completely flexible. Additionally, the operation of each of the VLANs is as a completely separate bridged network.

Figure 9.1

LAN switching without VLANs (single broadcast domain).

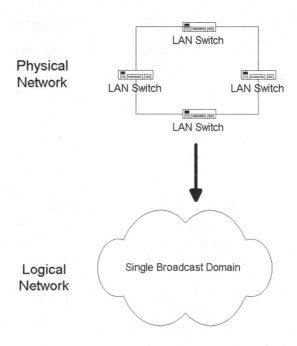

Figure 9.2

LAN switching with
virtual LANs (many
overlapping
broadcast domains).

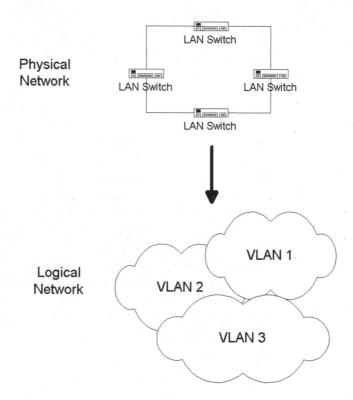

In Figure 9.2, the VLANs have allowed the single switched LAN to support several logical virtual LANs. Each VLAN would contain its own users and act as if it were a physically separate bridged network. This mechanism is very significant in that with VLANs, a common set of switches can build separate discrete LANs. Without VLANs, separate switches would be required to construct separate LANs. The best logical model of a VLAN network is shown in Figure 9.3.

This model defines a VLAN system as having a physical switched LAN infrastructure with layered logical broadcast domains, or VLANs, on top of the single set of switches. Each of the logical VLANs acts independent of the others in its handling of broadcast and multicast traffic.

Even though most vendors of VLAN-capable switches utilize proprietary mechanisms to implement VLANs, almost all of them would agree with this general definition of the term *VLAN*. With this definition in place, the next task is to understand why VLANs are of use to switched networks.

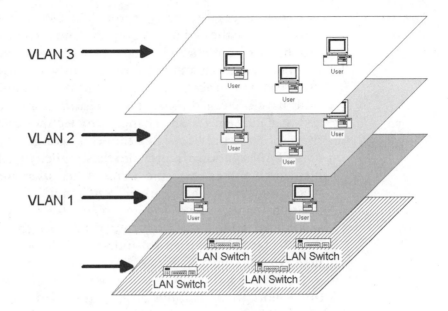

Figure 9.3
Logical VLAN
model.

VLAN 3

VLAN 2

VLAN 1

Reasons for VLAN Use

Given that a VLAN is a logical layer two broadcast domain, what service
will it provide to a switched network that makes it such an important
feature? Answering this question completely is impossible, since the basic VLAN can be used for an almost incalculable list of applications.
Even though there can be no absolute set of reasons to use VLANs, there
are several common reasons, which are seen in almost every vendor's lit-
erature and almost every analyst's report on the technology. These common goals of all VLAN systems provide an excellent framework for
evaluating a basic VLAN system. Given the fundamental goals we are
about to discuss, a network planner can determine which VLAN solutions offered by vendors will really provide a value to his or her network. Additional features and functions will always exist, but the
following core features must exist in a VLAN solution to justify its deployment.

Simplification of Adds, Moves, and Changes   The single most important reason for implementing VLANs in a network is to simplify the
process of adds, moves, and changes. It is well known that the cost of
moving end users in a corporate organization can be extremely high.

The cost comes from many factors. The costs include the personnel to actually move the end-user's computer and reconfigure it for its new location; the cost of changing network access lists on routers to reflect the user's new location; and, most importantly, the cost of having the end user be unable to access the network until the changes and reconfigurations have been made. Since most organizations today have significant end-user adds, moves, and changes, any technology that would simplify this process would be a significant cost savings.

A VLAN solution can provide this simplicity in any network that implements a router-based hierarchy. When users move in a routed network, they must change their configuration to adapt to their new location. If a user moved to a new area of the network and that new area was connected to a different router interface, that end-user's PC would have to be reconfigured to understand the logical network where it now existed. This type of movement is shown in Figure 9.4.

In Figure 9.4, the movement of user X from floor 2 to floor 3 will require more than just physical relocation. User X has an IP address of 172.16.2.100, which is only valid in the 172.16.2.0 subnetwork. Since the router connects to floor 3 using its 172.16.1.1 interface, all devices on floor 3's LAN require 172.16.1.x addresses. Even after user X has physically moved to floor 3, user X will not be able to use the network until that user is given a 172.16.1.x address from the system administrator. Beyond assigning this new address, the system administrator may need to change the router configuration to adjust any access lists or other con-

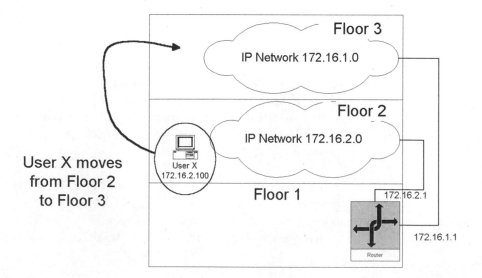

Figure 9.4

User movement example.

trols that are specific to user X in the 172.16.2.0 network. The result is that a simple move of this end-user's PC may require many additional tasks to adapt the end system to its new location within the router hierarchy.

Virtual LANs can simplify this process by changing the relationship between user and network. In the above example, the end user was required to adapt to the new location. In a VLAN system, the network is now able to adjust its configuration when the end users are moved. An example of utilizing VLANs to simplify this process involves using VLANs as containers for subnets. If the network were built using a single switched LAN and two VLANs, one VLAN would contain the users in the 172.16.1.0 network and another VLAN could contain the 172.16.2.0 users. These VLANs could be implemented in many ways, including making the ports on floor 2 equal the 172.16.2.0 VLAN and floor 3's ports equal the 172.16.1.0 VLAN. In more advanced VLAN systems, the actual end systems could be added to the VLAN regardless of ports. The actual mechanism is not significant and will be discussed separately.

Once the two VLANs were constructed, they would act just as two separate bridged LANs. The router would have one interface in the 172.16.2.0 VLAN and another in the 172.16.1.0 VLAN. At that time, the network would look logically exactly as it did when each floor had its own physical LAN. Now, when user X moved to the third floor, instead of reconfiguring the end user, the 172.16.2.0 VLAN could be reshaped to include the port user X plugs into on floor 3. This action is shown in Figure 9.5.

Figure 9.5

VLAN use in user relocation.

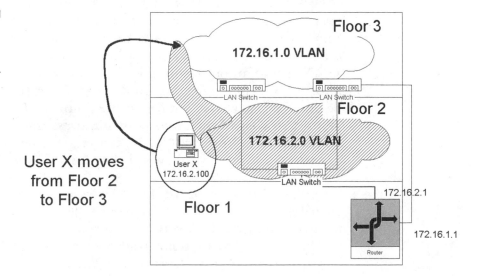

When the user moves to floor 3, the VLAN for subnet 172.16.2.0 is simply extended to include the user's new location. Since the user, now on floor 3, is still in the 172.16.2.0 VLAN, the user's IP address and other configurations are still valid and no end-user reconfiguration is required. Some VLAN implementations allow this process by changing the VLAN of the new location's port. Other, more advanced systems can dynamically adapt the VLAN to any location the user moves to without manual intervention. Either method is significantly better than the reconfiguration required without VLANs.

It is important to note that this example required end-user reconfiguration, or VLANs, because the network was constructed using a routed hierarchy. If the network were a flat IP network, as discussed in Chapter 4, the user would have been free to move anywhere without reconfiguration and without using VLANs. If you implement a flat logical IP network, your network inherently supports complete user movement without reconfiguration.

Control of Broadcast and Multicast Traffic   In addition to simplifying adds, moves, and changes, VLANs are expected to provide broadcast/multicast control over switched LANs. In Chapter 3, it was seen that the only real limit to the size of a switched LAN is based on the level of broadcast and multicast traffic. When that level becomes excessive and impacts the end users of the network, the network does not continue to scale in size. VLANs attempt to address that issue by providing broadcast control within the switched LAN.

Because there are many VLAN mechanisms offered by switch vendors, the degree of broadcast control provided could vary significantly. Simple port-based VLANs could be used to isolate broadcast-intensive users to one broadcast domain, while more advanced protocol-based VLANs could automatically group broadcast traffic of one protocol into a VLAN containing only those users. The actual mechanisms will be discussed later. In general, even the simplest VLAN mechanism can be used to control some broadcast/multicast traffic on the switched LAN. Because of this fact, VLANs can reduce overall broadcast/multicast traffic and, as such, allow switched LANs to scale to larger sizes.

Creation of Private Networks   VLANs can be used to create private virtual networks. By using VLANs, a single network is able to support many private virtual networks that operate independently of each other. This type of feature is not available with existing LAN technology, but with VLANs it becomes an option. The advantage of this private virtual network concept is that now providers of network infrastructure need only build one physical LAN. Then, as users of the network require connectivity, logical VLANs can be implemented for each group of users. Since all of the VLANs share the same physical topology but are logically separate networks, use of the single physical switched LAN is maximized.

As an example of this concept, consider an office building. Within the building many businesses exist. Normally the businesses would be forced to deploy their own networks or share a common building network. Since the businesses are not related to one another, the idea of sharing a common accessible network is not appealing. Alternatively, the cost of building their own network is usually not a cost-effective process if too few users exist or the users are located in different parts of the building. Using a VLAN system, it would be possible for the owner of the building to deploy a switched LAN connecting all offices. Then, using VLANs, each business could have isolated networks, which could exist anywhere in the building. This logical VLAN could be used to create a VLAN of one business with offices on several floors. For the owner of the building, this network is very cost effective, mainly because there is only one physical network deployed, and, since the VLANs are logical, network connectivity can be easily altered as areas of the building are used by different businesses.

These reasons for using VLANs are just some of the many possible uses of this technology. It is important to understand that these basic functions and goals are to be considered the minimum feature set of any VLAN solution. If a vendor has a technology called VLANs but is unable to simplify adds, moves, and changes and is unable to control broadcasts on your network in some way, then that vendor's VLAN solution is most likely too limited to be useful.

Basic VLAN Mechanism

The term *VLAN* is used to describe many different technologies. This section will attempt to describe the various VLAN mechanisms that exist in the industry today. In this discussion two major areas of functionality will be examined. The first will be the VLAN membership mechanism. This defines how a VLAN is created. The second will describe how the VLAN-enabled switched networks will operate with each other. This is known as the VLAN distribution mechanism. By examining the possible options for both VLAN membership and distribution, it will be possible to understand how a particular vendor-specific VLAN solution is implemented. After reading this section, the fact that all VLAN solutions are not equal should be evident.

VLAN Membership Options

VLAN membership defines how groups of MAC layer end users are associated with a particular VLAN or VLANs. There are many methods for this process, ranging from simple port association to complex protocol-based association. Before those methods are examined, a more fundamental categorization must be made. That categorization of VLAN membership is based on whether the VLAN is viewed as a collection of ports or a collection of MAC addresses.

VLANs as Port Groups or Collections of MAC Layer End Users
Before actual VLAN membership methods can be discussed, the more fundamental question of what a VLAN really is must be addressed. Our basic VLAN definition described it as a logical layer two broadcast domain. While all VLAN mechanisms meet that general definition, it is necessary to understand what elements make up that logical broadcast domain. Is the broadcast domain a collection of ports chosen through some logical interface, or is the broadcast domain a group of MAC layer end users using a logical interface? While this may not seem like a significant difference, it is critical in understanding the operation of any vendor's VLAN switch.

Most vendors treat a VLAN as a collection of switch ports. Those ports can be joined to form the VLAN by any number of criteria—for instance, all ports that see IP traffic could be made members of the same VLAN (e.g., an IP VLAN). The fact that the VLAN is a collection of ports does not prevent those ports from being joined using higher-layer protocols or other abstract rules. While defining a VLAN as a collection of ports that share common criteria is functional, it has some limitations. The first major limitation is that this type of VLAN is difficult to make dynamic. Dynamic VLANs are those that can adjust automatically to end-user adds, moves, and changes. Since this type of VLAN is based on switch ports being members, and switch ports do not usually get up and move across the network, it is difficult to handle end-user movement. In general, implementations that use this port model are only able to understand end-user movement by relearning the end-user's parameters when they appear at another port.

The second major issue with VLAN systems that treat VLANs as collections of ports is the inability of those systems to understand shared segments or end users using several protocols. While this type of system could identify the presence of several protocols on a port, or even several end users, that information would then be used to add the port to the VLAN or VLANs defined by the criteria. Once the port is added to those VLANs, all end users and packets sent are considered as being from that port and as such are sent to all VLANs of that port. In order to address this issue, most vendors using this model allow only one VLAN per port. Other vendors either implement the VLAN system with this functioning as designed or implement complex filtering mechanisms to prevent unnecessary packet flooding. This function is shown in Figure 9.6.

Figure 9.6 demonstrates that if the switch builds VLANs as collections of switch ports, the presence of multiple users requiring separate VLANs or the presence of a single user using several VLANs results in the entire port being joined to all of the VLANs present. In this figure, once the port is made a member of the IPX and AppleTalk VLANs, all users on that port are considered members of both VLANs, regardless of whether they individually meet the VLAN criteria. To avoid this, most vendors would recommend a single VLAN per port or at least a single user per port.

The second option for VLAN grouping is to consider a VLAN as a collection of MAC layer end users. This option requires that the switches keep track of their locally attached users and use their individual mem-

Figure 9.6

VLANs as collections of switch ports.

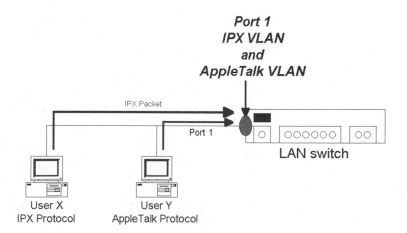

berships in VLANs to flood out the end-users' broadcasts or forward other VLAN users' broadcasts to that user. To make this happen, the switch must keep track of all directly attached users. As those users send packets into the switch port they are attached to, the switch examines the packets to determine if those users belong to any defined VLANs. If a user does, the switch adds the user's MAC address to a table associating it with the known VLAN. The switch also floods that individual broadcast/multicast packet to other switches and ports that contain at least one user in that VLAN. If a different user on the same port then sends a broadcast or multicast packet into the switch, that user's MAC address is added to the table associating the individual end user with a VLAN. The second user's packet is also flooded out to other switches and users sharing its VLAN. At this point, two users on one port are associated individually with different VLANs by simply associating their MAC address to the VLAN. Now, if either user sends a broadcast into the switch, it will be flooded out based on the specific sending station—not based on the entire port, as was the case with the port-based model. Figure 9.7 shows this concept.

Figure 9.7 shows that the switch has a table mapping individual MAC layer end systems to VLANs. The table is used to determine what VLAN or VLANs a packet from that user should be sent to. In this example the broadcast sent from user X is sent to the IPX VLAN, while the broadcast sent from user Y is delivered to the AppleTalk VLAN. This mechanism allows users on a common shared segment to be treated as belonging to separate VLANs for inbound broadcast handling. One disadvantage of this system is that on a shared segment, all users will see the broadcasts

Figure 9.7

VLANs as collections of MAC layer end users.

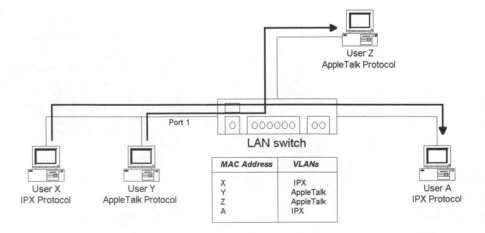

MAC Address	VLANs
X	IPX
Y	AppleTalk
Z	AppleTalk
A	IPX

sent to any user on the segment. This is generally not significant, in that this is the behavior of any shared segment and could be avoided where necessary by placing the users on separate switch ports.

VLAN Membership by Port Inheritance   The first mechanism to create VLANs is known as port inheritance, or port-based VLANs. This mechanism works by simply stating that the switch port is associated with a VLAN. Then all users on that port will also be associated with that VLAN by inheritance from the switch port. If the system using the VLAN equals the collection of ports, this type of association simply defines the ports' VLAN. If the system using the VLAN equals the collection of MAC addresses model, then all users on that port with no other VLAN associations are given a membership in this VLAN. Essentially the port association is the default VLAN for end users on the port.

This method of VLAN membership is most useful in grouping together physical areas of a network. By associating the VLAN with switched ports, the VLAN is also associated with the physical areas those switch ports connect to. An example of this type of service would be in a situation where a department of an organization exists on one floor of a building. The users in that department use desktop (nonmobile) PCs. In such a case, a VLAN for that department could be made simply by associating all switch ports for that floor of the building with the department's VLAN. Now, any devices plugging into a port on that floor become members of the department's VLAN. This method of VLAN creation is simple to deploy, because knowledge of the actual end users is not needed. This method is not dynamic, however, because if a user in the department moved to another floor, the VLAN will not automatically follow the user. Instead, the system administrator must change the port association of the port at the user's new location to match the department's VLAN. While this method is not completely dynamic, it is still easier than reconfiguring the end user or recabling the network.

VLAN Membership by MAC Address   The second level of VLAN association is based on end-user MAC address. Using this method, an end system or port is associated with a VLAN because a specific MAC address is present. If the VLAN equals the collection of ports model, the presence of a specific MAC address on a port associates the port with the VLAN. This results in all users on that port being part of that VLAN. If the VLAN equals the collection of MAC layer users model, the presence of the MAC address only affects that single end-user's VLAN membership. The use of MAC address as a VLAN membership rule is much more dynamic than the port association membership discussed previously. By associating the VLAN to the MAC address, the VLAN membership is able to move with the end user. If a true VLAN equals the collection of MAC layer users model, once a user is associated with a VLAN he or she is free to move anywhere in the network and keep his or her VLAN mappings without intervention. If the VLAN equals the collection of ports model, the new ports must be able to add the MAC address's VLAN to their ports' VLANs in order to support user movement.

This mechanism is most useful in situations where end users move around the network. By associating their MAC address to a set of VLANs, the user's PC can move anywhere in the network and keep its VLAN membership. In cases of laptops and other mobile computers, this feature is invaluable. The disadvantage of this model, however, is that there must be an initial configuration step provided. In that step the users must be associated with their VLANs. In networks of thousands of end users, this model may not be appropriate for all devices, based on the fact that users must be manually associated with their VLANs before they can use this feature. To use this type of VLAN effectively, the vendor must provide very intuitive and easy-to-use VLAN creation tools and graphical user interfaces.

VLAN Membership Based on Upper-Layer Protocol or Service

The third category of VLAN membership is based on upper-layer protocols and services. This type of VLAN is used to logically group the broadcast traffic of a particular protocol or service. The logical grouping should include only those devices requiring the particular protocol or service's broadcast/multicast traffic. VLANs based on protocol can be implemented using either the VLAN equals the collection of ports or VLANs equal a collection of MAC layer users.

In the VLAN equals ports model, a protocol VLAN is built by telling the switches to examine incoming packets for a particular protocol or service. If a match is seen, add that port to the VLAN. Once the port is added to the VLAN, broadcast and multicast packets will be sent out that port. Using this model, the port is then responsible for sending incoming broadcast and multicast packets to the appropriate ports, based on the protocol of the packets received into the switch port.

In the VLAN equals the collection of MAC layer users, the switch examines packets sent from each user. If the user's packet matches a protocol with a VLAN, the switch then associates the MAC address with the protocol VLAN. Once the MAC address of the user is associated with the protocol, the switch is then responsible for delivering all packets that belong to that protocol VLAN to the end-user's switch port. When the end user sends his or her own packets of this protocol type, the switch is responsible for delivering the packets to all other switch ports containing users within that VLAN.

This type of VLAN is most useful for broadcast/multicast control on switched LANs. By creating different VLANs for specific protocols, users utilizing those protocols are allowed to see the broadcasts of that VLAN, while users not in the VLAN are prevented from seeing that protocol. By isolating a protocol to only the users utilizing that protocol, the switched LAN is able to scale up to much larger sizes.

The actual protocols supported are entirely dependent on the switch vendor. Vendors that support this type of VLAN usually support the major layer three network protocols, such as IP, IPX, DECnet, Apple-Talk, Banyan, and so on. Some vendors will also support higher-level applications that use broadcasts such as IPX RIP and SAP and the various routing IP protocols such as RIP, OSPF, and so on. Since the mechanism usually works based on the switches being able to identify the protocol, any identifiable protocol or service is a VLAN possibility. The model of protocol VLANs is shown in Figure 9.8. There are three protocol-based VLANs. An IPX VLAN exists for the IPX protocol between the server and the IPX clients and the router. An IP VLAN exists between the router, the IP clients, and the UNIX server. The final VLAN is one based on the Novell Service Advertisement Protocol (SAP). This VLAN includes only the server and the router. Note that the router and many of the other devices exist in several protocol VLANs.

While protocol and service type specific VLANs are very useful in controlling the broadcasts and multicasts of a network, they have some deficiencies. First, since the implementation of such VLANs is based on specific vendors, interoperability is almost impossible. Second, even though a VLAN vendor may state support for this type of VLAN, the actual mechanism used for such a VLAN may have significant issues. Some of those issues relate to the ability of a user to belong correctly to more than one protocol VLAN. Some vendors allow end systems to exist in multiple protocol VLANs but then flood out any broadcast or multicast sent in the user's switch port to all VLANs it exists in, regardless of protocol. Other vendors have difficulty allowing users to even belong to multiple VLANs. A good protocol-based VLAN solution should support several concurrent protocol VLANs, based on the end-users' protocols. Those VLANs should be independent, meaning that if the user sends an IPX packet into the switch, it only goes to the IPX VLAN. One final re-

Figure 9.8

Protocol and
service type VLANs.

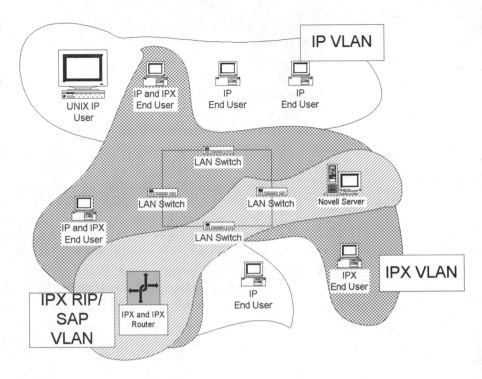

Figure 9.8

Protocol and
service type VLANs.

quirement with these types of VLANs is that they must coexist with
port and MAC VLANs. If they do not, the system is severely limited.

VLAN Distribution Options

Once VLANs have been established using any of the above methods, the
second function that must be supported is a VLAN distribution mechanism. The distribution mechanism is needed to allow VLAN criteria to
have the same definition on all switches. It would seem that this type of
service would be a requirement for any VLAN switch, but some vendors
do not include a VLAN distribution mechanism in their switches. By
not including any mechanism for VLAN distribution, the switch's
VLAN can only exist at that switch. Single-switch VLANs are usually of
no use in a real network consisting of multiple switches. If a vendor po-
sitions a VLAN-capable switch, be sure to ask how that switch will interact with other switches on the network. If the switch does not share
common VLANs with other switches, the switch is not suitable for a
multiswitch LAN. Be sure also to verify that the switch's VLAN distribu-

tion mechanism is not just layer three routing between switches, since that mechanism, which is used by some vendors, will isolate the VLANs on each switch with a router hierarchy. Since the router hierarchy is what we are trying to limit, any switch that enhances it is generally not suited for medium-to-large-sized switched LANs.

Frame Tagging The primary VLAN distribution mechanism in use is known as frame tagging. A frame tag is defined as an identifier within packets that describes the packets' VLAN membership. Frame tags can either be explicit or implicit. An explicit frame tag consists of an additional field or fields added to existing packets, marking them as belonging to one or more VLANs. An implicit frame tag is an existing field in the original packet that identifies its membership in VLANs. Figure 9.9 shows these two types of frame tags.

The explicit tag shown in Figure 9.9 modified the original packet to add the tag. This kind of tagging is done for packets that cannot support the concept of an implicit tag. Many vendors simply implement explicit tags on all packets. By doing this, the more complex analysis of implicit tags is not needed. The disadvantage with any explicit tagging is that it adds to the size of the original packet. Since most LAN technologies support packets only of sizes smaller than or equal to their Maximum Transmission Unit (MTU), it is very possible that oversized packets may

Figure 9.9

Explicit versus implicit frame tags.

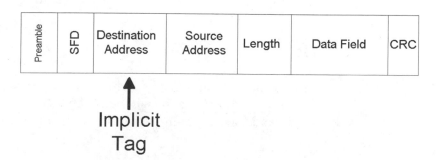

be generated on interswitch links. If this happens, there is no guarantee that the packets can be delivered. Because of this, some vendors have limited their use of explicit tagging to broadcasts, multicasts, and unknown packets. These types of packets are rarely of maximum size and as such pose almost no threat of becoming oversized.

The implicit tag is defined as the switch using some internal characteristic of the original packet to identify its VLAN. Some fields that can be used as implicit tags are the source or destination addresses and the type field and SAP fields of the LLC. An example of an implicit tag is a packet sent to the BPDU multicast address. This packet has a well-known destination address. If a VLAN switch created a BPDU VLAN, there would be no need to tag these frames in order to identify them and flood them out to only BPDU VLAN ports. Most vendors do not implement implicit tagging, since it is more difficult to utilize. If it is used, it eliminates the possibility of oversized packets and generally increases the overall efficiency of the switches' forwarding logic, since no packet modification is required.

Centralized Server Another option for VLAN distribution is a centralized VLAN server. This option creates a single entity that knows the VLAN mappings of all MAC layer users. When users enter the network, the server provides their VLAN mappings to the switches. If this model is not used with frame tagging to forward packets between switches, the server will need to tell all switches the MAC address to VLAN bindings for all users. By centralizing the VLAN definitions at a server, the network is much easier to manage, since VLANs really only exist on the server. The danger with this system is that if the server fails, the network may not continue to operate. For that reason, most vendors have moved away from this model. In almost all VLAN systems, a server will be present to create VLANs and view their operation, but it will generally not be a critical component. If the server fails in well-designed VLAN systems, the network will continue to operate.

Other VLAN Services

In addition to basic VLAN functions, most vendors' VLAN switches offer additional services to switched LANs. In addition to VLANs, some vendors add special troubleshooting tools and enhanced topology mechanisms to better design a switched LAN. This chapter will not examine these services, but when evaluating a VLAN system, it is important to know if the vendor's system can add any additional features beyond VLANs. The most common of those additional features are as follows.

1. Fully meshed topologies—the ability to use more advanced topologies beyond simple spanning tree. Some vendors offer multiple spanning trees for each VLAN, while others offer true active meshed topology algorithms. Any enhancement to the switched LAN topology that reduces or eliminates the spanning tree topology rules is desirable.

2. Directory information—some systems allow the known layer three information about end users to be accessed directly. This type of information, correlating MAC address to location to upper-layer protocol addresses (IP, IPX, etc.), can be invaluable in troubleshooting a switched LAN. If this directory is comprehensive and global, it can be viewed as an alternative to some of the RMON version 2 groups.

3. Logical topology views—a VLAN system that can display the logical and physical topology of the LAN is invaluable. Because the VLANs can change shape as users move, a VLAN system should be able to easily display the current location of a VLAN's members. This type of information is invaluable when troubleshooting or planning network capacity improvements.

4. Hybrid routing—since VLANs represent layer two broadcast domains, some form of routing must be used to connect them. Some vendors do not offer the VLAN interconnectivity methods internal to their switches. These vendors typically rely on external routers to connect VLANs. Other vendors will embed a real router in their switches. This is slightly better than the external router in that it does not require two separate devices. The real router embedded in the switch is a router and as such does force the network to be built around the router's hierarchy. The final option for routing is hybrid functions, which switch packets at layer two by understanding and resolving layer three flow to destinations in other VLANs. These devices are the most complex but usually also the fastest and most feature-rich, since they are true switches with some understanding of protocol. See Chapter 1 for more details on these layer three switching methods.

The 802.1Q Standard

As discussed previously, the term *VLAN* is used to describe a wide variety of vendors' LAN switching features. While all of the features attempt to create logical bridged networks, they do so using extremely different methods. In an attempt to standardize the definition and function of a VLAN, the IEEE 802.1Q working group has begun development of a specification for virtual bridged local area networks. This section will examine this evolving standard.

IEEE 802.1Q Introduction

VLANs are very powerful additions to a switch-based network. They allow a single switched infrastructure to support many logical LANs. They allow the separate networks to share a common backbone, and they provide the flexibility to reshape any of the logical LANs by simply changing logical rules through network management systems. Through the use of VLANs, the process of adds, moves, and changes should be significantly simplified. In large switched networks, the VLANs allow logical separation of the various types of broadcast and multicast traffic, enabling switched networks to solve the only issues preventing their further scalability. Because of these significant advantages, the VLAN has become a required feature in most networks. In order to allow this new feature to be implemented in a heterogeneous network consisting of many vendors' devices, the IEEE is developing the 802.1Q standard.

Since the IEEE 802 working group is primarily concerned with the standardization of technologies and not their market applicability, the IEEE 802.1Q standard is focused on defining only the mechanisms of the VLAN-capable switches. The standard does provide a set of functions that, if implemented as defined in 802.1Q, should allow interoperability with other vendors' 802.1Q switches. This limited scope of simply defining a basic model of VLAN-capable switches fails to provide a comprehensive VLAN definition that addresses the implementation of this technology in practical networks. This lack of practical implementation guidance and the narrow focus of addressing only a basic model of VLAN operation make this standard equal to a small subset of the features deployed by vendors years prior to this standard's ratification.

Features of 802.1Q VLANs

The general goals of the 802.1Q standard are simply to define an architecture for VLANs. This architecture includes the basic features of a VLAN system and the protocols and functional requirements of an 802.1Q VLAN switch. The actual specification is based on other IEEE 802.1 standards such as transparent bridging and spanning tree algorithm. The new feature introduced in 802.1Q is the concept of a virtual bridged network, or VLAN. In order to use IEEE 802.1Q VLANs, the standard defines an operational model of the VLAN-capable switch.

Switches implementing 802.1Q VLANs are essentially just 802.1D-compatible bridges with a modified set of ingress and egress rules, an additional protocol for identifying the VLAN capabilities of end systems or switch neighbors, and a VLAN transport mechanism based on a frame tagging implementation. Each of these three areas allows the switch some needed capability to create multiple logical bridged LANs over a common switch fabric.

New Ingress and Egress Rules   An 802.1Q-capable bridge must be able to properly deliver packets to a specified VLAN. Since the bridges are just devices with many interfaces and some forwarding logic, the VLAN switches will modify their forwarding logic to understand the concept of having multiple independent broadcast domains accessible via one bridge. The modification of the forwarding logic is based on the addition of new ingress and egress rules. These rules are used to define how to handle inbound and outbound packets. The 802.1Q-compatible switches handle inbound packets by classifying them based on the VLAN Identifier (VID) of the port they were received on. It is also possible that the switch will receive a packet on a port connected to another 802.1Q-compatible switch or an end user capable of categorizing his or her own packets into VLANs. This ingress categorization of packets involves the addition of a frame tag if needed. The frame tag indicates the VLAN ID of this packet, as well as other information related to the priority of the packet and the addressing format. This process is shown in Figure 9.10.

The packet received on port 1 in Figure 9.10 was associated with VLAN ID 12 at the ingress switch through the addition of an explicit frame tag. It is also possible that the switch could support implicitly tagged frames. An implicit tag is defined as some existing field in the

Figure 9.10

Ingress operation of
802.1Q.

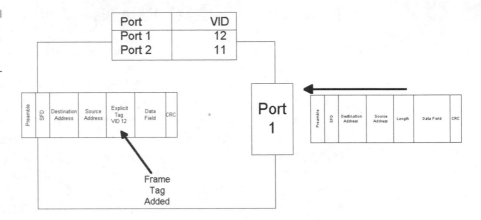

Port	VID
Port 1	12
Port 2	11

Frame
Tag
Added

packet that identifies its VLAN identity without need for modification.
Examples of such implicit tags include multicast destination addresses,
type fields, and source/destination address pairs. Once the packet is
identified as belonging to a VLAN using either implicit tagging or explicit tags, as shown in Figure 9.10, the packet must be delivered.

The delivery mechanisms of 802.1Q switches are known as the egress
rules. The switch will examine received packets and, based on their
VLAN membership, deliver them to ports that share that membership.
This process is made more complex by the fact that some ports require
that explicitly tagged packets be untagged before delivery, while other
ports, known as trunk ports, will accept explicitly tagged packets. In order for the switch to know what to do with a packet, the standard defines membership sets that specify the ports that a particular VLAN
should be delivered to. The membership set is created either through
management applications "coloring the ports" or through a dynamic
protocol called GARP VLAN Registration Protocol (GVRP), derived
from the 802.1P Generic Attribute Registration Protocol (GARP), initiated by other switches or end users supporting 802.1Q.

The membership set lists the egress ports for a particular VLAN.
Within the membership set is a subset called "the untagged set." This defines which of the ports in the membership set require that the packet
be delivered in an untagged format. Based on the list of ports in the
membership set and the untagged set, the switch will then relay the
packet to only the ports through which a particular VLAN exists. The
switch will also apply normal forwarding and filtering logic before delivering untagged unicast packets out to ports.

Figure 9.11

GVRP protocol
locations.

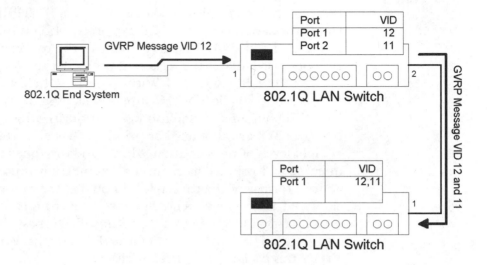

GARP VLAN Registration Protocol (GVRP) In order to support multiple switch topologies and VLAN-aware end nodes, the 802.1Q standard implements GVRP. This protocol is a signaling method used to identify VLAN membership to peer switches in the network. A switch or end system that supports specific VLANs will use GVRP to identify its capabilities to either other switches attached over the spanning tree topology or, in the case of GVRP end systems, the switch port it is attached to. Figure 9.11 shows the logical operation of GVRP in an 802.1Q network.

The communication between the end system and the 802.1Q switch uses GVRP to register that the end user supports VLAN 12. This allows the switch to forward received packets with VID 12 to the port with the end user. The communication between switches used GVRP to identify which VLANs are to be sent up or down the spanning tree link. Each switch should register with its neighbors the VLANs it supports, so that the packets with those VIDs are delivered to that switch.

Distribution Mechanism 802.1Q provides a tagging-based distribution mechanism to allow multiswitch VLAN networks. The tagging mechanism standardization is one of the most difficult areas in this standard. Since the frame formats of Ethernet, Token Ring, and FDDI are very different from one another, the 802.1Q standard has had to define several frame formats for tagging. Within the explicit tag of 802.1Q there are two major elements: a Tag Protocol ID (TPID) and a Tag Control Information field (TCI). The tag protocol ID is used in the existing Ethernet II and SNAP headers to identify the packet as a tagged packet. IEEE specified 8100 as the registered protocol type for 802.1Q tagging.

After the TPID is the TCI. Within the TCI, there are three fields. The first is a priority field. 802.1Q supports tagging of packets for not just VLAN ID but also to establish packet prioritization. Three bits of the two-byte TCI are allocated for priority. That gives the network a total of eight levels of prioritization, which can be mapped to vendor-specific queuing and priority mechanisms. The next bit is used to indicate the address format of the packet. It is known as the canonical format indicator and assists the switches in converting from Ethernet least significant bit first addressing to Token Ring/FDDI most significant bit first addressing. The final 12 bits of the TCI are the VID, indicating the VLAN this packet is associated with.

Using the GVRP mechanisms for identifying where a VLAN exists between switches, the tagging mechanism can mark a packet as a member of a specific VLAN. The packet can then be sent through the spanning tree backbone of switches and is assured of being delivered to the correct VLAN, as indicated by the VID. This tagging allows a common link between switches to transport many different VLANs' packets and still allow for correct identification of the VID of a packet.

Limitations of 802.1Q

From the above discussion about 802.1Q, we can see that the standard does provide a basic mechanism for creating multiple logical, virtual bridged LANs over a common switched LAN. The technology used is sufficient to achieve that goal. The standard is, however, less than sufficient in its goal of allowing vendor interoperability in a VLAN network, because it lacks any mention of how to use VLANs and how to agree on the use of VLANs between switches. This is illustrated in the example of two 802.1Q switches attempting to interoperate. If one switch defines VID 12 as the SALES VLAN, because members of a company's sales department populate its ports, there is no guarantee that VID 12 on other switches will have the same meaning. In reality, the other switch, possibly from another vendor, has defined VID 12 as a VLAN for all Apple-Talk users on that switch. Now, the same VID exists in a common network with two very different uses. Based on 802.1Q, the two user groups would be combined into one VLAN and thus see each other's packets.

This example could be avoided simply by making sure that each switch uses the same context for VLAN VID 12. Unfortunately, no mechanism is present in 802.1Q to identify the context of a VLAN. It is entirely up to the vendor providing the switch and then the system administrator to make sure that a particular VID has universally consistent significance on the LAN. That assumption highlights a major failing of this standard in addressing the most desired type of standard: a standard resulting in intervendor VLAN consistency.

The second major limit of 802.1Q is that it focuses only on VLANs as logical bridged networks contained in selected switch ports. From the discussion at the beginning of this chapter, we learned that many vendors have enhanced their own VLAN systems to solve other switch network issues. These include enhancing the switch topology with trunking and meshed topologies, adding intelligent broadcast control, and advanced troubleshooting interfaces. The 802.1Q standard does not address any enhancement to switched LANs other than the basic VLAN model. Because of this, almost every vendor shipping VLAN-capable products would have to disable very useful, but proprietary, features to be compatible with other vendors' 802.1Q switches. Most real-world customers will not sacrifice features that allow for better designed and implemented switched LANs just to implement an interoperable subset of what they already have.

802.1Q will be adopted by most vendors as a standardized frame tag format and as a protocol to allow end-system VLAN registration (GVRP). Some vendors may even utilize GVRP as a mechanism to share VLAN information with their peers. However, it is very likely that most vendors will not sacrifice their more advanced VLAN mechanisms to be fully compatible with this standard. Even if vendors do claim compatibility with 802.1Q, it is unlikely that they will transparently interoperate with other vendors' switches that also claim 802.1Q compliance.

Summary

The virtual LAN is a significant enhancement for switched LANs. Even though the term describes a wide variety of vendor-specific implementations and the IEEE standard for the technology is lacking, the technology is still very important to building larger switched networks. With the addition of VLANs, the switched LAN becomes more flexible and thus more useful. The VLANs can be used for services as simple as creating flexible boundary subnets in a router-based network or for more complex services such as categorizing and controlling protocol-specific broadcasts in a large-scale flat-switched LAN. Because of the lack of useful standardization of the technology, a switched network administrator should choose the most feature-rich VLAN solution that is the least proprietary to the existing systems on the LAN. A VLAN solution should solve the broadcast and adds, moves, and changes issues in your LAN in addition to any other features. If it does this and does not impact existing well-behaved devices on your LAN, it is a viable product.

RMON Introduction

Remote Monitoring, or RMON, is one of the most talked about technologies in networking today. It has become an almost mandatory part of every networking system. The interesting element of this demand is that few people know what RMON really is, and fewer still know how to utilize it effectively to manage their networks. The fact is that RMON is valuable and because of this should be one of the primary management tools utilized in networks today. This chapter will provide a complete description of RMON and an interpretation of how to utilize each facet of RMON to assist in managing a network. Through this understanding, the reader should have a much better perspective about utilizing RMON to assist in the baselining and monitoring of networks.

Standard

RMON is defined by the Internet Engineering Task Force (IETF) as several Requests For Comments (RFCs). The specific RFCs are RFC 1757 and RFC 1513.

These RFCs describe the framework for the RMON Management Information Base, or MIB. For those unfamiliar with the Simple Network Management Protocol (SNMP), a MIB is simply a listing of defined data elements and their appropriate syntax and identifier. One could view a MIB as the fields in a database. An example of a MIB is the IETF Bridge MIB, which defines all the information an IEEE 802.1D-compliant bridge should provide to a network management system if asked. MIBs provide some well-known structure to the information a particular system contains. The Bridge MIB, for instance, contains spanning tree information and information about the source address table. The MIB does not define how to collect data or how to use data. It simply specifies how to organize data so that other systems can access them.

The RMON MIB's main purpose is to facilitate a distributed management system consisting of two elements: RMON probes and RMON managers. The RMON probes are the devices attached to the physical network responsible for collection of real data. The RMON managers are usually computing devices that retrieve the RMON information and process and present it to the system administrator. The RMON MIB does not explicitly define how the probe should collect the data or how the manager should present these data. Instead, the RMON MIB defines how the information is to be categorized in a common fashion so that the manager and probe can exchange the data using a standard format. The overall goals of RMON are defined in RFC 1757.

- Offline operation: There are sometimes conditions when a management station will not be in constant contact with its remote monitoring devices. This is sometimes by design in an attempt to lower communications costs (especially when communicating over a WAN or dialup link) or by accident, since network failures affect communications between the management station and the probe. For this reason, this MIB allows a probe to be configured to perform diagnostics and to collect statistics continuously, even when communication with the management station may not be possible or efficient. The probe may then attempt to notify the management station when an exceptional condition occurs. Thus, even in circumstances where communication between the management station and the probe is not continuous, information regarding fault, performance, and configuration can be continuously accumulated and communicated to the management station conveniently and efficiently.

- Proactive monitoring: Given the resources available on the monitor, it is helpful for it to run diagnostics and to log network performance continuously. The monitor is always available at the onset of any failure. It can notify the management station of the failure and can store historical statistical information about the failure. This historical information can be played back by the management station in an attempt to perform further diagnosis regarding the cause of the problem.

- Problem detection and reporting: The monitor can be configured to recognize conditions, most notably error conditions, and to check for them continuously. When one of these conditions occurs, the event may be logged, and management stations may be notified in a number of ways.

- Value-added data: Because a remote monitoring device represents a network resource dedicated exclusively to network management functions, and because it is located directly on the monitored portion of the network, the remote network monitoring device has the opportunity to add significant value to the data it collects. By highlighting those hosts on the network that generate the most traffic or errors, the probe can give the management station precisely the information it needs to solve a class of problems.

■ Multiple managers: An organization may have multiple management stations for different units of the organization, for different functions (e.g., engineering and operations), and in an attempt to provide disaster recovery. Because environments with multiple management stations are common, the remote network monitoring device has to deal with more than one management station, potentially using its resources concurrently.

Elements of an RMON System

An RMON system consists of two basic elements: probes and managers. Any number of either can be utilized, but it is common to have RMON probes attached to each segment of the network and one or two managers displaying the probes' information. Figure 10.1 illustrates a typical RMON configuration.

RMON probes can exist as dedicated devices or can be a software application embedded in other types of networking hardware. It is not unusual today to find RMON probe functions as part of many vendors' LAN switches. This combination of switching and RMON provides a cost-effective method of incorporating RMON into a switched network. The RMON managers are software applications that either operate as stand-alone applications or are integrated into any of the various network management platforms, such as HP OpenView, SunNET Manager, Spectrum, and NetView 6000.

One of the most significant advantages of RMON as an architecture is that by standardizing the definitions of the probe data, any vendor's RMON-compliant probe should be able to communicate with any vendor's RMON-compliant management applications.

Ethernet RMON Groups

RFC 1757 defines the RMON MIB for Ethernet networks. The MIB is divided into nine groups, based on functionality. In order to be RMON compliant, a probe or manager need not implement the entire MIB; instead, the probe or manager can implement any combination of the

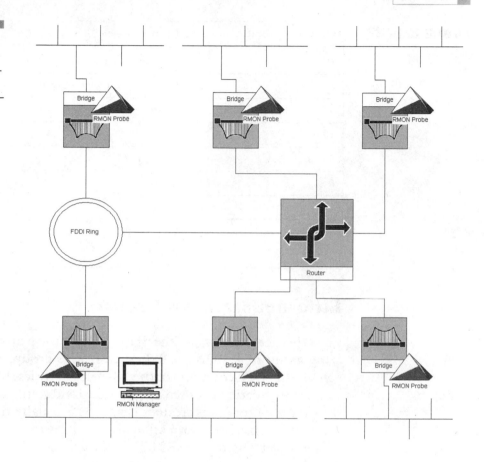

Figure 10.1

Sample RMON probe and manager placement.

nine groups, as long as the groups that are implemented are implemented fully. The nine groups are shown in Table 10.1.

Each of these groups provides some service to manage or monitor a network segment. On RMON probes, it is common to see only a portion of the RMON groups implemented. On simple RMON probes, groups 1, 2, 3, and 9 are implemented. On more complex probes, groups 4, 5, and 6 may be added. On the most complex RMON probes, groups 7 and 8, and even some vendor-specific additional proprietary groups, are added. It is important to note that in most cases, only the basic four RMON groups will be needed, while in other situations all nine groups may be needed. In the following sections, each group will be discussed and its applications examined. By understanding the function of these groups, choosing which groups are appropriate will be far more understandable.

TABLE 10.1

RFC 1757 RMON
Groups

Group Number	Group Name
1	Ethernet statistics
2	Ethernet history (and history control)
3	Alarm
4	Host
5	HostTopN
6	Matrix
7	Filter
8	Packet capture
9	Event

Ethernet Statistics Group

The Ethernet statistics, or EtherStats, group is the primary statistics gathering group of RMON for Ethernet. In this group, a table is defined containing 32-bit counters for the Ethernet statistics shown in Table 10.2.

The information counted in this group is absolute data starting from the time the group was created. That time is usually the time the probe was turned on. This information accumulates for as long as the probe operates; to be useful, the RMON manager should be able to show not just the absolute counters but also the difference between samples (called delta) and the peak values seen. By having delta information, a rate can be seen; and by having peak values, absolute maximum values can be determined. In switched networks, this group can provide at-a-glance data showing if the error rates, packet rates, or load is potentially excessive—for instance, if there are very few errors in the statistics group, there is usually no error issue on the network and there is no need to look in other groups for more details.

Ethernet History Group

The Ethernet history group is actually defined in RMON as two groups: the history control group and the Ethernet history group. The history

TABLE 10.2

RMON
EtherStats
Group

Statistic	Definition
Drop events	This counter defines the number of times that the RMON probe was unable to accurately count incoming packets. If this counter is incremented, the probes' data are to be considered inaccurate. The degree of inaccuracy is not measured in this counter, because each dropped event could have consisted of any number of packets not being analyzed. There is no counter indicating how many packets were not analyzed. Normal causes of dropped events are high bursts of traffic, high sustained traffic levels, or a lack of resources (CPU capacity primarily) on the RMON probe.
Octets	This counter displays the number of bytes received by the RMON probe. Both bytes of good and bad packets are counted. This counter is an absolute measure of the traffic level on the network segment. Some RMON managers use this statistic to calculate the percent utilization of a segment, using a simple formula defined in the RFC: $$Utilization = \frac{Packets \bullet (9.6 + 6.4) + (Octets \bullet 0.8)}{Interval \bullet 10,000}$$
Packets	This counter displays the total number of packets received by the probe. All packets processed are counted here, including bad packets. This counter is not a good measure of overall utilization, based on the fact that the size of the packet is not specified. A 64-byte packet is counted just as a 1,500-byte packet would be.
Broadcasts	This counter shows the total number of packets seen at the probe with a broadcast destination of 0xFFFFFFFFFFFF. This counter is extremely useful in measuring broadcast rates and peaks of a segment. It is critical to note that this counter should not be used in relation to the packet counter above to gauge broadcast load. Some RMON manager applications will display a breakdown of packets seen percent by type (broadcast, multicast, and unicast). This view is deceiving in that it may show 30 percent broadcasts on a network, which could be taken inadvertently to mean 30 percent of network capacity is being used by broadcasts. Instead, the counter really is saying that of the total packets seen, 30 percent were broadcasts. The total could have been ten packets with three being broadcasts.

TABLE 10.2

(continued)

Statistic	Definition
Multicasts	This counter shows the total number of packets seen at the probe with a multicast destination (any address with the group bit set but not the broadcast address). This counter is extremely useful in measuring multicast rates and peaks of a segment. It is critical to note that this counter should not be used in relation to the packet counter above to gauge multicast load. Some RMON manager applications will display a breakdown of packets seen percent by type (broadcast, multicast, and unicast). This view is deceiving in that it may show 30 percent multicasts on a network, which could be taken inadvertently to mean 30 percent of network capacity is being used by multicasts. Instead, the counter really is saying that of the total packets seen, 30 percent were multicasts. The total could have been ten packets with three being multicasts. This counter, combined with the broadcast counter, provides some measure of the total nonunicast packet count on the network.
CRC alignment errors	All packets seen having a length in bytes ranging from 64 to 1,518 that contain a bad frame check sequence (also known as the CRC) are grouped into this counter. RMON does not distinguish between a true Ethernet CRC error and a true Ethernet alignment error. True CRC errors are valid size frames with a bad CRC but an integral number of octets, while true alignment errors are frames not having an integral number of octets, resulting in a bad CRC calculation. In most cases, these two errors simply mean a valid frame was corrupted during transmission via some physical layer fault. Examples of this kind of failure include external noise and fractured fiber cables caused by exceeding the bend radius' of the cable. This counter is an excellent measure of the overall error rate on the segment.
Undersized packets	RMON does not define packets violating Ethernet frame size limits as "runts" and "giants." Instead, RMON defines four errors, which specify valid frames that violate the Ethernet maximum or minimum size limits and invalid frames that violate these rules. Undersized packets are defined as valid Ethernet packets that are simply less than 64 bytes in size. This means that these packets were generated as valid by a real end user and have not been corrupted in transition. If a network has a large number of undersized packets, there is usually an application violating the Ethernet minimum size limits.

TABLE 10.2

(continued)

Statistic	Definition
Oversized packets	Oversized packets are simply valid packets greater than 1,518 bytes in size. These packets were generated by a valid end system and are usually the result of an application ignoring the maximum Ethernet frame size. In some cases, transitional devices such as FDDI or Token Ring to Ethernet bridges could fail and inadvertently forward larger FDDI or Token-Ring packets onto the Ethernet. This failure is very rare.
Fragments	The fragment counter specifies how many invalid (bad CRC) undersized frames were seen on the segment. Fragments are usually the result of a collision late in the packet transmission but can also be caused by external noise damaging frames beyond recognition.
Jabbers	Oversized frames that fail their CRC check are categorized as jabbers. Usually this is the result of a transmitter failure, which generates an invalid data stream. As such it is usually an indication of an adapter card failure on the segment.
Collisions	This counter defines the count of collisions seen on the segment. Ethernet's access method, CSMA/CD, allows for collision events as a normal part of an operating Ethernet. As the physical size of the segment grows or the number of users increases, it is usual to see higher collision rates occur. Do not view this counter as an error condition. What is important to note is the relationship between the number of packets and the number of collisions. In an operating network under low load, a collision rate of less than 1 percent should be the norm. However, in the same network under high load, a collision rate of 20 percent might not be unusual. Monitoring this counter for obviously high percentages based on packet load is a useful tool in detecting physical layer failures, such as failing terminators in 10Base-2 and 10Base-5 coaxial networks.
Pkts 64 octets	This counter shows the number of analyzed packets 64 bytes in size. Usually a packet this size contains less than 64 bytes of relevant data but was padded to meet the Ethernet minimum size limit. This counter usually indicates the amount of negotiation and acknowledgment type packets seen, such as IP ARP packets. The counter is not very useful in troubleshooting but is useful in determining how much of the total packet rate is made up of small frames. Small frames are usually indicators of overhead on the network, not real data transfer such as file transfers.

TABLE 10.2

(continued)

Statistic	Definition
Pkts 65 to 127 octets	This counter indicates the number of packets sized 65 to 127 bytes. Usually these packets are associated with negotiation and acknowledgments but not to such a degree as 64-byte packets are.
Pkts 128 to 255 octets	All packets between 128 and 255 bytes in size are counted here. Usually this size of packet is used for real data transfers. This is not an optimal size to move large files, since larger-sized packets will transfer more data with less overhead.
Pkts 256 to 511 octets	All packets between 256 and 511 bytes are counted here. Usually this size packet is related to real data transfer.
Pkts 512 to 1,023 octets	This counter defines the number of 512- to 1,023-byte packets counted. This size of packet is used for real data transfer. A large percentage of packets in this size range are a good indicator that your network is using reasonable size packets to move data. This results in a relatively efficient network.
Pkts 1,024 to 1,518 octets	All packets counted that are between 1,024 and 1,518 bytes in size are listed here. In most cases, packets of this size are desirable when moving data, since they transfer a great deal of data with minimal overhead of headers and framing.

*Bend radius is a term used to describe the maximum curve a fiber cable can tolerate and still operate. If fiber cable is bent further than the bend radius, there is a possibility that the fiber core can break apart or fracture and lead to excess dB loss or even loss of connectivity. Ethernet alignment errors are usually seen in the case of a fractured fiber that is still marginally operational.

control group defines the parameters the history group is to operate under. The main purpose of the history group is to provide a long- or short-term sampling of statistics internal to the probe. This group gathers statistics similar to the Ethernet statistics group but does so in terms of time-specific samples. The advantage of the history group over the statistics group is that the history group provides statistics describing the operation of the segment in terms of when the actual statistics took place. The statistics group only provides absolute statistics about the network with no time reference. Having an understanding of when a particular statistic took place is invaluable when trying to gauge the behavior of a network or determine what condition the network was in when a failure occurred.

The history group allows a view into the segment's health, showing times of peak and low values and trends on the network. An example of this kind of information is the broadcast rate measurement of a network. If RMON history shows that the broadcast rate is always about ten packets per second, it is most likely that those broadcasts are periodic advertisements from routers and servers. On the other hand, if the rate is usually two packets per second, but the history shows a peak of 30 packets per second every morning, that is most likely the result of users logging in and finding their servers. This kind of information is extremely useful if you are trying to understand the cause of broadcasts on a segment so that you can reduce their rate or at least control their growth as you increase the size of your switched network.

The history group operates based on a fixed-size database. When you enable this group, you must specify two parameters: duration and interval. The duration is the total time the RMON probe is to store statistics. The interval is the time between successive samples. RMON requires these parameters because the RMON probes have limited memory space for data storage. By fixing the size of the RMON history database, the probe can guarantee that it will always have space to store and deliver the requested historical data. If the probe does not have enough memory to create the specified history, it will create a history of the requested duration but with a larger interval. An example RMON history setup is shown in Figure 10.2. It shows a history of two hours' duration with samples every minute.

In Figure 10.2, it can be seen that this RMON history database is fixed at 120 samples, each showing one minute of statistical information. As time goes by, the database remains fixed at 120 samples but slides. At any given time, if you examine this RMON history, you can see the last 120 samples. All older information is discarded. This concept is very important to understand, because, when RMON history is configured, the proper duration must be chosen to ensure that data of interest will not be discarded by the time they are needed. RMON history configuration will vary, based on the use of the information, but, as a general guideline, each segment should have a short-term and a long-term RMON history configured. Table 10.3 lists a typical history configuration.

The RMON history group gathers statistics similar to that of the Ethernet statistics group. Table 10.4 lists the actual statistics gathered in each RMON history sample.

Figure 10.2
RMON history
operation over time.

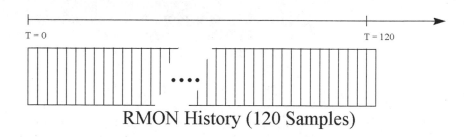

RMON History (120 Samples)

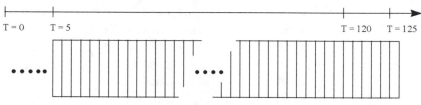

RMON History (120 Samples)

TABLE 10.3

Sample RMON
History
Configuration

Interval	Duration	Uses
1 minute	4 hours	This history provides very detailed statistics at one-minute intervals. It is best used to react to network problems immediately after they occur. The four-hour duration is based on the average response time needed from when the issue occurs to when the system administrator can go to the RMON manager and view the RMON statistics at the time of the failure. If your response time is different, this duration can be adjusted.
1 hour	2.5 days	This history provides a long-term analysis tool. By gathering statistics in one-hour intervals for 2.5 days, the system administrator can gain an understanding of the behavior of the network. This kind of history is most useful when determining when traffic peaks occur, when error rates rise, and how broadcast and multicast rates fluctuate over time. Based on the memory of the RMON probe, this duration can be extended or reduced as needed but should always be at least one average workday.

TABLE 10.4

RMON History
Statistics

Statistic	Explanation
Drop events	The number of dropped events in this sample. This indicates that the probe could not process all packets seen during this sample. If absolutely accurate statistics are required, this sample should be discarded.
Octets	The count of bytes seen in all frames processed during the sample. Note that even byte counts for bad packets are added to this statistic.
Pkts	All packets counted by the probe are shown here for this sample.
Broadcast pkts	This counter shows the number of broadcast (destination = 0xffffffffffff) packets seen during the sample period. This is very useful in trending broadcast rates on a network.
Multicast pkts	All multicast packets are counted here. This counter, combined with the broadcast packets counter, provides an indicator of the total nonunicast packets seen on the segment during this sample.
CRC alignment errors	This counter is incremented for each valid packet with a bad CRC seen in this sample. When troubleshooting error conditions in the physical network, it is very helpful to know when the physical errors occurred. If the problem is consistent, a faulty component or cable is likely to be the cause. If the errors occur only in some samples, the problem is more likely to be a noise source.
Undersize pkts	Any valid packet under 64 bytes in size is counted here.
Oversize pkts	Any valid packet over 1,518 bytes in size is counted here for each sample.
Fragments	Any invalid CRC packet under 64 bytes in size is counted here for each sample.
Jabbers	Any invalid CRC packet over 1,518 bytes in size is counted here for each sample.
Collisions	The total number of collision events seen in this sample is counted here. This counter is not an indicator of errors, since collisions are a natural part of the CSMA/CD access method of Ethernet. If the collision rate is excessive in relation to the total packet count seen, there may be a physical problem on the network.
Utilization	This counter is new in the history group. Using the formula introduced in the statistics group, the history group stores the calculated utilization of the network during this sample. This counter allows for examination of network bandwidth usage over time.

RMON Alarm Group

RMON probes are valuable tools for automatic monitoring of your network. The alarm group of RMON, in conjunction with the event group (group 9), allows the probe to be configured to watch for any statistical condition and automatically notify the RMON manager of its occurrence. This is extremely valuable to a system administrator, because it is simply impossible for a support staff to watch all statistics on all segments to detect error conditions. By using the RMON probe's alarm and event groups, the responsibility of constant monitoring is given to the RMON probe. If a specified condition occurs, the RMON probe will either log the event locally for future examination or send an SNMP trap message to the RMON manager. The trap should then be used to trigger some indication to the support staff that there is an error condition occurring. The actual indication the manager will provide is not specified by RMON. Most current management software packages will at least flash the probe's icon yellow or red, but some implementations can automatically generate trouble tickets or even page a support person.

The actual operation of the alarm group is based on a hysteresis mechanism. This allows a more accurate indication of when a condition begins and ends. Figure 10.3 illustrates this hysteresis mechanism's operation.

From Figure 10.3, it is obvious that the RMON alarm group only activates an alarm indication if the statistic being counted crosses either a high- or low-point mark called rising and falling thresholds. It is also important to note that once a rising threshold is crossed and an alarm generated, another rising alarm cannot be set until the corresponding falling alarm is activated. This process defines the start of an error condition and the end of an error condition, based on that condition being defined as the statistic being monitored between the rising and falling value. In the example in Figure 10.3, the error condition is defined as a broadcast packet rate between 350 and 500 in a ten-second time frame. The rising and falling alarms indicate the beginning and end of this condition. Even though the rising threshold was crossed twice, only the initial rising alarm is valid.

To use the RMON alarm group, several parameters must be configured for each alarm. Table 10.5 lists the parameters defining a specific RMON alarm.

Figure 10.3

RMON alarm operation for broadcast packets— 10 seconds.

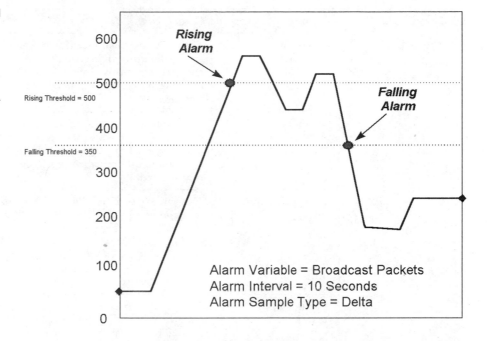

Rising Threshold = 500

Falling Threshold = 350

Alarm Variable = Broadcast Packets
Alarm Interval = 10 Seconds
Alarm Sample Type = Delta

TABLE 10.5

RMON Alarm Group Configuration Parameters

Parameter	Description
Alarm interval	This variable specifies the time data will be sampled to determine if a threshold has been crossed.
Alarm variable	The RMON alarm group can set thresholds against any statistic in the probe's MIB. Typically the alarms will be set against values in the Ethernet statistics group, but there is no restriction limiting alarms to only RMON values. If the probe supported other MIBs based on vendor-specific counters or even other standards (such as FDDI SMT or MIB II), an alarm could be configured against any statistic counted by the device. Alarms can only be set against statistics that are counted as integers.
Alarm sample type	This variable specifies whether the sample counted will be analyzed for the change since the last sample (delta value) or analyzed as an absolute number. If the statistic is a counter, such as those in the Ethernet statistics group, a delta value is appropriate because the counter will always increase. If the statistic is one that shows a current rate, such as load, the absolute value is better used.

TABLE 10.5

(continued)

Parameter	Description
Alarm rising threshold	The rising threshold specifies the value this statistic must cross in an upward direction for the rising alarm to be triggered. Once this value is crossed, a falling threshold must occur before a second rising alarm can be generated.
Alarm falling threshold	The falling threshold specifies the value this statistic must cross in a downward direction for the falling alarm to be triggered. Once this value is crossed, a rising threshold must occur before a second falling alarm can be generated.
Alarm rising event index	This variable specifies the RMON event that will occur once the rising threshold is crossed. The actual event is defined in the event group of RMON. Usual events are the logging of this alarm in a local table on the probe, the generation of an SNMP trap to a network management station, or both of these actions. See the following section for more details.
Alarm falling event index	This variable specifies the RMON event that will occur once the falling threshold is crossed. The actual event is defined in the event group of RMON. Usual events are the logging of this alarm in a local table on the probe, the generation of an SNMP trap to a network management station, or both of these actions. See the following section for more details.

Through the use of the alarm group, RMON probes can be configured to watch for almost any measurable condition on the network. This feature allows system administrators to focus only on the events being seen from the RMON probes rather than the actual statistics in question. A properly configured RMON alarm system could generate alarms when broadcast and multicast rates seem high, when error rates increase, and when utilization grows beyond a comfortable level. All of this monitoring could be done without any of the system administrator's time being dedicated to the tasks. All the system administrator must do is watch for new events (traps) from the network's RMON probes.

Host Group

In addition to examining packets for statistical data related to the Ethernet statistics and history groups, the RMON probe has the capacity to examine packets in terms of the stations sending or receiving the data. The host, HostTopN, and matrix groups are generally implemented together on more advanced RMON probes to allow this kind of station-specific analysis.

The host group defines a database consisting of all MAC layer addresses seen by the probe and the corresponding statistics related to that station's activity. Using the host group, a system administrator can view the activity of any end station in terms of the statistics listed in Table 10.6.

TABLE 10.6

RMON Host Group Statistics

Host Group Statistic	Description
Host address	The Ethernet, Token Ring, or other physical layer address of the host whose statistics are listed in the remaining counters.
Host creation order	This value indicates the relative order of creation for the host address. The lower the number the older the address. An entry of 1 would indicate that this address was the first host address seen by the RMON probe. It is important to note that the probe can discard old entries in this table if it is running out of memory in order to add new addresses.
Host in pkts	The number of good packets sent to this address. Who sent them is not the function of the host group. The matrix group will provide that information.
Host out pkts	The number of packets (good or ones with errors) sent from this address onto the segment. This also does not indicate their final destination; that is the role of the matrix group.
Host in octets	The number of bytes contained in good packets sent to this address.
Host out octets	The number of bytes contained in all packets sent from this address. This counter is a good measure of relative utilization of this segment by address. If the system administrator is curious about which devices generate the most traffic, the ones with the greatest value in this counter are a rough estimate. That kind of information is useful in determining which stations should be connected to the network using faster technology such as a dedicated switch port.

TABLE 10.6

(continued)

Host Group Statistic	Description
Host out errors	This counter indicates the number of bad packets sent by this address. This counter is useful in determining the source of errors once the Ethernet statistics or history groups indicate that the segment error rate is unacceptable. It is important to note that there can be many causes of errors and packet corruption before the packet reaches the RMON probe. The cable could be faulty, external noise could be affecting the signal, or the adapter card could be defective. If this counter is indicating errors, all of these possibilities must be examined to determine the actual cause of the errors.
Host out broadcast pkts	This counter shows the total good packets sent from this address to the broadcast address of 0xFFFFFFFFFFFF. This and the multicast out counter are excellent measures of which stations are the cause of the segment's broadcast rate. It is usual to see traditional routers and servers generate the majority of the broadcast and multicast traffic on any segment.
Host out multicast pkts	This counter provides the total number of multicast packets sent from this address. Used with the broadcast counter above, these counters can show the absolute number of nonunicast packets sent from any station on the network.

It is important to realize that this group is showing all addresses seen on this physical segment, not just the actual devices connected to this segment. Figure 10.4 shows a typical host table on one RMON probe's port in a network consisting of several segments.

Examining the data seen in the host table of RMON probe 1, it is obvious that this table includes information about end stations on the probe's physical segment (X and Y) and end stations on other segments (Z, B, and A). What also must be noted is that only stations attached directly to the probe's segment will have absolutely accurate counters in this table. Devices such as user Z may show up in this table as they send broadcasts and multicasts or if they participate in a conversation with a user on the probe's segment. The data in the probe's host table, however, would only reflect those situations and would know nothing about the communications this address was involved in that did not cross the probe's segment. The conversation between Z and B is an example of information that probe 1 would never see and thus never count.

Figure 10.4
Example RMON
host data.

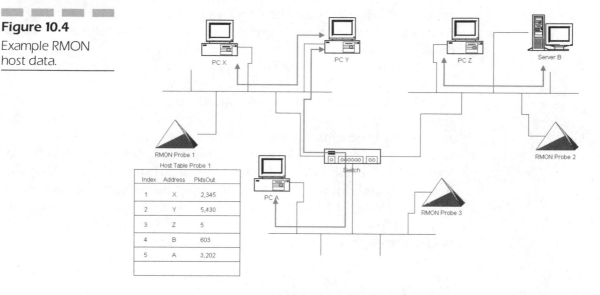

Figure 10.4
Example RMON
host data.

Host Table Probe 1

Index	Address	PktsOut
1	X	2,345
2	Y	5,430
3	Z	5
4	B	603
5	A	3,202

The function of this group is to gather general statistics about the activity of end users on the network. Even though any one probe cannot count the traffic seen on all segments involving an address, it can count the total inbound and outbound communications for users on its local segment. Additionally, the broadcast and multicast counters must be accurate for all users on the entire switched network. This is simply due to the fact that nonunicast packets are flooded to all segments in a switching system and thus to all RMON probes in the switched network. This fact makes the host group a very valuable tool in determining the source of broadcast and multicast traffic on a network.

RMON HostTopN Group

The HostTopN group operates as an enhancement to the host group. The purpose of this group is to generate reports based on the host group's data. The reports generated specify a listing of the top N devices generating a specific statistic. N is a number specified when configuring this group. An example of a HostTopN configuration could be to find the top ten addresses for the broadcast out statistic over the next 60 minutes. Once the group is configured by specifying the statistic, time frame, and number of hosts N, the RMON probe examines the host table for the specified duration. No information can be seen until the duration is met. At that time, the RMON probe provides a list of the top N addresses generating that statistic. The list should be in order and should display the rate of the statistic, not the absolute value.

The main purpose of the HostTopN is to add some time reference to the statistics in the host group. While the host group provides information about each address, it does not specify any time frame for those statistics. Using the HostTopN, the system administrator can now automatically generate answers to questions such as, "Which stations are generating the most broadcasts per second on the network over the next eight hours?" These data could be obtained manually by resetting the host group and extracting the statistics eight hours later and then manually calculating the top broadcast out addresses; however, it is automated in HostTopN. This group makes the answers to questions about end-system activity much more accessible.

RMON Matrix Group

The RMON matrix group is a tool similar to the host group in that it provides statistics about end systems. It is more advanced than the host group in that, while the statistics of the host group identified the packets that were sent to *or* from any address, the matrix group defines the statistics in terms of the addresses they were sent to *and* from. The actual form of the matrix group is a table listing all source to destination pairs and the associated statistics. Table 10.7 defines the statistics provided in the matrix group.

It should be noted that the actual form of the matrix group internal to the RMON probe is really two tables. One table counts statistics from source to destination, while another counts statistics from destination to source. This fact is not particularly important, because most RMON management software displays this information in one large table listing source to destination pairs and their statistics. Based on this format, if a system administrator wanted to see the total statistics between two addresses, two entries would need to be used: one from source to destination and one from destination to source.

The matrix group can be useful in gauging the total activity between users. There are many other tools that also provide this capability and can do so based not just on hardware addresses but on protocols and applications. Because other tools, such as network analyzers, can give more details about the communications between a pair of users, RMON matrix is not widely used for this purpose.

TABLE 10.7

RMON Matrix
Group
Statistics

Matrix Group Statistic	Description
Source address	The source of this particular pair of addresses.
Destination address	The destination address of this pair of addresses.
Pkts	The total packets (valid and invalid) sent from the source address to the destination address. This counter describes the one-way communication between these two devices.
Octets	This counter shows the total number of bytes transmitted from the source address to the destination address. This statistic is a good measure of relative utilization of the network between these two devices in one direction. To provide a realistic perspective of how these two devices are used the network, it is important to also find the matrix group entry showing the destination to source information.
Errors	This counter shows the total number of bad packets sent from the source to the destination address. This counter is useful in troubleshooting connectivity issues between two devices. An example would be if an end user had difficulty communicating to a server. If the RMON matrix between the two addresses showed a great number of packets with errors, there is a physical layer issue, which may be the real cause of the connectivity problems.

RMON Filter Group and
Packet Capture Group

The RMON filter group is usually only implemented on dedicated RMON probes, due to the large amount of processing that must take place to use this group effectively. The purpose of the filter group is to allow the RMON probe to monitor for packets matching any user-defined filter. If the packets match, they may be counted and optionally captured in a buffer defined by the packet capture group for further analysis. This is exactly the same operation that a network analyzer such as a Network General Sniffer would provide on a network. The advantage of using the filter group to do this analysis and potential capture is based on the fact that the RMON probe is already on the segment performing other functions. The RMON probe and its management software are usually not as sophisticated as a true network analyzer. If all that is necessary is simple analysis, then the RMON probe's filter and packet capture groups may be sufficient. If advanced decoding and analysis are required, then a true network analyzer is the better option for the task.

The filter group operates through the use of bit-masked filters. The bit masks are the binary representation of the value the filter is looking for. Since the filter is a bit mask, any sequence of binary digits can be filtered and thus any type of data packet can be filtered. It is possible to set filters on any protocol, such as IP, IPX, and Banyan. It is also possible to filter on fields internal to the protocols such as IP addresses, IPX sockets, or even subprotocols such as User Datagram Protocol (UDP) and Sequenced Packet Exchange (SPX). In fact, any uniquely identifiable data can be filtered. This may sound like a tremendously powerful tool, and it is, but with that flexibility comes the complexity of configuration. In order to set a filter, one must know the necessary bit mask for the data in question. RMON does not provide any guidance as to what specific filters to use; instead, it provides a very flexible mechanism to do bit-masked filtering. Because of the complexity in determining a properly offset bit mask to find a particular protocol or application, the RMON management applications are usually preconfigured with several common protocol and application filters. It is usually the case that the more complex and sophisticated the RMON management application, the more useful the filter and packet capture groups will be.

Once a filter is defined, the RMON probe will evaluate all packets seen for either a match or no match against the filter. The filter group can be configured to count the number of matches and mismatches seen by the probe for all filters. It is then optional whether or not to implement the packet capture group to store packets that either match or do not match the filter. The packet capture group operates using a fixed-size, predefined buffer. Before using the packet capture, the probe must be configured to specify the buffer parameters listed in Table 10.8.

Once the buffer is configured, the actual operation of the RMON filter and packet capture groups can begin. The process is shown in Figure 10.5.

In Figure 10.5, the process involved in filter and packet capture is shown. This process can be resource intensive, because each packet seen by the RMON probe must be compared to all filters defined. Additionally, the probe must dedicate memory to store the captured packets. Because of the resource requirements needed to operate these groups, only the most advanced probes will implement them. These groups can be

TABLE 10.8

Configuration
Parameters for
RMON Packet
Capture Buffers

Packet Capture	Description
Control channel index	Identifies the source of packets being sent to this buffer. This should match a defined channel in the filter group. It is usual, when configuring the filter in the RMON management application, that the packet capture buffer be configured at the same time.
Control full action	The RMON probe can be set to lock the buffer when it becomes full so as not to lose any packets. It can also be configured to allow the buffer to wrap when it becomes full. This wrapping action will overwrite the oldest packets stored as new packets are received from the filter group. It is usually recommended to use the lock option if you are looking for the first instances of a particular packet. An example of this is if the first-time login process always failed for a particular device but subsequent retries were successful. By locking the buffer, there is a guarantee that the first packets will be in the buffer when the management application retrieves the packets for analysis. A wrapping buffer is useful if the packets being watched for are not dependent on time or the required packets are to be the most recently seen. An example of proper use of a wrapping buffer is the capture of router and server updates. The most recently generated server advertisements and routing table updates are usually the ones of interest, since they reflect the current state of the network. A wrapping buffer set against filters for RIP or SAP packets would allow immediate retrieval of the most recent instances of those packets.
Capture slice size	This value defines how much of the captured packet is to be stored into the buffer. In most troubleshooting situations, only the first several hundred bytes are important, since they contain the header information listing protocols and addresses. This setting allows the packet capture to truncate the packet storing only the number of bytes specified here. When using this value, it is important to recognize that by selecting a portion of the packet to be stored, some data may be lost on long complex packets; but usually this provides for a significant number of additional packets that will be able to fit into the buffer. Based on the type of analysis the probe is performing, this trade-off between packet size and quantity of packets must be decided. If the analysis is looking for obscure packets or packets whose entire data field is significant (such as routing updates), the full packet size should be captured. If the analysis is concerned with packets whose header information is the only necessary data, then a truncated packet should be stored.

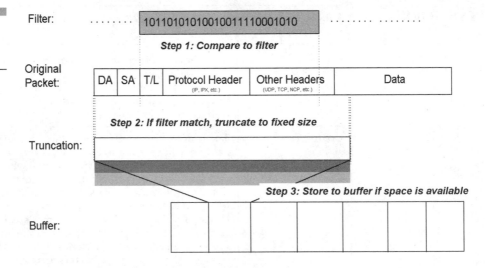

Figure 10.5

Filter and packet
capture operation.

very useful in certain situations but are generally viewed as less capable
than traditional dedicated LAN analyzers.

Event Group

The RMON event group is defined as the last group of RMON RFC
1757. It is best to discuss this group in term of its relationship to the other
three basic RMON groups: Ethernet statistics, Ethernet history, and
alarm. This group does nothing without the alarm, filter, or packet capture groups. Its job is to send indications of events in the RMON probe
to some external interface. That interface can either be a log on the
RMON probe or an SNMP trap message sent across the network to a
management station. Additional types of events are also implemented as
vendor-specific extensions to this group. Those proprietary events include enabling and disabling ports.

Token-Ring RMON Differences

RFC 1757 defines RMON version 1 operation with an emphasis on
Ethernet networks. RMON has been extended through RFC 1518 to also

include 802.5 Token-Ring LANs. RFC 1518 is not a completely different RMON standard. In fact, most of the RMON groups are unchanged when implemented on a Token-Ring network. The major changes are in the Ethernet statistics and Ethernet history groups. Since these groups in RFC 1757 define Ethernet-specific statistics, they must be replaced with relevant Token-Ring-specific statistics. RFC 1518 also adds an additional group called the Token-Ring group. This new group defines several areas of Token-Ring-specific statistics and network-configuration-specific values.

The host, HostTopN, and matrix groups are essentially unchanged. The error counters in the host and HostTopN groups are tied to the line, burst, A/C, congestion, internal, and abort errors. In the matrix group, the error counter is not used. The filter and packet capture groups are unchanged, with the exception of an additional flag in the filter group defining information about the status of the packet being examined. The alarm and event groups are unchanged for Token Ring.

Token-Ring Statistics Group

The Token-Ring statistics group is actually two separate groups of statistical information. The first is the Token-Ring MAC layer statistics group and the second is the Token-Ring promiscuous statistics group. The need for two groups is based on the complexity of Token-Ring's error isolation and identification functions. An 802.5 network is much more detailed in defining various error conditions, when compared to the basic error identification of an 802.3 Ethernet network. In order to accommodate the larger amount of information, the RMON statistics group is divided into two groups: one group dealing with ring operation–related errors and statistics and another dealing with user-to-user data packet statistics. The values of the Token-Ring MAC layer statistics group are shown in Table 10.9.

The second subgroup under the statistics group of Token-Ring RMON is the promiscuous statistics group. This group defined the statistics related to the user-to-user communication on the ring. The MAC layer group did not record any information about packets used by applications and therefore is of no use in trending the overall utilization for the network. In order to gain a perspective into the actual usage of a Token Ring, the promiscuous statistics group should be utilized. Table 10.10 defines the elements of the Token-Ring promiscuous statistics group.

TABLE 10.9

Token-Ring
RMON MAC
Layer Statistics

802.5 MAC Layer Statistic	Description
Drop events	The number of dropped events on this probe. This indicates that the probe could not process all packets seen. If absolutely accurate statistics are required, this information should be discarded.
MAC octets	The total number of bytes used on the network for MAC layer operations. These operations include normal ring operation functions, such as insertions, error reporting, neighbor notification, and ring recovery. This counter does not include the bytes used for user-to-user communications, since they will be recorded in the Token-Ring promiscuous statistics group.
MAC pkts	The total number of packets used in all ring operation processes.
Ring purge events	The number of times the ring has entered a purge condition. The ring purge is a normal event after the token is lost due to a token error. This counter is useful in determining overall stability of the ring, based on the fact that frequent token errors are a sign of an unstable ring. Other statistics can then be used to determine the actual cause of the instability. It should be noted that the RMON probe does not count the ring purge events caused by the monitor contention process or the beacon process.
Ring purge pkts	The total number of ring purge frames seen by the probe.
Beacon events	The total number of times the ring has entered a beacon state. This is the indication that the ring has had to begin physical layer recovery. The actual cause of the beacon is not significant to this counter. If this counter is nonzero, the Token Ring being monitored has had a physical failure since the probe began monitoring.
Beacon time	The total time the ring has spent in a ring recovery state using the beacon process.
Beacon pkts	The total count of beacon frames seen by the probe involved in all beacon events.

TABLE 10.9

(continued)

802.5 MAC Layer Statistic	Description
Claim token events	This counter indicates the total number of active monitor elections seen on the network. When the current active monitor (the elected station responsible for ring operation) fails or leaves the ring, a new station must be elected. The monitor election or contention process uses the claim token frame to determine the next active monitor. If monitor contention fails, the ring recovery, or beacon state, will begin. A high number of claim token events over a short time is a good general indication of an unstable ring.
Claim token pkts	The actual number of claim token frames used in the claim token events. In order to become the new active monitor it is necessary for a station to successfully send three claim token frames around the ring. Given this fact, the claim token pkts counter is usually at least three times greater than the claim token events counter.
NAUN changes	This counter indicates the total number of nearest active upstream neighbor changes seen on the ring. All Token-Ring stations must know what station is immediately upstream of them on the ring. This station is known as the NAUN. When the NAUN changes, the station seeing the change must send a report NAUN change to the configuration report server of the ring. When this happens, the RMON probe logs a NAUN change. This is a good measure of the number of insertions and deinsertions seen on the ring. On a backbone ring with very static servers, bridges, and gateways, this counter should be very low. On a client ring the counter will usually be high, based on the stations being turned off and on each day.
Line errors	The total number of soft isolating line errors seen on the ring. This error count is usually an indication of physical layer problems on the ring. Normal insertion and deinsertions can, however, cause a small number of line errors.
Internal errors	The count of internal errors reported by stations on the ring. When a station fails an internal operation, it will report that failure as an internal error. Any number of internal errors is a clear indication that this ring has or had at some time a failing adapter card inserted.

TABLE 10.9

(continued)

802.5 MAC Layer Statistic	Description
Burst errors	The total number of soft isolating burst errors seen on the ring. This is usually an indication of physical layer issues on the ring. Normal insertion and deinsertions can, however, cause a small number of burst errors.
AC errors	The number of A/C errors seen on the ring. If this counter is nonzero, an end station on the ring has failed to set the A/C bits of neighbor notification packets properly. If this is the case, an end system most likely is failing or has failed in hardware.
Abort errors	The total number of abort delimiter messages seen by the RMON probe. The abort delimiter is a special two-byte data unit consisting of the start and end delimiter fields of a Token-Ring frame only. It is used when a station fails to transmit successfully and is able to notify the ring of this failure by aborting the transmission. If a station is receiving a valid frame and then sees an abort delimiter, it will disregard the current frame.
Lost frame errors	This counter logs the number of lost frame errors reported on the ring. A lost frame error occurs when a station transmits a packet and fails to see the packet return within 4.1 ms. This error usually indicates that the frame's ending delimiter field was destroyed elsewhere on the ring by a line or burst error. As long as the total lost frame error count is less than the total line and burst error count, there is usually no real problem on the ring. If this counter is increasing without corresponding line or burst errors, the ring is having a potential failure. In this case, further investigation must be performed using tools that provide details about which stations are seeing these errors. The RMON Token-Ring station group and LAN analyzers are appropriate tools for further examination of excessive lost frame errors.

TABLE 10.9

(continued)

802.5 MAC Layer Statistic	Description
Congestion errors	The total number of receiver congestion errors seen on the ring. This error is not uncommon on Token-Ring networks during periods of high traffic. The error indicates that a receiving station was unable to copy frames being sent to it. The station could not copy these frames due to a lack of resources such as buffer capacity and CPU cycles. Large Token-Ring networks should try to minimize this error, because it is a measure of network inefficiency, since each congestion error usually results in a retransmission of the failed packet. By increasing the CPU and buffer capacity of the end systems and controlling the flow of protocols it is usually possible to reduce the total congestion error rate on a ring. Please note that this error does not indicate any physical layer error condition on the ring. It only indicates that a receiving station could not copy a valid packet into its buffers.
Frame copied errors	The total number of frame copied errors seen on the ring. When a station sees a packet destined to its address, that station changes the A/C bits in the frame status field at the end of the packet to ones. This change indicates that the station it was destined for copied the frame. This error occurs when a station other than the destination station changes these A/C bits. Causes of this error include bridges and switches that modify these bits when forwarding unknown packets, duplicate addressed multiple interfaces on one device (for redundancy), and failing adapter cards. In general, this counter should be zero unless some device on the ring has a valid reason for modifying another station's packet A/C bits.

TABLE 10.9

(continued)

802.5 MAC Layer Statistic	Description
Frequency errors	This counter shows total frequency errors seen on the ring. A frequency error is a serious condition, because it indicates that the ring could not be clocked successfully. It forces monitor contention to elect a new active monitor and can lead to a beacon condition and ring failure. If this counter is nonzero, the ring has experienced clocking failure and was most likely unstable. Causes of this error include a failing active monitor and the physical ring being too large from a timing and jitter perspective. Note that ring size is measured in terms of jitter resulting from stations and cables building the ring. For each cable type and category, the station's count maximum and cable distance will differ. A very common cause of excessive frequency errors on new rings is the use of low-quality media filters. A media filter is a passive device used to convert a shielded twisted-pair connection to unshielded twisted-pair cable. Since the filter is part of the physical ring, it adds to the total accumulated jitter of the ring. If the filter is low quality, it may introduce excessive jitter into the ring and cause frequency errors to occur when the rest of the ring expands in size with the addition of new stations.
Token errors	The total number of token errors seen on the ring is counted here. A token error is logged every time the active monitor detects that the token passing process fails. The failures include a breakdown of the priority mechanism, the presence of any packet passing the active monitor twice, a corrupt or damaged token, and the absence of any token or packet for 10 milliseconds. These failure conditions have two real causes usually. The corrupt or absent token situations are usually caused by line or burst errors elsewhere on the ring destroying the token. The priority breakdown is caused by applications failing to operate properly on the ring. To differentiate between the two conditions, examine the line and burst error counters. If they are incrementing as the token error count increments, the condition is related to frame corruption. If the line and burst error counts are not increasing as the token error count increases, there is most likely an end-system application issue involved.

TABLE 10.9

(continued)

802.5 MAC Layer Statistic	Description
Soft error reports	The total number of times that a report soft error MAC frame has been generated on the ring. Each station on a Token-Ring network is responsible for detecting and reporting errors to the network ring error monitor or monitors. This counter indicates how many times the station on the ring reported errors. In each error report frame, up to 255 of each error could be reported.
Ring poll events	This counter indicates how many ring poll processes have occurred on the ring. The ring poll process, also known as neighbor notification, occurs every seven seconds on a functional Token Ring. This counter should see one ring poll event every seven seconds. If that is not the case, the ring is potentially unstable or the ring poll process is failing.

*Jitter is the measure of clock deviation seen on the ring. The active monitor station on any ring measures the difference between the transmitted clock and the received clock after the signal circulates the ring. The active monitor is required to compensate for this difference using a buffer called the elastic buffer. If this buffer cannot compensate because the difference is too great, the ring has a frequency error.

The two statistics groups of RMON for Token Ring define a great deal of information. By understanding the definitions of each statistic and having a basic understanding of Token-Ring operation, a system administrator of a Token-Ring network is armed with a tremendous amount of information. These data are critical in monitoring the operation and measuring the growth of the network.

Token-Ring History Groups

Just as the statistics group for Token-Ring RMON defined two subgroups, so too does the history group. RFC 1513 defines a MAC layer and a promiscuous statistics group to fully count all statistics involved in a typical 802.5 network. The process used is identical to the Ethernet history group defined in RFC 1757: a sliding window defined by an interval and a duration used to define the logging of statistical data. The Token-Ring MAC layer history group logs time-sampled statistics based on all the values seen in the Token-Ring MAC layer statistics group. The only additional statistic included in this group is the ML history active

TABLE 10.10

Token-Ring RMON
Promiscuous
Statistics

Promiscuous Group Statistic	Description
Drop events	The number of dropped events on this probe. This indicates that the probe could not process all packets seen. If absolutely accurate statistics are required, this information should be discarded. This counter should be the same as the dropped events counter in the MAC layer statistics group.
Data octets	This counter shows the total bytes seen on the ring for user-to-user communication. This is a good measure of absolute utilization on the network.
Data pkts	The total number of valid user-to-user data packets seen on the ring. This includes unicast and nonunicast packets.
Data broadcast pkts	This counter shows the number of non-MAC layer packets seen destined to one of the two Token-Ring broadcast addresses (0xffffffffffff or 0xc000ffffffff). This is a good measure of the total broadcast rate on the ring for use in baselining and broadcast analysis.
Data multicast pkts	All multicast destined packets seen by the probe are counted here. The multicasts counted include functional addressed non-MAC layer packets and protocol-specific multicasts. This counter, combined with the data broadcast pkts counter, provides a total count of non-MAC layer nonunicast packets on the network.
Data pkts 18 to 63 octets	The number of Token-Ring non-MAC layer packets seen ranging in size from 18 to 63 bytes. This size packet is usually used as acknowledgment messages or other overhead. A high percentage of traffic in this range is an indication of excessive overhead on the ring. If the applications are mostly character echoing types, such as terminal emulation (TN3270, VT100), there will be more smaller-sized packets seen. If the network applications are used mostly to transfer files, larger-sized packets should be the more common.
Data pkts 64 to 127 octets	All packets between 64 and 127 bytes are counted here.
Data pkts 128 to 255 octets	All packets between 128 and 255 bytes are counted here.

TABLE 10.10

(continued)

Promiscuous Group Statistic	Description
Data pkts 256 to 511 octets	All packets between 256 and 511 bytes are counted here.
Data pkts 512 to 1,023 octets	All packets between 512 and 1,023 bytes are counted here.
Data pkts 1,024 to 2,047 octets	All packets between 1,024 and 2,047 bytes are counted here. This counter may indicate that packets created on the Token Ring are larger in size than an attached Ethernet network could support. If the network contains both Ethernet and Token-Ring elements, the switches, bridges, or routers may have difficulty passing these packets. Some devices support IP fragmentation to allow large IP packets to be broken down into several smaller packets and forwarded. This feature will not exist in IP version 6 (the next-generation Internet Protocol) and does not exist for other protocols. In general, mixed Ethernet/Token-Ring networks should attempt to limit the maximum frame size to about 1,500 bytes, so that no fragmentation or forwarding issues will be experienced.
Data pkts 2,048 to 4,095 octets	All packets between 2,048 and 4,095 bytes are counted here.
Data pkts 4,096 to 8,191 octets	All packets between 4,096 and 8,191 bytes are counted here. This counter represents the presence of packets on the Token Ring that are larger than can be supported by an FDDI network. If a mixed FDDI/Token-Ring network is built, the issues discussed under the data pkts 1,024 to 2,047 octets counter are applicable.
Data pkts 8,192 to 18,000 octets	All packets between 8,192 and 18,000 bytes are counted here.
Data pkts greater than 18,000 octets	All packets over 18,000 bytes are counted here. These are considered oversized packets in most cases and should not be seen unless some application has justification for their use.

stations. This statistic counts the total number of active stations on the ring during each sample interval. When this number increases, a station insertion has occurred, and when it decreases, a station has left the ring. This value is extremely useful in determining the overall stability of a ring, based on the fact that insertions and deletions cause line and burst errors, which can cause minor frame loss.

The Token-Ring promiscuous history group counts the statistics listed in the promiscuous statistics group with no additions. The counting of those statistics in time-specific samples is useful in trending the network's operation and utilization. As an example, a high number of packets—1,024 to 2,047 bytes in one sample—could be an indication of a large file transfer, while a consistent number of packets—256 to 511 bytes—may be an indication of periodic routing table updates. These statistics are not extremely useful in troubleshooting a Token-Ring network but are helpful in gauging the overall operation of the network for capacity planning.

Token-Ring Station Groups

RMON for Token Ring adds an additional group not seen in RFC 1757. This group, the Token-Ring station group, is a collection of Token-Ring-specific information defining ring- and station-specific parameters. A basic Token-Ring RMON probe will usually implement this additional group with the statistics, history, alarm, and event groups. The usefulness of this addition is in associating MAC layer details with Token-Ring stations. The host, HostTopN, and matrix groups associate utilization statistics and traffic details with user addresses but do not define how that station is operating at the MAC layer. This group defines this missing piece through several tables, outlined in Table 10.11. This group represents the second level of Token-Ring statistics used when troubleshooting. Once the statistics or history table shows a potential error rate or ring problem, this group is used to define which particular stations are involved in the issue. If a high line error rate is seen in the Token-Ring MAC layer statistics group, the RMON Token-Ring station group could be used to find the two stations defining the fault domain where the line errors are occurring. Once that area is defined, troubleshooting is a simple matter of determining which adapter of the two stations or which cable belonging to the stations is failing or being affected by noise. This is a much simpler method of troubleshooting than having to suspect any component on the ring of being the cause. Table 10.11 explains the various parts of the Token-Ring station group. This table breaks the station group into several functional groups for descriptions rather than defining each element separately.

TABLE 10.11

RMON Token-Ring Station Group

Station Group Element	Description
Station control table	This table defines the overall ring status. The information contained in this table provides an overall assessment of the condition of the ring. The number of active stations, the current active monitor, the number of order changes (inserting or deleting stations), the current ring operational state, and details of the last beacon condition (sender and destination of the beacon frames) are listed here. This table should be monitored closely to watch for changes of state from normal to a purge, claim token (monitor contention), or beacon state. An RMON alarm against this value would be a good application of the alarm group.
Station table	This table defines the details about stations on the ring. The details are similar to the MAC layer statistics group but are tied to a single station. The major elements are: • Station address: The MAC address of the end station. • Station last NAUN: The last upstream neighbor of this station. • Station status: The current status of this station. The possible states are active, inactive (not seen in the ring poll), or forced removal (removed through management station's actions). Some RMON probes will only list active stations, so inactive and forced removal stations may never be seen. • Station last enter and exit times: The time (sys uptime) when the station last inserted and deinserted from the ring. This provides an indication of how long an active station has been on the ring. • Station duplicate address: The number of times a station has had duplicate address test errors during insertion. If this counter is nonzero, there is most likely another station with the same MAC address in existence. This counter does not indicate that there are two stations with the same MAC address on the ring, since that condition is prohibited by the insertion process. It normally means that another user could not insert, because the address that station has is already on the ring..

TABLE 10.11

(continued)

Station Group Element	Description
Station table *(cont.)*	• In and out line/burst errors: These four counters list the number of line and burst errors seen by this station (line/burst in) and the number of line and burst errors seen by the nearest downstream station of this station (line/burst out). This is a useful format, because if the current downstream station's line/burst in errors and the upstream station's line/burst out error counters do not match, they were not always adjacent. If they do match, then it is likely that all of the counted errors occurred between these two stations. • Other errors: Internal, A/C, abort, lost frame, congestion, frame copied, frequency, and token errors seen by this station are counted here. This is useful when trying to find more detailed information about a ring error rate. An example would be if the ring had a high congestion error rate. This group could specify which stations were congested. That would allow a focused troubleshooting of those stations to determine how to improve their performance to reduce overall congestion. • In and out beacon errors: The total number of beacon frames sent from this station to its upstream neighbor to recover the ring from failure is defined as the beacons out. The beacons in are the total frames sent from another station (the downstream neighbor) to this station during ring recovery processes. Participation in any beacon process as either a beaconed or beaconing station is an indication that the station or its downstream neighbor's fault domains have had physical failures. • Station insertions: The number of times this station has inserted into the ring. On probes that only track active stations, this counter is not useful, because once the station leaves the ring, all statistics are deleted.
Station order table	This table shows the current logical order of the ring. The only real information contained in this group is a listing of all the active stations seen on the ring in their logical order. This is useful in determining the nearest active upstream neighbor of a station.

	Station Group Element	Description
TABLE 10.11 (continued)	Station configuration table	This table lists configuration information of the stations on the ring. Through this table, the station's adapter card can be queried for the following configuration details: • Location: The physical location parameter given to the device on insertion by the ring parameter server. If this parameter is not supported or not used, the value should be zero. • Microcode: The microcode level of the adapter card's processor. This parameter is meaningful only in engineering-level troubleshooting where new microcode may be required to fix internal adapter card issues. In general this information is meaningless. • Group address: The last four bytes of the group address this station uses. This group address is not a functional address such as the addresses used for the active monitor and ring error monitor. • Functional address: The functional addresses recognized by the station. This is a bit mask allowing up to 31 different functional addresses defining logical entities (active monitor, RPS, REM, CRS, etc.) supported by this adapter.
	Source routing group	This area of the Token-Ring group defines specific statistical information about the operation of source route bridging on this ring. The information provided includes: • Ring number: The source route ring number of this ring. This value should be unique. • Frames in/out/through: The total number of source-routed frames sent to devices on this ring (in), from devices on this ring (out), and between devices on different rings using this ring for transit (through). This is useful in determining where the backbone areas of the network are. Rings with a high number of through frames are generally considered backbone rings and are the best suited for performance improvements, such as replacement by a Token-Ring switch.

TABLE 10.11

(continued)

Station Group Element	Description
Source routing group *(cont.)*	• All routes broadcast frames and octets: The total number of all routes' broadcast frames seen by the RMON probe and their total byte count. It is normal to see some all routes broadcasts on a Token-Ring network, since they are a part of path determination. If the number of all routes broadcasts is a large percentage of the total packets seen on an active ring, there may be an application-related issue misusing the all routes broadcasts message. To further troubleshoot that issue, a LAN analyzer should be used to determine the source address of the all routes broadcasts and its application.
	• Single route broadcast frames and octets: The number of single route broadcast messages seen and their total byte count. These packets are also needed for path determination. Excess amounts of this type of packet should be handled just as excess amounts of all routes broadcasts are.
	• In/out/through octets: The total byte count of the in/out/through packets counted above.
	• Local LLC frames: The total number of frames that did not include a source Routing Information Field (RIF). These frames can be described as being sent to and from devices on this local ring. This does not include MAC frames such as beacons and error reports.
	• 1–8 hop frames: The number of packets seen by the probe based on the number of hops in the RIF. A separate counter tracks each hop count value. These counters only increment for packets whose source or destination are on the probe's local ring.
	• More than 8 hops frames: Any packet with an RIF containing more than 8 hops. This is an important value, because IBM networks usually limit the RIF size to 8 hops, while IEEE 802.5 allows space for 14 hops.

The Token-Ring RMON group provides the same basic functions for 802.5 networks as RFC 1757 provides for Ethernet networks. The goals of proactive management, off-line operation, problem detection and reporting, value-added data, and multiple managers are consistent in RMON for Token Ring and Ethernet. By understanding the application of these RMON tools, the system administrator is much better prepared to monitor, manage, and troubleshoot the network.

RMON Version 2 (RFC 2021)

RMON as discussed previously is focused on the management of OSI layers one and two systems. This means that RMON is designed to monitor and manage Ethernets and Token Rings. RMON has done an exceptional job of standardizing the network monitoring functions for these types of networks and has become the single most useful tool in dealing with their operational issues. What RMON does not attempt to manage is the actual protocols and applications operating over the Ethernet or Token-Ring infrastructure. The management and monitoring of protocols such as IP, IPX, and AppleTalk have usually been left to complex network analyzers such as Network General's Sniffer system. In general, these analyzers have complex software capabilities in order to understand the format and operation of a specific protocol on the network. A basic RMON probe would be overwhelmed if asked to identify and monitor specific protocols in addition to the statistical information discussed previously.

The difficulties in using vendor-specific network analyzers are the same issues faced in managing Ethernet and Token-Ring networks prior to RMON. Each vendor had a good set of statistical information, but there was no real way to share it in a nonproprietary way. With RMON, Ethernet and Token-Ring monitoring devices could now format and share data with other vendors' management applications. Obviously, a standardization of the data format used to examine protocol and application-specific data could be helpful in exactly the same way. In order to make this possible, RMON version 2 has come into existence.

RMON 2 is not a replacement for RMON 1. RMON 2 is a new RMON standard for monitoring networks for protocol- and application-specific information. It can work cooperatively with RMON 1 even on the same RMON probe. The significant disadvantage of RMON 2, however, is that it requires a tremendous amount of CPU processing power on the probe to do the required analysis. Because of this, RMON 2 will usually be implemented on dedicated RMON probes rather than integrated into other network devices such as switches and hubs.

RMON 2 Structure

The RMON 2 MIB contains nine functional groups. An RMON 2 probe does not need to implement all groups in order to comply with this MIB, but it must implement all elements of any groups supported. Table 10.12 describes the functions of each of the nine RMON 2 groups.

TABLE 10.12

RMON 2 Group Definitions

RMON 2 Group	Description
Protocol directory	This group defines all protocols that the probe can identify. The actual definitions of the protocols are not defined in RFC 2021. RFC 2074 provides some guidance to assist in configuring this group to identify specific protocols. This directory will list layer three protocols, such as IP, IPX, DECnet, etc. It will also list higher-layer protocols supported, such as UDP, TCP, SPX, DDP, etc. There is no requirement as to how many protocols can be supported by a specific probe. If the probe has sufficient resources, a great number of protocols may exist in this directory. No real statistical information is stored in this group, but the group is mandatory if any other protocol-specific groups such as host and matrix are to be implemented.
Protocol distribution	This group collects raw statistics for each of the protocols in the protocol directory group. The actual statistics gathered are the packet count and byte count on the segment seen for each protocol. This group can be useful in determining how much of a segment's bandwidth is being used by each protocol. It can also be used to detect potentially invalid network usage. An example of this use would be this group seeing IPX protocol packets on a network segment that should only contain IP protocol users. This could be an indication of an unauthorized Novell NetWare communication or other IPX-driven applications, such as various network-based games. In order to use this type of analysis for monitoring, the system administrator must baseline the network to determine what protocols are present when the network is functioning as desired.

TABLE 10.12

(continued)

RMON 2 Group	Description
Address mapping	The address mapping group tracks the physical address to network address mappings for all protocols supported. This group will develop a listing of all network addresses seen and the most recent MAC layer address seen using that address. This is useful in determining which physical device is using which network layer addresses. This group could be used to determine the presence of duplicate network addresses, since each entry has a time of creation associated with it. If that time is constantly being reset, there may be two or more physical devices using the same network address. As each of the duplicates speaks, the table is changed to reflect the most recently seen MAC address. This mechanism is not as advanced as some network analyzers' processes, which can provide listings of the physical addresses sharing the network address. Because better means are available in existing LAN analysis tools, RMON 2's address mapping group is not the first choice of tools in troubleshooting duplicate network addresses.
Network layer host	This group builds a table listing each network layer address seen by the probe. Associated with the address are several counters. They include: • In packets: Packets sent to this network address. • Out packets: Packets sent from this network address. • In bytes: Total byte count of all packets sent to this network address. • Out bytes: Total byte count of all packets sent from this network address. • Out MAC nonunicast packets: The total number of broadcast and multicast packets sent from this network address. • Created time: The system uptime when this network address was added to this table. This group is used primarily to determine the amount of protocol-specific traffic generated by specific end systems. As a troubleshooting tool, this group can be used to determine if an end system is even using a specific protocol. It is not unusual for an end-station's protocol stack configuration to be invalid. The end station then is unable to even use that protocol. Unfortunately, the applications trying to use that protocol usually provide the user with cryptic error messages, which do not immediately identify that the protocol is not even operational. Using this group, identifying if the end-system's network address is present and active can prove whether the protocol is operational or not.

TABLE 10.12

(continued)

RMON 2 Group	Description
Network layer matrix	This group creates a table listing all network layer conversations by source and destination network address. Associated with each conversation pair are the network addresses of the two stations involved, the packet count and byte count in both directions, and the time this entry was added to the table. This group can be used to determine which protocol-specific conversations are using the most network capacity. An example would be if this table showed a very large byte count between two IP addresses. This could be the result if one of the addresses existed on the switched network but the other was on another interface of the local router. This situation should be examined to determine if these two IP devices might be better located in the same switched network. If that relocation is possible, the overall performance of that IP communication will be improved, since the router would no longer be in the path. This group also defines a HostTopN function allowing automatic reports listing the top N address pairs generating a statistic over some fixed time. The top ten byte count over eight hours would provide a good listing of the top ten active conversations on the network.
Application layer host	The function of this group is to count all traffic statistics by application layer protocol from each network layer address. Each application layer protocol is counted by packets in and out and bytes in and out. This table could provide insight into the actual networking applications in use on a particular device. This group could, for example, show how much FTP traffic versus SNMP traffic is coming from a network management station.
Application layer matrix	This group defines a table listing the network traffic by application layer protocol between network layer address pairs. The statistics counted include the byte count and packet count in both directions between the two network addresses for each protocol identified. This table could potentially be used in situations where the system administrator is attempting to identify how much traffic from a server is related to NFS operations versus other IP-based applications. This group also includes a HostTopN function, allowing automatic reports listing the top N address pairs generating a statistic over some fixed time.

	RMON 2 Group	Description
TABLE 10.12 (continued)	User history	The user history group provides a very flexible historical statistic logging mechanism. This group allows the system administrator to create a table of statistics to be logged using a fixed interval and duration. This mechanism is exactly the same as the RMON 1 history group, except that the statistics being logged can be any MIB variables on the device. This group could be viewed as a customizable history group. This mechanism allows for much more flexible statistics gathering. Instead of a network management station having to poll the probe for values not in the Ethernet or Token-Ring history groups on some interval, the probe can simply be configured to use this user history group to log those statistics locally. Possible statistics could be MIB II values, RMON 2 protocol distribution values, and even vendor-specific MIBs. The log can store either absolute values or delta values and define the start and end times of each sample.
	Probe configuration	This group is used to standardize the configuration and access to RMON 2 probes. No real statistics involved in managing a network are included in this group. Instead, the group contains configuration settings for the probe's operation, firmware upgrade process, SLIP configuration, network configuration, SNMP traps, and other parameters. This group attempts to provide a common set of configuration parameters to RMON 2 probes, so that any RMON 2 network management software can be used to configure any vendor's RMON 2 probe. This group can be used on dedicated probes but will usually not be used on probes embedded into switches or other networking devices, since those devices already have their own configuration systems.

Summary

Overall, RMON 2 adds a standardized format to the statistical analysis of protocol-specific traffic patterns on networks. It does this by a flexible but complex mechanism of protocol identification. When implemented on stand-alone probes, RMON 2 could add significant insight into the operation of protocols and applications on a network. However, when added to switches and other networking hardware, the overhead needed to fully implement all RMON 2 groups could significantly impact their overall performance. Most networking hardware vendors will find a balance between implementing RMON 2 and impacting network performance. That balance will most likely result in low-end switches having only basic RMON 1, while backbone high-end switches may include some of the RMON 1 and RMON 2 groups. Additional RMON 1 and RMON 2 functions will be reserved for stand-alone probes.

When managing a switched network, RMON 2 adds some interesting information but is usually not a requirement for managing or monitoring this type of network. LAN switches operate at OSI layer two and as such have a much closer relationship to RMON 1. The implementation of RMON 1 should be considered vital to managing and monitoring a switched LAN. The implementation of RMON 2 or a good set of LAN analyzer tools should be considered for further examination of the network's operation and for troubleshooting the switched network.

BIBLIOGRAPHY

World Wide Web Resources

LAN Technology Scorecard—Shows updated summary information about most LAN technologies:

http://web.syr.edu/~jmwobus/comfaqs/lan-technology.html

DHCP Frequently Asked Questions Web site:

http://www.syr.edu/~jmwobus/comfaqs/dhcp.faq.html

Books

ANSI/IEEE. Std 802.3, ISO 8802-3:1993. *Information Technology—Local and Metropolitan Area Networks. Part 3: Carrier Sense Multiple Access with Collision Detection (CSMA/CD) Access Method and Physical Layer Specifications.*

———. Std 802.1D, ISO 10038:1993. *Information Technology—Telecommunications and Information Exchange between Systems—Local Area Networks—Media Access Control (MAC) Bridges.*

———. Std 802.5, ISO 8802-5:1992. *Information Technology—Local and Metropolitan Area Networks. Part 5: Token-Ring Access Method and Physical Layer Specifications.*

———. Std 802.2-1989, ISO 802-2:1989. *Information Processing Systems—Local Area Networks. Part 2: Logical Link Control.*

Comer, D. *Internetworking with TCP/IP.* 2d ed. Englewood Cliffs, NJ: Prentice Hall, 1991.

Huitema, C. *Routing in the Internet.* Englewood Cliffs, NJ: Prentice Hall, 1995.

Martin, J. *Local Area Networks.* Englewood Cliffs, NJ: Prentice Hall, 1994.

Miller, M. A. *Troubleshooting Internetworks.* Redwood City, CA: M&T Books, 1991.

———. *LAN Protocol Handbook.* Redwood City, CA: M&T Books, 1990.

Naugle, M. G. *Network Protocol Handbook.* New York: McGraw-Hill, 1994.

Norton, P. *Programmers Guide to the IBM PC and PS/2.* Redmond, WA: Microsoft Press, 1988.

Perlman, R. *Interconnections: Bridges and Routers.* Reading, MA: Addison-Wesley, 1992.

Rose, M. T. *The Simple Book.* Englewood Cliffs, NJ: Prentice Hall, 1991.

Sidhu, G., et al. *Inside AppleTalk.* 2d ed. Reading, MA: Addison Wesley, 1990.

Siyan, K. S. *Windows NT Server 4 Professional Reference.* Indianapolis, IN: New Riders Publishing, 1996.

———. *NetWare Professional Reference.* Indianapolis, IN: New Riders Publishing, 1995.

Windows NT Server Networking Guide. Redmond, WA: Microsoft Press, 1996.

RFCs

RFC 2074. "Remote Network Monitoring MIB Protocol Identifiers." A. Bierman and R. Iddon, January 16, 1997.

RFC 2021. "Remote Network Monitoring Management Information Base, Version 2, Using SMIv2." S. Waldbusser, January 16, 1997.

RFC 1920. "Internet Official Protocol Standards." J. Postel, Internet Architecture Board, March 1996.

RFC 1918. "Address Allocation for Private Internets." Y. Rekhter, R. Moskowitz, D. Karrenberg, G. de Groot, and E. Lear, February 29, 1996. (updates RFC 1627) (obsoletes RFC 1597)

RFC 1757. "Remote Monitoring Management Information Base." S. Waldbusser, February 1995.

RFC 1700. "Assigned Numbers." J. Reynolds and J. Postel, Information Sciences Institute, October 1994.

RFC 1631. "The IP Network Address Translator." P. Francis and K. Egevang, May 20, 1994.

RFC 1541. "Dynamic Host Configuration Protocol." R. Droms, October 27, 1993.

RFC 1534. "Interoperation between DHCP and BOOTP." R. Droms, October 8, 1993.

RFC 1533. "DHCP Options and BOOTP Vendor Extensions." S. Alexander and R. Droms, October 8, 1993.

RFC 1513. "Token-Ring Extensions to the Remote Monitoring MIB." S. Waldbusser, September 1993.

RFC 1122. "Requirements for Internet Hosts—Communication Layers." R. Braden, Internet Engineering Task Force, October 1989.

RFC 985. "Requirements for Internet Gateways." R. Braden and J. Postel, Information Sciences Institute, June 1987.

RFC 925. "Multi-LAN Address Resolution." J. Postel, October 1, 1984.

RFC 791. "Internet Protocol." Information Sciences Institute, September 1981.

INDEX